THE Organic
Lawn Care
MANUAL

THE Organic Lawn Care

MANUAL

A Natural, Low-Maintenance System for a Beautiful, Safe Lawn

Paul Tukey

Foreword by
Nell Newman
President of Newman's Own Organics

Storey Publishing

To my mother, Charlotte, the fertile soil so full of life
To Katie, my sunshine
And to Christina and Duke, my roots

The mission of Storey Publishing is to serve our customers by publishing practical information that encourages personal independence in harmony with the environment.

Edited by Carleen Madigan Perkins

Art direction by Mary Winkelman Velgos

Cover design by Kent Lew

Text design and production by Mary Winkelman Velgos and Kristy L. MacWilliams

Indexed by Susan Olason, Indexes & Knowledge Maps

Cover Photography © Image Source/Getty Images

Back Cover Photography © John Ewing, bottom; © Adam Mastoon, top

Interior Photography © Scott Calhoun/Zona Gardens: 157, 248; © John Ewing: 8, 14 top and bottom right, 16, 18, 21, 32–34, 36, 37, 43, 45, 48 bottom, 50, 67 left, 69 all except center left, 72 top and bottom right, 73, 74 left, 77, 79, 82–84, 87, 89 top right, 90, 91 top and middle, 92, 93, 95, 97 bottom, 98, 100–103, 104 left, 109, 112, 115, 116, 122–127, 132–134, 137, 147, 152, 160–164, 168 bottom, 169, 175, 176, 178–180, 183, 214 top, 215, 220, 222, 224, 225, 226 bottom, 227, 228, 231, 232, 235, 241, 255; Todd Harrington: 233; © Christine Hoffman: 88; © Image Source/Getty Images: 48 top; © iStockphoto: Greg Nicholas 23, Shane Link 147 top, David Elfstrom 147 bottom, Wolfgang Melle 168 top, Melissa Carroll 252, Mitch Aunger 253, Dan Roundhill 254; © Adam Mastoon: 2, 5, 14 bottom left, 22, 49, 104 right, 106, 226 top, 236; © Bill Beatty/Painet: 198 top right; Carleen Madigan Perkins: 80; © Newman's Own Organics/ Nikki Brooks: 7; © Paul Boardway Tukey: 11, 13, 15, 20, 27, 40, 52, 64, 65, 67 center and right, 69 center left, 70, 71, 74 right, 76, 81, 85, 91 bottom, 94, 96, 97 top and middle, 105, 107, 108, 114, 119, 128, 130, 141, 142, 167, 170, 174, 181, 182, 198 top left and bottom, 199–201, 216–219, 221, 233, 234, 237, 242–247, 249, 250; Paul Tukey, Jr.: 72 bottom left; Katie Hoffman Tukey: 89 all except top right

Illustrations © Elayne Sears

Text © Paul Boardway Tukey

The information in this book is true and complete to the best of our knowledge. All recommendations are made without guarantee on the part of the author or Storey Publishing. The author and publisher disclaim any liability in connection with the use of this information. For additional information please contact Storey Publishing, 210 MASS MoCA Way, North Adams, MA 01247.

Storey books are available for special premium and promotional uses and for customized editions. For further information, please call 1-800-793-9396.

Printed in China by R.R. Donnelley

10 9 8 7 6 5 4 3 2 1

Library of Congress Cataloging-in-Publication Data

Tukey, Paul Boardway.
  The organic lawn care manual : a natural, low-maintenance system for a beautiful, safe lawn. / Paul Boardway Tukey.
    p. cm.
  Includes bibliographical references and index.
  ISBN 13: 978-1-58017-649-1; ISBN 10: 1-58017-649-6 (pbk. : alk. paper)
  ISBN 13: 978-1-58017-655-2; ISBN 10: 1-58017-655-0 (hardcover : alk. paper)
  1. Lawns. 2. Organic gardening. I. Title.

SB433.T74 2007
635.9'647—dc22
                                                        2006033373

contents

I consider myself to be one of the lucky ones; I've always felt connected to our earth and able to live in harmony with it. My mother, an early environmentalist, was a big influence for me. We recycled and had apple trees and kept a couple of chickens. There was a river near my house in Connecticut, and, growing up, I'd run through the woods with my fishing rod, our pack of dogs following, and I'd fish and bird-watch all day. The natural world was always part of my life, part of my awareness.

My interest in organic products probably also stems from the fact that I was something of an ornithologist early on. I was fascinated by birds as soon as I could walk. I read about the peregrine falcon and was amazed by its qualities, including the fact that it can stoop at up to two hundred miles per hour. Of course, in my studies I also learned that the use of DDT has made falcons extinct east of the Mississippi. That's a mind-boggling concept for a little kid — extinction.

These days, disturbing environmental facts can still boggle the mind and hit very close to home. I have friends with mercury poisoning, probably acquired by eating fish caught in contaminated waters. Bird and insect populations are waning, due at least partially to the pesticides people put on their lawns and gardens in the interest of creating "beauty." In an age when we know fossil fuel resources are very limited, North Americans use on average the equivalent of eighteen gallons of gasoline maintaining their lawns each year. For many people, pursuing the "perfect" lawn appears to be an obsession. Good people who are making unfortunate decisions about tending their grass are contributing to air and water pollution, global warming, and, especially, compromised human and animal health.

As credible scientists make direct links between higher rates of childhood cancers and increased use of lawn pesticides, I hope that every state develops laws at least as restrictive as those in Connecticut, where it is illegal to apply pesticides near schools and day care centers. Given that veterinarians have proof that lawn chemicals are partly responsible for a 30 to 40 percent increase in the mortality of dogs and cats, I can't imagine why any of my fellow dog owners would ever risk using chemicals on their lawns.

This is where *The Organic Lawn Care Manual* can help. Author Paul Tukey gently educates us about a better way to care for our lawns: Using organic methods, we can still achieve great results. In addition to giving us a great deal to think about, he gives us the tools to be successful.

It's an approach that will work. I know that early on, my dad was skeptical about organic products and methods. In 1992, during Thanksgiving in Connecticut, I decided the proof was in the pudding: Without telling him, I arranged for an organic farm in California to ship to me a three-pound box of organic salad greens, peas, and potatoes, and I managed to find an organic turkey as well. I made Thanksgiving dinner exactly the way Dad loves it — but with all organic ingredients. Only when he had wiped his plate clean did I ask, "So, how did you like your organic meal, Pa?" And he got the picture, which convinced him that organics could really take off.

And it can all begin with how we care for our lawns.

Nell Newman
President of Newman's Own Organics

Preface

It has long been said we learned everything we needed to know in kindergarten, yet I suspect many of us still spend most of our lives trying to figure it out anyway. I know I have.

I often joke that I've been at a disadvantage since I grew up in an era — the '60s — in the state of Maine, where kindergarten was not a prerequisite for first grade. My journey in life began on a dairy farm in the small town of Bradford, where my hero was my grandfather, a sixth-grade graduate named Henry VanDyne, who milked cows and hayed fields for his livelihood. My heroine was his wife, Clarida VanDyne, who grew all the family's food and for whom "store-bought" was a scornful phrase. By requirement, I rode with Gramp to the fields to align his tractors with their trailers, and I shoveled out manure from his cows' stalls. I lugged Gram's "swill pails" to the garden and planted her peas and beans. By the time I was 10, I was mowing the lawn and running the "Trojan horse" (our Troy-Bilt tiller).

Amusement, in those days, was seasonal and simple. Summer was always the best. I couldn't wait for June, when the back lawn by the corner of their yellow house would come alive with tiny red strawberries that I could forage while Gram and Gramp took their afternoon naps. In the evening, just after the dew fell, I'd jack the lawn for night crawlers in hopes that Gramp would take me fishing, or I'd trap the lightning bugs that put on their nightly fireworks display atop the grass. Gram always seemed to appreciate the collection of flowers I'd gather from around her lawn, the daisies and clover, the orange hawkweed and Johnny-jump-ups of my primitive bouquets.

Though maybe never a typical teenager, I did have a typical teenage need: money. So I always mowed lawns, lots of them, having learned the work ethic and technique from Gramp. Mowing lawns each summer also helped put me through college, and working with all that equipment, gas, and fertilizer helped maintain my connection to Gramp. Scientists tell us scent is the most powerful, primal sense, and to this day the smell of a freshly cut field or lawn reminds me of that magnificent, gentle man.

In a roundabout way, that brings me to today and the publication of this book about natural lawn care. After many years as a lawn care professional, after another decade as the publisher of the gardening magazine *People, Places & Plants,* I considered writing a book primarily about *why* you should care for your lawn organically. I thought of citing myriad scientific studies and other alarming information about the convoluted way we have come to care for our lawns in the generations since weed 'n' feed was introduced in the late 1940s.

Instead, I have opted to keep the book simple, presenting straightforward how-to methods for safe, effective lawn care. I could probably write an entire book about why you should avoid lawn chemicals, about all the reasons the time is right to change your ways. It's probably better, though, to simply give you the tools and information to make the change in your own life and landscape. The ultimate decision is your own.

Before I begin, I'll share two more motivating moments that led me to this book. In the early '90s, when my lawn care company had grown to 27 employees and more than 800 customers, I was fined by the Maine Board of Pesticide Control for applying the herbicide Roundup without a license. Who knew you needed a license to apply Roundup, I asked? Professionals, I discovered, must be licensed before they can legally apply synthetic fertilizers, herbicides, and fungicides to other people's lawns.

Passing that lawn pesticide test was a big moment, meaning I could call myself a licensed pesticide applicator and charge even more money for spreading synthetic chemicals on my customers' lawns.

The following year was the most profitable for my company, but it also brought another defining moment. When a new colleague, a Maine botanist named Dr. Richard Churchill, came to visit me at a job site, I showed him my progress with eliminating weeds from the lawn at a local Maine hospital where recovering cancer patients took a daily stroll. Instead of being impressed with my lawn care prowess, Dr. Churchill scoffed at me and scurried away.

It was the first time anyone had ever questioned my use of lawn chemicals.

Within a year, my doctor also began asking difficult questions. In 1993, after a spring of frequently applying weed 'n' feed, I began suffering nosebleeds and shortness of breath at the end of each workday. "Do you work with chemicals of any kind?" he asked.

"No," I replied. "I mow lawns for a living, the same thing I've been doing off and on since junior high school."

My doctor immediately ordered me to cease applications of lawn chemicals, and coincidentally or not, my health problems went away. My company ended all lawn chemical applications by the spring of 1994, and it has been part of my mission in life ever since to research and present alternatives.

As I offer this book to you, my disclaimer is that I'm not a scientist. For the past few years, I have not even been a lawn care professional. What I am is a gardening communicator, a magazine editor and publisher, a television commentator, a keen observer, and a passionate backyard gardener who, within reason, loves a beautiful lawn. I'm a Little League baseball coach who can't wait to get out in the grass each spring to toss a ball with my son. I'm still addicted to mowing, to the sight of straight-line patterns of turf and to the scent of freshly cut grass. I am utterly certain you can have a beautiful lawn, however, without a synthetic chemical program.

Some scientists believe that synthetic lawn care products will come under increasing scrutiny in coming years, much as the pesticide DDT did in the 1960s. Just as Rachel Carson predicted in her landmark book *Silent Spring* in 1962, the environmental and health effects of DDT have been catastrophic. Since DDT was banned in 1972, dozens of other pesticides have been restricted or eliminated now that scientists have a greater understanding of their effects.

"We are seeing only the tip of the iceberg," says Dr. Michael Surgan, the lead environmental scientist for the New York State attorney general's office. "In the coming years, many more lawn care products that are currently on the market will be proved to be dangerous."

With this book, I hope to offer proof to you that the risk is simply not necessary. You can grow a beautiful lawn without synthetic chemicals; I've done it, and so have many, many others. The advances in natural lawn care — from fertilizers to new grass varieties — have been breathtaking in recent years. The truth is that making the transition is not easy, but in the end it is tremendously effective.

Call this your organic lawn care kindergarten book . . . everything you need to know to grow home turf safely, efficiently, and effectively. As you read the book, I suspect you'll ask deeper questions about your lifestyle that may take longer to contemplate. It's a process, I've found, that never ends.

The Language of Organics

FOR ANYONE CONSIDERING organic lawn care, one of the most daunting tasks can be understanding the associated terms and phrases. For readers' convenience, a glossary is included starting on page 257. Before you even turn to the first page, however, here are two of my personal definitions I'd like you to consider. That will put us on the same page, so to speak, before you begin to read.

Organic. To chemists, the word *organic* describes any compound from any natural or laboratory source that contains a carbon molecule. In this book, *organic* refers to elements within a natural system of horticulture. Products and soil amendments within the system must be derived from plants, animals, or minerals; actions should be considered for their impact on soil, water, and air quality and on the health of the earth. This approach requires careful observation and strives for a balance that gives us the results we desire while not overriding nature. A successful organic system improves life, both above- and belowground.

Chemical. Everything contains chemicals, whether derived from nature or the laboratory. In this book, the word *chemical* refers to a synthetic system of horticulture. Products and amendments may have been created in a laboratory; actions may be considered only for their impact on the plant, while overlooking their influence on soil, water, and air quality. This approach often follows formulaic instruction, and often treats the symptoms of plants rather than the underlying cause of the problems. A chemical lawn system has a greater potential than a natural system to harm life, both above- and belowground.

We can't help ourselves. We love them, those great swaths of luxuriant green. Lawns have been inspiring poetry and passions for many North Americans for as long as we have claimed these United States and Canadian provinces. We might have tried to extract ourselves from Great Britain more than two centuries ago, but we brought many British sensibilities to this side of the watershed, none more telltale than our innate desire to keep our grass properly mown.

In 1806 the first book on gardening in the New World, *The American Gardener's Calendar,* advocated a "grand and spacious" lawn. In 1830, the British engineer Edwin Budding invented and exported the first mechanical lawn mowers, and by the mid-1800s our nation's first widely read horticultural author, Andrew Jackson Downing, began to associate tidy turf with social status. "We hope every day," he wrote, "as the better class of country residences increases, to see this indispensable feature in tasteful grounds becoming better understood and more universal." By 1875, keeping up with the Joneses was already in full swing, at least in the view of social activist Peter Henderson: "We occasionally see some parsimonious individual, even now, who remembers that in the grandfather's days, grass was allowed to grow for the food of the critters, and he leaves it for food for his critters still . . . it is gratify-ing to know that such neighbors are not numerous, for the example of the majority shall soon shame them into decency."

Modern psychologists tell us that the desire for lawns is largely a male passion; studies show men are subconsciously comforted by the color green and that maintaining grass heightens our senses of security and success. I'm sure that's true, but I also know that Gram kept riding and smiling atop her John Deere lawn tractor into her early 80s. A well-kept lawn was second only to her highly productive vegetable garden on the scale that measured her satisfaction.

The Synthetic Lawn

Other than a few robust octogenarians who still get outside on their own, scarcely anyone is left alive who has not had access to the luxury of the ultimate lawn care contrivance known as weed 'n' feed. What a seemingly great tool it was when it became available to

It was troubling to see that this baseball field, where my son's Little League team plays, received an application of chemical fertilizer just before practice started.

the masses in 1948, courtesy of the heirs of a hardware store owner from Ohio named O. M. Scott. With one pass of a lawn spreader, we could feed the grass, kill the weeds, and still have time for a round of golf at the course we so envied. Mr. Scott, in fact, got his start in the lawn business by mechanically separating weed seeds from grass seeds for the golf course superintendents of the late 1800s. Throughout the mid-1900s, golf champions were hired to endorse lawn care products by asking us: "Want a lawn that's fairway smooth?" Of course we did! In the 1960s, when television began to bring Arnold Palmer's swing and swagger into living rooms every weekend, we were hooked on lawns for good. In just a generation, golf and good ole American marketing conspired to increase the size of the lawn industry more than tenfold, from 35,000 mowers sold in 1942 to more than 4 million in 1962, the year Palmer won his second consecutive British Open title.

Fast-forward to the Tiger Woods generation, and we love our lawns more than ever. In the United States, homeowners now blanket more than 30 million acres in turf, making grass a multibillion-dollar industry and a bigger agricultural crop than corn and soybeans combined. Whether we play games on our grass or simply paint our landscape inside a pristine green frame for the sake of beauty, we're collectively covering an area the size of the entire state of New York — from Long Island to Buffalo — in just 12 or so different species of plants.

All that mowing, blowing, watering, planting, and weeding requires all sorts of tools, some of them new and some of them not all that different from the gadgets Edwin Budding and others created more than a century ago. In this age of environmental awareness, however, all of that gasoline, exhaust, water, fertilizer, and pesticide require new evaluations of old habits. This may simply build awareness or, I hope, cause quantum changes in behavior.

Moving toward Organic

We are at a remarkable time in American and world history as a movement associated with the word *organic* is sweeping the planet. Sales of organic food products are increasing at more than 20 percent annually in the United States and people are beginning to understand how organics, in all aspects of life, can play a significant role in improving our quality of living. Organics, especially as it relates to lawn care, is a primary means of thinking globally and acting locally.

The reasons for natural lawns are many. They're safer for families, pets, and the environment. They use fewer fossil fuels, water, and fertilizer. They can be less expensive and, in time, require less of your time — which allows you to enjoy your lawn rather than fret about its upkeep.

You might have heard, though, that organic lawn care doesn't work, or that going organic in your landscape inevitably leads to a field of weeds. Maybe you've tried organic lawn care in the past and it didn't meet your expectations. That's where this book comes in. Organic lawn care can, and does, work well.

It's not my goal to belabor the argument about health and environmental risks associated with traditional synthetic lawn care. Plenty of other books already offer that perspective, including several in the suggested reading list, page 261. In the same way pundits of this once young nation exhorted us to mow our grass, a modern generation of writers has lined up in a camp behind best-selling author Michael Pollan, who would have us swap our mowers for trowels and our lawns for gardens. "Lawns, I am convinced, are a symptom of, and a metaphor for, our skewed relationship to the land," he writes. "They teach us that, with the help of petrochemicals and technology, we can bend nature to our will."

A bending of nature, whether for a lawn or a garden, is in fact always necessary. Left to her own devices, Mother Nature will re-create a meadow and then a forest from even the most developed of lots. I know of a once pristine professional baseball stadium in Maine, abandoned for a decade, that is now barely recognizable through the trees and shrubs filling the parking lot and outfield. Not many of us want to live in a forest.

The bending of nature in our landscapes, however, need not be overly forceful or wasteful. Proper organic lawn care, in fact, shouldn't waste much of anything. When you read the pages that follow, I'll show you how to achieve your own luxuriant swath of green, if that's your goal, in a way that keeps your family and this planet safe from toxins. I'll talk about lawn alternatives and lawn reduction strategies. I'll also show you that organic lawn care is based in solid, proven science that is being supported by the work of soil biologists, plant breeders, educators, researchers, engineers, and leading turf professionals.

This book, as promised, will not be a highly technical presentation of these breakthrough technologies. From experience, I know you can grow a reasonably successful natural lawn by simply understanding and following this one long sentence: Treat your soil well with compost and natural fertilizers, pick the right grass for your climate and sunlight situation, water well, use the right tools, and mow properly with a sharp blade. This book, if read thoroughly and followed carefully, can also help you have a great lawn, the best in the neighborhood if that's your goal, as it is mine. I want you to love your organic lawn, in whatever form it takes, when you're finished using this information.

The organic lawn in the foreground handled drought far better than the synthetic lawn in the background.

1 Evaluate Your Lawn Care Needs

a lawn, by simple definition, is an area of short grass. For some of us, though, it's much more. Whether we use the turf as a place to play with our children, entertain our friends, frame our gardens, encourage or discourage wildlife, or privately lounge with a book and a beer, our lawns often have a great deal to say about who we are.

In my first few homes I never thought much about the lawn, and I suspect many folks are the same. I simply mowed whatever grass was in place already and did little to make my lawns any bigger or smaller, better or worse. That was, I suppose, natural lawn care in one of its simplest forms. At least I wasn't running out to purchase and apply products I did not yet understand.

As I have aged, as a parent, homeowner, gardener, and landscaper, I have begun to pay far more attention to the lawn and its place in my daily life. I wish I'd started sooner; in retrospect, it was amazing how much I wasted time, resources, and opportunities along the way. When I recently moved into a new home, I realized I had accumulated a mental checklist for my lawn. I encourage all of you to make a similar list for yourselves before you get started with lawn care. Even if your lawn is already established at a longtime home, taking yourself through the 12-point list will likely be a valuable exercise. Many of these topics are covered in far more depth later in this book.

How Will You Use Your Lawn?

Do you *use* your yard, or is it only your benign gateway to the outside world? If you're like me and you play games with your children on the grass, you'll want to define a needed area and keep it regularly maintained. Do you have a primary spot where guests often congregate? This space, too, will require definition, since guests rarely like to party in knee-deep wildflowers. Keep in mind, though, that this space does not need to be turf; terraces, a deck, patio, gazebo, or porch may cost more than grass initially, but they'll often pay you back in time, aesthetics, and property value.

As for those areas where no games are played nor guests wined and dined, consider the alternatives. Later chapters focus on ground covers and wildflowers. Trees, surrounded by ground covers or mulch, require far less maintenance than turf in the long run. Many shrubs, which offer varied points of interest throughout the different seasons, can grow for years

with little attention once established.

Even if you want to stick with turf as your primary landscape feature, you can vary the maintenance program depending on usage and location within your yard. In front of my home, an area measuring about 100 feet by 40 is mowed fairly regularly for baseball, football, and all the other lawn games my family enjoys. I am certain to grow types of grass that can withstand plenty of foot traffic. I top-dress this area with compost, fertilize it in spring and autumn, and keep it regularly aerated and dethatched. The work is substantial, but worth it.

Behind the house, around the deck where we barbecue, I mow a broad path once a month at most so we can freely walk to other areas of the property. Farther out from the paths, I mow just twice, in early spring and late fall. The rest of the year I enjoy whatever wildflowers come up naturally . . . or I help out nature by scattering a few seeds from time to time. In these areas, I don't fertilize, aerate, or think twice about weeds.

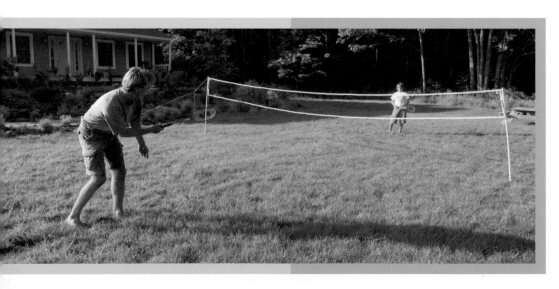

With a teenage son at home, our front lawn serves as a constant playing field.

The result has been a semi-controlled environment that gives my family the functional outdoor space it wants, while providing a place for a vast diversity of other plant and animal species to coexist. If the only time you visit certain areas of your property is atop or behind a lawn mower, ask yourself why you need to bother.

How Much Time Do You Want to Spend?

When I was just out of college, I considered mowing my own lawn a nuisance, even though mowing became part of my profession. I guess it's part of that cobbler's-children-have-no-shoes phenomenon. When I did get around to mowing, the grass was often so tall that I'd cut off more than I should and then the lawn would suffer and turn yellow (more on that in chapter 11). I'd also have to rake areas where the clippings were so thick they'd smother the grass or get tracked into the house.

It's far better to make a realistic assessment of your time in the beginning and don't grow more lawn than you have occasion to maintain. A standard rule is that a 5,000-square-foot lawn takes about an hour to mow with a 21-inch rotary mower and up to a half-hour longer with one of those manual push-type reel mowers. You could mow an entire acre in an hour with the right piece of equipment, but then you're getting into significant expenditure.

Is Your Lawn a Welcome Mat for Animals?

Will cats and dogs be running across the lawn and tracking it into your house on a regular basis? Do you put out the welcome mat for birds, deer, and other wildlife, or would you really rather they stay away? Both of these answers should dramatically impact your lawn care decisions.

Numerous studies have shown that cats and dogs are far more susceptible than adult humans to health risks associated with synthetic lawn fertilizers and pesticides. A study in the April 2004 edition of the *Journal of the American Veterinary Medicine Association*, for example, concluded that certain breeds of dogs are four to seven times more likely to contract bladder cancer when exposed to chemically treated lawns.

Lawn care products that come into the home on the bottom of paws is also of great concern. Synthetic fertilizers and pesticides will, in time, break down in contact with soil, sun, and rain, but

Parents Beware

IF YOU HAVE KIDS playing games on the lawn, consider all the factors before applying any unnatural lawn additives. According to numerous studies, children have been proved to be significantly at risk from many lawn and garden chemicals. "Parents can make a big difference in their homes," says Dr. Philip F. Landrigan, of the Mount Sinai School of Medicine. "They have the power over the decision whether or not to use chemicals."

these same materials may never break down if they become lodged in cracks in your flooring or in the weave of your indoor carpeting.

When it comes to wildlife, natural lawns attract more birds, insects, and other critters than a synthetically treated lawn of the same size. Large open swaths of any kind of turf, however, are not as welcoming to wildlife as gardens of trees, shrubs, and flowers. If you grow grass right up to the foundation, with no trees or shrubs nearby, you'll have a hard time attracting birds to a feeder. They like to have the cover of a tree or shrub close by. Similarly, deer and some other critters will generally stay off a lawn unless an apple tree or a juicy yew shrub invites them in.

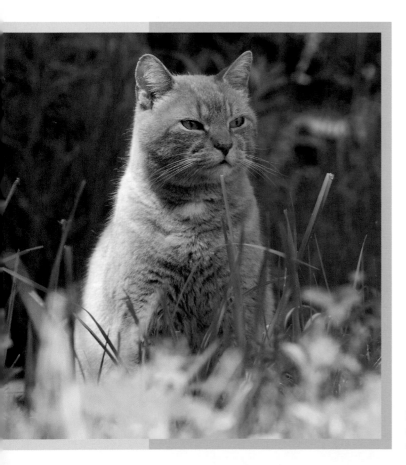

Pumpkin, the Tukey family cat, can roam safely in an organic lawn.

How Much Sun Does Your Yard Receive?

One of the most important evaluations you can make, right up front, is an honest assessment of sunlight throughout your yard. This will become a tremendous consideration in chapter 4, when we examine turfgrass varieties. Full sun, needed by the majority of grasses, is defined as at least six hours of direct sunlight between the hours of 8 a.m. and 4 p.m. Full shade, not favored by any lawn grasses, is two hours or less of full sun during those hours. Homeowners who have yards with heavy shade should consider planting a shade-loving lawn alternative (see page 242), installing hardscape, or laying down mulch, rather than watch a patch of sun-loving lawn grass struggle to survive. Remember: not all bare ground needs to be covered by grass, especially if the site isn't conducive to it.

Although this is a book celebrating lawns, I encourage everyone to also think of trees as a major part of the landscape. If you do have more than six hours of full sun, you may be thrilled to have a nice tree cast shade over at least part of your property during the heat of the day. I happily avoided planting a lawn on a section of my property in favor of a hammock hung between a sugar maple and an old pine. My son loves to lounge in the hammock, bemused or confused that his father gets so much joy from tending the grass and garden nearby.

What Is Your Soil Profile?

I'll address this in depth in chapter 3, but it's worth stressing again and again that lawn care, and any other kind of gardening, begins with the soil. Take the time to do a full evaluation of your soil type, pH, and fertility. This can be done with a relatively simple and affordable soil test, either from your local Cooperative Extension Service branch or a certified soil lab.

You're also about to read more on a new test known as a bioassay, which measures the life in your soil in terms of bacteria, fungi, protozoa, and other microscopic organisms. You probably haven't thought about those things since high school biology class, but they're all integral to a healthy, natural lawn. This type of test is more expensive than a simple soil test. Depending on the size of your lawn and your goals for its appearance, however, the one-time cost may be well worth it.

How Much Water Do You Have Access To?

This subject also gets its own chapter, but you'll need to think about access to water early on in the landscaping process. Many communities throughout North America now place restrictions on lawn irrigation; does yours? Many towns, like mine, are still on backyard well systems. Does your well provide enough water to even think of irrigating grass? Periods of drought are typical just about everywhere, and as much as I love my lawn, I'd still rather be able to shower and keep the kitchen tap flowing.

If you're on a municipal water system, chlorine and fluoride are also factors in lawn care. Some communities routinely add fluoride to the water supply to keep teeth healthy, but this has shown to negatively impact the vitality of lawns and soil. Chlorine is less of a concern but can, in some cases, contribute to an unhealthy lawn. I'll talk about ways to mitigate the potential negative side effects of chlorine and fluoride later on, in chapter 8.

Saving water is certainly an option with gutter systems pouring into rain barrels or through recycled household discharge known as gray water. Any water that has been used in the home, except from toilets, kitchen sinks, and dishwashers, can often be used for landscape irrigation. This is a great way to reclaim fluids from your clothes washer, bathtub, shower, and bathroom sink — which comprise 50 to 80 percent of water used in most homes. Using this water will require some rerouting of your plumbing, but it is an expense that gets paid back quickly.

Can You Handle the Gear?

The decision to do your own lawn care requires the ability to purchase and stow 20 or so different items. You'll also need a shed or a significant portion of your garage to keep the mower, rakes, edging spade, trimmer, ear and eye protection, garden hoses, and other equipment discussed in chapter 11. Take a look around your home to see if you can accommodate the tools of the trade.

Do You Want to Increase Your Curb Appeal?

Real estate experts tell us that a nice lawn and overall landscape can significantly increase the value of a home, by as much as 10 to 15 percent in some cases. In other words, the time and expense of a lawn are often well justified. The first things any real estate agent will tell sellers are paint the house, inside and out, and mow the lawn.

If selling your property isn't in the cards anytime soon, your landscape's outward appearance may not be a high priority. Keep in your mind, however, that a nice lawn does add value . . . to a point. Too many gardens and too much lawn can actually be a negative for buyers; more than a few hours of required maintenance each week scares away some people.

A well-maintained organic lawn and landscape adds to your property value.

Do You Care What the Joneses Say?

You may find that some folks in your surrounding area have strong opinions about how your landscape should look. Some communities may even legislate what you can and can't grow and how high or low you should mow your lawn. I have a friend who gets nasty notes from neighbors in his country club community when he misses a mowing or two.

In an ideal democratic setting, you should be able to have a flowery mead right out to the roadside if you'd like. If neighbors do affect your decisions, though, be sure to make your voice heard. Some communities, for example, hire landscape contractors to care for all the yard maintenance around everyone's home. In this scenario, make yourself aware of the products they're using, and be certain those products are not harmful to your family, pets, or water supply. Don't be afraid to let the contractors know about the natural alternatives you read about in this book.

Who's Going to Do the Work?

Whose job will it be to mow, rake, weed, fertilize, and add any other soil amendments? Who will need to understand the process required? These are both significant questions if the goal is to have a great lawn.

At many homes, Dad may send a reluctant Johnny out behind the lawn mower every Sunday afternoon. Dad might even trust Johnny with the power string trimmer or the lawn spreader. If Johnny doesn't get it right, though, he can cause serious damage to the lawn by scalping the grass or applying too much synthetic fertilizer. He can also harm himself by using equipment improperly or by not using recommended eye and ear protection. A great benefit of natural lawn care is that it minimizes many health hazards, but even natural systems can carry certain risks from power equipment or improper use of organic insect killers. Think about these risks and talk them over. At the very least, you may save a few family squabbles.

With a lightweight reel mower, my 13-year-old son manages the mowing chores just fine.

2 Grass Anatomy

Called the blanket of the earth, the grass plant in its many forms is one of the most remarkable survivors on the planet. It can be cut off and will regrow. It can go dormant if it is too hot, too cold, or too thirsty, and then bounce quickly back to health when conditions improve. It can be walked on, poured over with water, dug up and put back, and still come back for more.

Before you delve further into this book, it may be useful to review the basics of how grass grows. I'll also review the all-important process of photosynthesis, which allows plants to create food by using the sun's energy. It's simple stuff, but important.

A single grass plant survives because it has minimal needs and multiple built-in protection mechanisms. It takes up water and nutrients through its roots, controls growth through its crown at ground level, and conducts photosynthesis and its breathing operations through aboveground shoots. Unlike many plants that have a long recovery time after pruning or shearing, grass readily repairs itself over and over again. And unlike plants that might die during drought or freezing temperatures, grass plants simply shut down and wait for better days.

A Lawn of Many Plants

A lawn, of course, comprises millions of grass plants growing in proximity. They shade each other in the heat; collectively resist invasion from weeds, insects, and diseases; and generally support each other year-round. Within the roots and shoots are specialized areas that may allow plants to creep together, either above- or belowground, to protect the lawn from trampling. Each section of the plants has a specific role, from the stem parts known as rhizomes that travel underground and weave together to form sod to the aboveground sheaths that help the plants stand tall. Before attempting to grow a lawn of your own, it's useful to study the grass anatomy chart on page 25, and even skip ahead to the glossary, on page 257. The language of lawns isn't overly complicated, but it does have a few nuances all its own.

The Life Cycle of a Grass Plant

Although we rarely allow it to reach this point, the grass plant has the same goal as all other living beings — to reproduce. Some grasses are annual, meaning they germinate from seed, grow, set their own seeds, and then die all in the same growing season. Some are perennial, meaning they grow and set seed each year and come back every year. Seasonal growth in lawn grasses varies widely, from just a few inches to a foot or two. Because we want our lawn to be a permanent part of the landscape, and not something that

has to be replanted every year or two, lawns are usually grown with any of several perennial grasses (see chapter 4).

Our goal for the lawn is at odds with the grass plant's goal for itself. Unlike the gardens we plant, we're usually not after a lawn of grass that goes to seed. We don't want it to reproduce; we're growing it for sustainably green foliage. The grass plant puts a tremendous amount of energy toward seed production. It's best, therefore, to mow the grass before it gets tall enough to set seed; it's better to allow the plant to store this energy so it can produce even more stems and blades.

Food from the Sun

All grass plants grow by using the sun's energy to turn water and carbon dioxide into carbohydrates and simple sugars that can be used to fuel their growth processes (with some oxygen and water left over, as well). It's the green pigment in plant leaves, known as chlorophyll, that makes this process — called photosynthesis — possible. Inside the chloroplasts is the important element nitrogen, which must continually be replaced or else photosynthesis cannot continue. Other elements, at least 15, are also absolutely necessary in varying amounts for grass growth. Some stimulate roots. Others help in processing the sugars or in building plant structures (see chart, page 28).

Grass blades, then, play an important role in food production. They have pores, known as stomata, that allow carbon

Grass Anatomy: A Basic Lesson

LAWN GRASSES are of three basic types: rhizomatous (spreading by underground stems), stoloniferous (spreading by aboveground stems), and clump-forming. Because of their ability to cover ground quickly, the former two are often the most desirable types.

Rhizomatous

Stem
A generally stiff, erect part of the shoot that supports leaves

Rhizome
Underground "running" stem capable of originating new shoots

Collar
The point where the blade and the sheath meet

Stoloniferous

Sheath
Part of the base of the blade that wraps around the stem and gives the grass plant strength and resiliency

Node
Swollen point on the stem where new buds develop into new leaves or seed heads

Stolon
Above ground "creeping" stem capable of originating new shoots

Clump-forming

Blade
The upper portion of the leaf

Crown
The point, usually at ground level, where roots and shoots originate

dioxide to get in and oxygen to get out in a breathing process called transpiration. Other parts of the grass, the crown and root structures, have the essential ability to store some of the excess carbohydrates and sugars created during photosynthesis. Maximizing the efficiency of this food production, breathing, and storage are the goals of the natural lawn care system. For example, if we cut off too much of a plant's blades all at once, we take away much of the plant's ability to conduct photosynthesis. That's why lawns that are cut from, say, 6 inches down to 3 inches will temporarily turn brown. (You'll learn more about mowing in chapter 11.)

It's important to understand, too, that grass plants can grow and store energy only during daylight and times of year when moisture levels and temperatures are appropriate. If the grass doesn't have enough stored sugars and carbohydrates during the off-season or in times of drought or stress, it will suffer and have a hard time recovering. Our inclination might be to try to help the lawn through these stressful times by adding more fertilizer, but "feeding" the grass during periods of stress — especially with fertilizers made from a high concentration of synthetic nitrogen — will usually make things worse. The result will be further browning, or "burning," of the lawn.

Water Makes It Happen

Because levels of sunshine and carbon dioxide are often fixed by nature, water becomes the most important variable in photosynthesis and often the one where we, as lawn growers, have the most influence. If we apply too little water, the lawn will suffer when photosynthesis declines. If moisture is too abundant, air pockets may collapse around the roots and, in effect, drown the plants. All sorts of lawn diseases affect lawns that have either too little water or too much.

As you'll see in the chapter on grass choices, some grasses require far less water than others. Matching the right grass with the right climate or water availability will be critical for the success of your lawn.

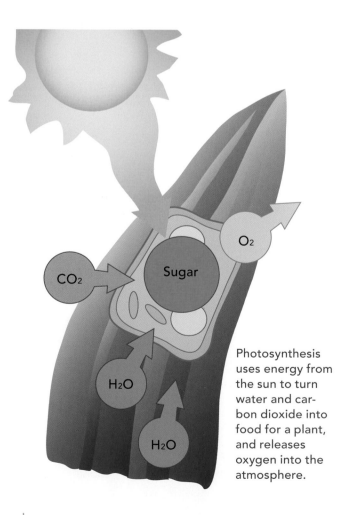

Photosynthesis uses energy from the sun to turn water and carbon dioxide into food for a plant, and releases oxygen into the atmosphere.

Todd Harrington

GROWING UP AS THE CHILD of a landscaper, Todd Harrington could identify the names of most trees and pesticides as a young boy. Having worked for his father's company, known as Mushroom Landscaping, for most of his life, he said he never had any doubt that working with plants would also be his life's calling.

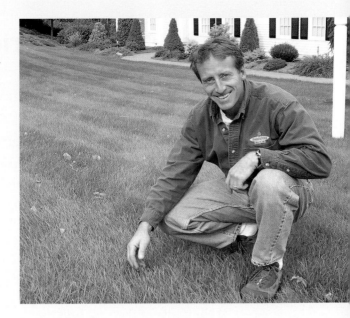

The chemicals, however, left him with a bad taste.

"It's something that, to this day, really bothers me to be around," said Harrington, who eventually took over his father's company, and changed the name to Organicare in 1989. "I really thought there had to be a better way to care for plants."

In an industry where the father-knows-best philosophy is still prevalent, Harrington's refocus of the family business was not immediately well received.

"People laughed at me," he said, laughing himself. "The chemical mind-set is so ingrained that no one believed you could really do it without insect killers, weed killers, and fungicides."

His early efforts, he admits, were hit or miss. Sometimes the organic treatments worked on trees and lawns; other times they didn't. The key was finding a scientific basis for organic gardening — and looking at soil through a microscope.

"I don't think I could ever get tired of looking at magnification of a healthy soil sample," said Harrington, who now treats more than 1,200 lawns organically in the area of Hartford, Connecticut. "Healthy soil, treated organically, is so alive with microorganisms it's incredible. Soil that has been treated with the chemical pesticides really looks, by comparison, like a dead zone. Soil scientists who use a microscope are just like a doctor who takes a blood sample to diagnose a disease in people. You can learn so much about a soil problem, and find a solution, by looking at the soil under a microscope."

A disciple of soil scientist Elaine Ingham, Harrington has helped pioneer the use of compost tea extracts in lawn care. By brewing specific kinds of compost tea, he can add more bacteria or fungi, or help the soil create its own nitrogen through the addition of microorganisms known as protozoa.

If it sounds complicated, it can be. The premise, though, is quite simple.

"You know the old saying about people: 'You are what you eat'?" he said. "Well, soil is the same way. The idea is to feed the soil a good, natural diet. When you do that, good things start to happen."

The Plant Nutrient Pyramid

WE ALL LEARNED AS CHILDREN that we need portions from all the major food groups to remain healthy. Remember the pyramid with fatty foods and sweets on top and grains and vegetables on the bottom? Well, soil has its own version of the pyramid, with six macronutrients at the bottom, three secondary nutrients in the middle, and at least seven micronutrients at the top. Although plants use some of the micronutrients in only very small amounts, they are nonethe-less essential. A common problem with many synthetic soil additives is that they contain only the three major mineral elements of nitrogen, phosphorus, and potassium (N-P-K) and none of the other nutrients. Lawn diets can get out of whack very quickly.

At right are the elements necessary for plant growth, with their percentages in a typical plant composition and a description of their roles in a natural lawn care system (for nutrient sources, turn to chapter 7). Some soil scientists believe nickel and silicon are also involved, but the following information is generally accepted by leading researchers.

Major Macronutrients

Oxygen (45%). Comes from either water or carbon dioxide; also bonds with carbon in the plant skeleton.

Carbon (44%). Derived from carbon dioxide; the major structural element in all visible life-forms.

Hydrogen (6%). Comes from water; bonds with carbon to the plant skeleton.

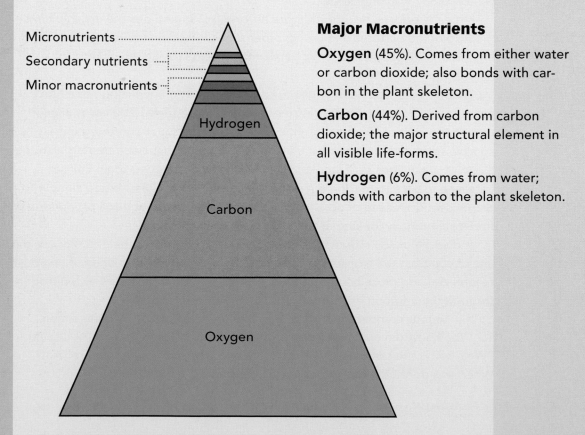

Micronutrients ....
Secondary nutrients ...
Minor macronutrients ...

Hydrogen

Carbon

Oxygen

These three air and water elements form the carbohydrates (sugars, starches, cellulose, and so on) for the basic building blocks of cells, and also join with other elements to form the complex plant molecules such as amino acids, proteins, and enzymes that allow plant growth.

Minor Macronutrients

Nitrogen (2%). A by-product of soil decomposition and atmospheric sources and necessary for photosynthesis; a primary constituent of amino acids and proteins that feed plants.

Phosphorus (0.4%). A natural component of soil and soil organisms; gives the plant energy and facilitates growth.

Potassium (1.1%). A naturally occurring soil salt; promotes plant vigor and disease resistance.

Secondary Nutrients

Calcium (0.6%). Naturally available in soils and subsoils; stabilizes pH levels and biological activity, loosens soil, is a major component of plant cell walls.

Magnesium (0.3%). A natural soil mineral that holds soil particles tightly together; a major component of chlorophyll, which promotes plant growth.

Sulfur (0.5%). A component of organic matter; a component of certain amino acids and plant proteins.

Micronutrients

Boron (0.005%). Usually available in manures and soils; promotes flowering, fruiting, and growth.

Chlorine (0.01%). Available in most soils in trace amounts; stabilizes organic matter.

Copper (0.001%). Clings to organic matter in soils; a component of chlorophyll, which promotes plant growth.

Iron (0.02%). An element of most soils; a catalyst in chlorophyll formation.

Manganese (0.05%). Widely varied content in soils; essential for photosynthesis, production of chlorophyll, and nitrate reduction.

Molybdenum (0.0001%). Usually available in trace amounts; promotes nitrogen fixing in legumes and pollen formation on blossoms.

Zinc (0.01%). Clings to organic matter; promotes starch formation for plant energy.

The Natural Lawnkeeper: A Gentle Guiding Hand

Differences in lawn systems really boil down to how we help our grass support photosynthesis. Do we apply medication in the form of synthetic chemicals? Or do we apply nutrition in the form of organic, naturally occurring foods? Do we allow our grass to become addicted to what is commonly known as the synthetic four-step program — weed killer, insect killer, another weed killer, and then a winterizing fertilizer? Or do we build toward a self-sustaining, beautiful lawn, one that can conduct photosynthesis year after year without much help or expensive additives from us?

People who grow lawns tend to fall into three distinct camps: those who do nothing to a lawn but mow whatever grows up from the soil; those who try to grow a lawn by synthetic means; and those who want a nice lawn, but try to achieve it through natural methods. This book is written, of course, for the last group . . . and in hopes that the second group will see the light and convert.

Since the 1950s, and especially in the last two decades, the second group has been by far the largest. Synthetic lawn care programs have supplied nitrogen, phosphorus, and potassium to grasses in vast quantities. This method has been tremendously successful in making grass appear green, but often sicker on the

In healthy organic soil (left), earthworms and other organisms quickly break down thatch and clippings. Lawns managed with chemicals (right) can quickly build up thatch, and roots may struggle to become established.

inside and more vulnerable to attack from outside forces such as insects and diseases. To cure the grasses' ills, people have found it necessary to apply synthetic pesticides and fungicides. Since synthetic lawns become dependent on multiple applications of fertilizers, as well as on more pesticides and fungicides year after year, a self-perpetuating multi-billion-dollar industry has emerged. It is, quite frankly, an addictive cycle not unlike that of a human being who becomes dependent on medication to get by.

A natural lawn system doesn't function in terms of feeding grass. Instead, it nurtures the life inside the soil. In this symbiotic relationship — that is, beneficial to all parties — healthy soil supports lush, green grass, which in turn also provides the soil with all sorts of nutrients. A natural soil environment is loaded with bacteria, fungi, nematodes, earthworms, and other soil organisms, all of which have vital roles in the process of recycling nutrients. Many of these soil organisms break down grass cuttings and any natural fertilizers that you may add into mineral forms that the living grass can then use to make carbohydrates and sugars during photosynthesis.

To some people, the drawback of the natural system is that it does not appear to work as quickly as the synthetic system. A natural fertilizer applied today may not turn your grass green tomorrow. In time, though, the natural system detailed in this book will function better and get your grass just as green. Most important, you'll be helping the environment around your home. Think of it as building a living, breathing underground community. The beneficial soil organisms that are neglected and often killed in the synthetic system will protect your grass, purify the groundwater, and keep your property safe for pets, children, and you.

Balancing Nutrients

IT WAS A GERMAN scientist, Baron Justus von Liebig, who in the mid-nineteenth century helped the world understand the delicate balance involved in plant growth by proving that multiple nutrients are essential for plant life. He authored something known as the "Law of the Minimum," which states that "plants will use essential elements only in proportion to each other, and the element that is in shortest supply — in proportion to the rest — will determine how well the plant uses the other nutrient elements."

In other words, if one element is missing or deficient, plant growth will be poor, even if other elements are abundant. If you think about it, von Liebig's law was really one of the first scientific justifications for organic gardening. By their nature, synthetic fertilizers give plants quick bursts of nutrients that disrupt the delicate balance. An organic lawn care system strives for a balance.

3 Building Good Soil

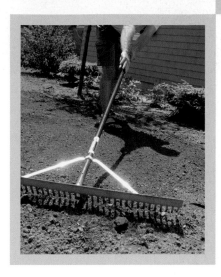

Perhaps because the word means so many things to so many people, *soil* may be the vaguest, most confounding concept in all of horticulture and gardening. On our hands, in the cracks of our floors, and on the soles of our shoes, soil is often reviled as "dirt." As a verb, it equates with all manner of negatives. To soil your enemy is to ruin his or her reputation. To soil your clothing means you've got work to do to make it clean. Even the top line in most dictionary definitions refers to *soil* as "the earth's crust," yet the last thing any gardeners want is crusty soil.

I prefer to think of soil as the batter of a delicious cake made from scratch. No matter how good the frosting may look and taste, the cake is a failure without good ingredients on the inside. Good soil is a resilient sponge, capable of absorbing, expanding, contracting, filtering . . . and coming back for more. Healthy soil is *alive,* just like your own body! You might be amazed to look at a speck of soil under a microscope; millions of organisms live in a single teaspoonful of healthy earth.

This is, simply, where it all begins and ends in lawn care (and all gardening, for that matter). If you have good soil, you can grow good grass. If you don't have enough soil — enough *healthy* soil — then your lawn will forever be a battleground of expense, frustration, and even environmental hazard. This is a chapter in which I feel almost apologetic. A proper discussion of soil can fill volumes; a full understanding of soil's complexities can take years of field trials and university study.

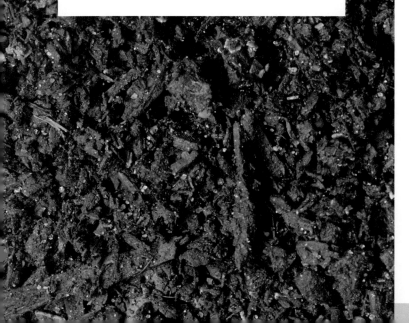

12 Steps

Understanding Soil

1. Soil is alive and should be treated with the respect afforded any living thing.

2. Within soil are colonies of organisms, large and small, that are all interconnected in the "soil food web."

3. As gardeners, we should nurture the soil, which in turn benefits plants.

4. Soil responds best to natural additives and amendments.

5. Any soil maintenance program should be based on a soil test.

6. Soil's pH is a critical measure of acidity and alkalinity.

7. Lawn soil needs proper texture.

8. Lawn soil needs proper structure.

9. Human activities such as lawn trampling and rototilling can impact soil structure.

10. At least 16 elements in soil combine to make plants healthy.

11. A lawn should be well drained.

12. A lawn's topsoil should be deep, at least 6 inches.

Soil Components

If lawn soil were drawn on a pie chart, it would consist of four sections: minerals (decaying rock and glacial material), water, air, and organic matter (any carbon-based materials, living or dead). It's no coincidence those four factors, plus sunlight, make plant growth possible. All four need to be in the right proportion, but when all you're looking at is a mass of brown, black, gray, red, yellow, or greenish material, how do you know?

Understanding soil may begin, for a number of you, with learning some new vocabulary. For a basic understanding, you'll need to know about soil texture and structure and the soil components of clay, sand, silt, and organic matter. To probe slightly deeper, you'll need to know about pH and its effect on the soil's available nutrients, as well as what makes soil breathe. When I really delve into what makes soil — and therefore turf — as healthy as possible, I'll talk about the secrets inside compost and compost tea. They are beneficial microscopic organisms known as bacteria, fungi, algae, protozoa, ciliates, flagellates, nematodes, arthropods, and amoebas, and they're magic when you allow them to flourish.

Texture

Grasping the concept of texture begins with utilizing your sense of touch in the texture test. In a lab, technicians can tell us exact percentages of the different sizes of soil particles known as sand, silt, and clay. They refer to soils by various categories such as "sandy loam" and "silty clay." You can make an educated guess about soil texture based on feel (see page 36).

When you walk across the soil or move soil around in your hands, is it heavy, medium, or light? Heavy soils generally contain a lot of tiny particles compressed together that we recognize as the clay used in pots and adobe houses. When moist, they'll ball up easily in your hands. Medium soils comprise a blend of different-size particles of clay, silt, or sand and tend to crumble readily even when moist. We refer to the largest soil particles as sand, and probably instinctively know from our childhood days in the sandbox that water passes quickly through light, sandy soils.

Most lawn grasses prefer medium texture, which allows for reasonable passage of air, water, and nutrients in and around the root systems. If soils are too heavy, grass struggles; if they're too light, water and nutrients drain off quickly and waste our efforts and resources. When you get to the next chapter, on different lawn grasses, you'll see how important it is to match grasses with the appropriate soil texture.

Structure

Soil structure is another physical property, one often confused with texture. Whereas texture refers to the sizes and proportions of the individual particles that make up the soil, structure refers to how these particles stick together to form crumbs or larger clumps known as aggregates. Good structure is essential; organic matter — in other words, compost, ground-up leaves, decaying roots, manures, and so on — is the glue that makes structure possible. Without organic matter, clay becomes impervious to water and air, and sand becomes a lifeless sieve. Without organic matter, clay and sand combine to make cement.

Your lifestyle, gardening, and lawn care choices can have a significant impact on soil structure. Driving on your lawn or playing sports repetitively in the same spot, for example, causes compacted soil structure by crushing soil aggregates together. Compulsively rototilling your soil (see page 177) breaks apart clumps and ultimately encourages crusting and compaction of the soil. Trying to use a rototiller in an excessively wet or dry soil is a definite no-no. Wet soils will turn to brick; dry soils will become dust.

Inappropriate applications of nutrients, synthetic or organic, also damage soil structure. Numerous studies have shown that applying excessive nitrogen, phosphorus, and potassium can actually reduce the organic matter in the soil and therefore negatively affect soil structure. Your grass won't grow as well and your soil may become overly susceptible to erosion during heavy rains or intensive windstorms.

Other studies have shown that the relationship between two other nutrients, calcium and magnesium, also affects soil structure. For a lawn, the ideal ratio is about 7 parts calcium to 1 part magnesium. These nutrients are most typically supplied to the soil in the form of limestone, but you need the proper type of limestone — preferably

Soil Texture: A Language All Its Own

FROM SOUTHERN NEW YORK TO NORTHERN ALABAMA, the locals call their heavy soil "Piedmont." Along the Mississippi River, folks refer to rich "delta" soil. In Georgia, growers are famous for their sweet onions grown on sandy "Vidalia" soil. People in all locales are fundamentally describing their soil's texture, a characteristic that is difficult to change without radical amendments.

Before you consider any major changes to your lawn's soil, or try to talk turkey with a soil supplier, you need to speak the language of texture, which refers to the percentages of sand, silt, and clay particles. Texture doesn't generally consider percentages of organic matter. Here are just a few of the designations:

Coarse sand. Gritty and loose, even when wet. Contains mostly sand particles of larger sizes.

Sandy loam. Will hold together slightly when wet but crumbles easily. Sand is about half the content, with silt about a quarter and clay another quarter.

Moist clay soil will form a ball when squeezed; sandy soil does not hold together, even when wet.

Clay loam. Feels heavy and holds together when wet. Contains about a third clay, a third silt, and a third sand.

Silt loam. Clumps together easily, but will break apart when rolled in the hand. Contains little clay or sand.

Clay. Forms extremely hard clumps when dry and feels sticky or plastic when wet. May contain very little sand or silt.

calcitic limestone rather than dolomitic limestone, because calcitic limestone contains very little magnesium. See page 135 for more information.

The bottom line to remember is that soil, like your own body, needs a balanced diet to sustain a healthy green lawn: that diet requires far more than the three nutrients indicated by the N-P-K numbers on the front of a fertilizer bag. Utilize the natural soil amendments outlined in chapter 7 to build structure; you, your soil, and our planet will be far better off.

Changing structure. If you're starting from scratch, it is possible to create a good soil structure by blending clay, sand, and silt with organic matter such as compost. The best way to do this is with a soil-blending machine, a contraption that looks something like a cement mixer. Although blending soil can also be done on a small scale inside a wheelbarrow, it's impractical for an entire lawn renovation.

If you do not have access to a soil blender, or are not attempting a full-scale renovation of your lawn, do not try to change your soil structure by adding straight clay, silt, or sand to it. Sand added to clay, for example, can create cementlike conditions. For the best results, add compost or other organic matter, which will improve the soil's overall structure.

When purchasing topsoil to add to your existing soil, look for a soil with a similar texture. Experiments have proved that sudden changes in soil texture can interrupt water flow and root growth.

The Ideal Lawn Soil

Even if you don't want to take the time to understand all the nitty-gritty details of soil biology and chemistry, here is one tenet of lawns you can't ignore: You must have adequate soil depth and drainage for a lawn to be successful. *Depth* simply refers to the amount of good soil available for the grass plants to develop roots. *Drainage* is soil's ability to keep water moving. Well-drained soil has plenty of pores, or spaces between the soil aggregates. Ideally, half of those pores will contain air and the other half water. If too much water fills the pores for prolonged periods of time, the soil can't breathe. This is often called "saturation" or "poor drainage."

Roots of the grass are evident well down into the soil in a healthy organic lawn.

Depth

The biggest recurring problem I see with lawns, especially in new home construction, is that a contractor didn't leave behind enough viable topsoil. Folks are lucky to get 3 inches in many cases, and lawn grasses need at least 6, preferably up to 12, to really thrive during every season.

It's easy to tell if your soil is deep enough. Simply dig down and examine the soil profile, which is a cross section of your soil that is easily obtained by sinking a shovel into the ground and taking a look. If you have just a few inches of brown, loamy material and then all sand or gravel, your lawn will easily leach water and nutrients and have a hard time enduring drought and extreme heat. If you have a bit of soil on top of heavy clay, your lawn may hold too much water and suffer root-rotting diseases.

Problem-solving. The only real solution is to build up the soil gradually with a top-dressing of screened compost every year, half an inch at a time during spring and fall, or to do a large-scale soil and lawn renovation. For this second option, you'll need to call around to excavation contractors or a soil supplier to get price quotes on soil. Ideally, they will have had their soil tested ahead of time and will be able to show you the results. If the soil test isn't available, test the soil yourself by sending a sample to your local soil lab (see soil tests, page 45). You're looking for good texture, structure, and a content of between 3 and 5 percent organic matter.

One hugely beneficial additional step is to blend compost with the topsoil you get from the contractor, even before you spread the soil on your property. I was able to find a contractor with a soil-blending machine; if you're a do-it-yourselfer, blend the soil in the wheelbarrow in a ratio of 2 parts soil to 1 part compost, or even 1 to 1, but as I stated in the last chapter, this isn't practical for a large-scale project. Take this step, though, if at all possible. Your lawn will grow like gangbusters if you start off right by adding compost in the beginning.

Improve Your Drainage

- To promote surface drainage, be sure to grade soil away from the house or surrounding structures.
- Add compost to your soil to improve drainage as well as the soil's capacity to hold water. In lay terms, compost increases the "sponge" factor, allowing soil to absorb more water. In more scientific terms, organic matter increases something known as cation exchange, which is the soil's ability to hold on to nutrients and water more efficiently.
- Evaluate your entire property to see where excess water will naturally want to flow. Will it flow off to a storm drain or culvert? The woods? A neighbor's property? Or will it form a pool somewhere on your property? Do you have a surface erosion problem every time it rains heavily? Depending on the answers to these questions, you may need to take action.

Drainage

Because I'm from a region where heavy clay soils are common, I've seen many instances where excess water becomes a major problem on lawns and in landscapes. In some cases, water pools up or puddles; in other situations, free-flowing water erodes the soil. A mottled gray color or even a musty stench that occurs because the soil can't breath may indicate poor drainage.

If pools of water often form on your lawn or surface soil erosion is evident on a frequent basis, you may need to move the water to a low point, or at least move it belowground. Basins or drainage ditches are the primary tools, although a new tool known as a rain garden has gained popularity. Turn to chapter 12 for details.

Install a basin. This is basically a hole in the ground within which water collects. It is best sited off the lawn, but can also be useful at a low point in the lawn if necessary. To install one in an existing lawn, cut away the top layer of sod with a sharp spade and set it aside on a tarp, in the shade if possible. Then dig the hole as deep as you reasonably can and place this soil on a tarp next to the hole so you don't disturb the rest of the surrounding lawn (you'll cart away some of this soil later). An ambitious homeowner's basin would be 4 feet in diameter dug 4 feet deep; it would hold about 200 gallons of water and, depending on the situation, help drain significant moisture from the surface.

Once the soil is removed from the hole, line the hole with landscape fabric, which you'll find at a landscape supply store or garden center. Refill the basin with crushed stone or brick refuse up to about 8 inches from the original

A basin installed in the middle of a lawn can allow hundreds of gallons of water to seep from the soil's surface.

soil surface. Cover the stone or brick with landscape fabric before filling in the next 6 inches with the original topsoil from near the soil surface; don't use subsoil from the bottom of the hole. Lay down the original sod (check chapter 5 for sod-laying instructions), and within a couple of weeks the evidence of your basin should be gone. Every time it rains, though, water will seep through the soil covering the basin and fill the cavern you've created.

You can also construct much larger drain basins, but will be better off renting a backhoe or hiring a contractor for

the job. The size of the basin needed will depend on the volume of your water problem. Some homeowners will also install underground water tanks equipped with pumps; rather than draining water away, these hold the excess water and can be tapped as irrigation sources during periods of drought.

Install a drainage ditch. If water is pooling or constantly running off aboveground and creating a surface erosion problem, then creating an underground canal may be the best action plan. You'll first have to decide your beginning and end points; in other words, what is the final destination of the water? You'll need to determine your energy level for digging and a budget for the perforated

One edge of our property needed aggressive action to correct poor drainage, so my neighbor came with a backhoe to dig a drainage ditch.

pipe, crushed rock, and landscape fabric needed for a durable drainage system. Many different drainage systems can be modified to fit the needs of your lawn and landscape, and depending on the scope of the project, you may want to hire a landscape contractor or excavation specialist.

I recently installed a drainage system around my house in an area where water was pooling on the lawn and in the nearby garden. It's commonly known as a French drain, yet it's not French at all. The phrase was reportedly coined for Henry French, a farmer from Concord, Massachusetts, who wrote about moving water from point A to point B in 1859.

The Importance of pH

Just as people have a blood count and a blood pressure, a living, breathing soil has its own quantitative measurements of health. The most basic of these is pH, which is the scale from 0 to 14 that measures acidity and alkalinity. The next chapter, on grass types, will detail the ideal pH for each species, but it's usually somewhere between 6 and 7.

Many longtime gardeners from the North, where soils are naturally acidic, automatically add limestone each year to "sweeten" the soil, or make it less acidic. Many gardeners in the West, on the other hand, add sulfur to make the soil more acidic. Having the proper pH is absolutely necessary for lawns to perform well. Without the proper pH level, nutrients are either trapped in the soil or they leach out too readily. At a pH of 5.5, for example, a soil may contain

plenty of nitrogen, but it won't be available to the grass until the soil chemistry is improved by raising the pH.

Obtaining the proper chemistry is highly improbable without a soil test (see page 45). Blanket fertilizer recommendations from books, magazines, Web sites, and even product labels are useless without a true soil analysis from a qualified lab. Sure, you can purchase a kit or tool from the garden center that gives you a pH reading, but you'll never know exactly how much lime or sulfur to add until you factor in your soil's texture and percentage of organic matter. If you're the stubborn type who prefers to soldier on without a lab test, add only small amounts of lime or sulfur each spring or fall, and take frequent pH readings so you know when you're getting close to the ideal. Adding too much lime, sulfur, and especially fertilizer all at once can quickly kill off soil microorganisms, which don't like sudden environmental changes.

Getting beyond N-P-K

For a true breakthrough in the way you think about your soil, you'll need to start thinking less about those three big numbers, known as N-P-K, on the fertilizer bag. Generations of gardeners have been brought up on 10-10-10 and 39-9-12, but as we learned in chapter 2, nitrogen, phosphorus, and potassium are just three of many nutrients that plants need to survive. How you deliver those nutrients to your lawn is at the core of natural lawn care.

Feed the Soil, Feed the Plant

Proponents of traditional lawn care, which utilizes large amounts of synthetically based chemicals to fertilize grass, will explain accurately that plants can't tell the difference between synthetic and natural fertilizers. Plants are like my son at mealtime. He's hungry and will eat huge quantities of whatever is in front of him. Given his choice, he'd eat pizza, fried chicken sandwiches, and gummy bears, washed down by a sugary carbonated beverage. Even he has learned, though, that too much of a good-tasting thing at the dinner table ultimately turns bad. Lawns are no different. When they are blanketed with instantaneous doses of synthetic fertilizers, they'll try to eat like crazy — and suffer all the bloated aftereffects associated with a human overeating: disease, addiction, and shoddy appearance.

Soil, unlike plants, can definitely tell the difference between synthetic additives that are created in a laboratory and natural foods, which often contain not only the necessary macro- and micronutrients for plant growth, but other beneficial ingredients as well. Healthy soil is living and breathing with organisms,

Fixing Nitrogen Naturally:
The Cornerstone of the Organic System

ALL LIVING THINGS need the element nitrogen. An atom of nitrogen lies at the heart of *all* amino acids and DNA in animals and *all* photosynthesis in plants. Since nitrogen gas comprises about 78 percent of the Earth's atmosphere, you might think we would have plenty of nitrogen anytime we needed it. However, much of that atmospheric nitrogen is inactive, or inert. How we convert it into a form available to grow our grass plants is one of the primary differences between synthetic and natural lawn care.

Nitrogen fixing is defined as any natural or industrial process that combines nitrogen gas with other elements to form nitrogen compounds useful to plants. These compounds are typically ammonia, nitrates, and nitrites.

Nature, of course, has its own methods of fixing nitrogen for plants to use through special microorganisms that live in soil and water. These invisible creatures ingest and excrete nitrogen sources in the soil, allowing the plants to use the nitrogen.

Certain plants known as legumes feed this nitrogen-fixing process. By taking nitrogen from the atmosphere and attaching it to their roots in baglike nodules, plants such as peas, beans, clovers, trefoils, and vetches become nitrogen warehouses for the soil. When the bacteria digest this stored nitrogen, the roots of other plants can then have access to the nitrogen. The key terms related to this phenomenon, and used interchangeably, are "nitrogen cycling" and "mineralization." Every time you add compost to the soil, leave your clippings on the grass, or apply a natural fertilizer rather than a synthetic fertilizer, you're supporting nitrogen cycling. Synthetic fertilizers not only bypass nitrogen cycling; they often slow the mineralization process by killing many of the microorganisms involved.

both large and small. In this natural environment, many nutrients become available to plants only after they've been consumed by soil organisms. When protozoa eat bacteria, or nematodes devour fungi, gases and by-products are slowly but surely released during this process. Those by-products then become food for our lawns.

When this system is working well, nothing is wasted and, in time, little needs to be added into the system in the way of expensive fertilizers. That is, ultimately, the holy grail of natural lawn care. When we reach the point with our soils that no more inputs are necessary, we have achieved freedom. If, on the other hand, we add a lot of unnatural materials to the soil, the delicate balance is lost. Soil organisms don't like synthetic inputs, especially synthetic nitrogen, which can burn everything in sight before it leaches into the subsoil and groundwater. Numerous studies have shown a significant reduction in soil organisms in the presence of synthetic fertilizers; the differences are readily visible under a microscope. Most soil is simply not equipped to hold large doses of foreign substances. A USDA study in 2001 showed that nearly 80 percent of synthetic fertilizer is wasted when they leach through the soil, get washed off from rainwater, or vaporize.

Healthy, organic soil is teeming with earthworms and other organisms.

It's Alive!

An organic way to give lawns what they need, therefore, is to nurture and balance the soil. When you give those microorganisms an organic food source such as compost, their digestion converts these natural foods into carbon dioxide, nitrogen, and other essential elements that the grass can then use to grow. That's why you'll always hear the organic lawn

Nematodes
Root-feeders

Arthropods
Shredders

Arthropods
Predators

Birds

Fungi
Mycorrhizal
fungi,
saprophytic
fungi

Nematodes
Fungal- and
bacterial-feeders

Nematodes
Predators

Organic Matter
Waste, residue, and
metabolites from
plants, animals,
and microbes

Bacteria

Protozoa
Amoebae, flagellates,
and ciliates

Animals

It's All Connected: The Soil Food Web

IN HIGH SCHOOL BIOLOGY we all learned about the food chain. Humans are at the top and every other life-form lies beneath us in descending order, from other mammals, to birds and fish, to insects and worms, down to microscopic life. Claiming no such hierarchy, the "soil food web" — a term coined by Elaine Ingham, a soil scientist in Oregon — offers another explanation for life and its cycles: Everything on Earth is connected. Everything feeds everything else.

"An incredible diversity of organisms make up the soil food web," says Dr. Ingham. "They range in size from the tiniest one-celled bacteria, algae, fungi, and protozoa to the more complex nematodes and microarthropods, to the visible earthworms, insects, small vertebrates, and plants. As these organisms eat, grow, and move through the soil, they make it possible to have clean water, clean air, healthy plants, and moderated water flow."

In the food chain, when one source is in short supply, it can often be replaced — or at least that is how man has approached the issue. When one element in the soil food web gets out of balance, the entire system visibly suffers. Natural lawn care programs, done properly, support all forms of life.

"There are many ways that the soil food web is an integral part of landscape processes," says Ingham. "Soil organisms decompose organic compounds, including manure, plant residue, and pesticides, preventing them from entering water and becoming pollutants. They sequester nutrients that might otherwise enter groundwater, and they fix nitrogen from the atmosphere, making it available to plants."

community talk about adding compost to lawns: quality, finished compost is a great readily available soil food teeming with beneficial organisms. If all you do is coat your lawn with about half an inch of good compost each year, you will eventually have decent turf if you also follow this book's pointers about watering, mowing, and overseeding.

If you're a do-it-yourselfer who just wants to maintain a healthy lawn without synthetic chemicals, keep in mind that your soil is alive with things we can see — earthworms, beetles, and grubs — and a lot of things we cannot see. The more alive your soil becomes, the better suited it will be to grow grass, eliminate weeds, and keep insects and diseases from getting out of control. We'll review specific programs for adding soil life in chapter 7.

Though it's an emerging and complicated area of science, soil life can be measured. Certain kinds of soil tests (see page 47) provide a simple gauge of soil activity by measuring emissions of carbon dioxide. Other soil tests are even able to measure the relationships between fungi and bacteria in the soil. Though these tests can be expensive, consider having the activity of your soil tested if you're going to spend money on a large-scale lawn renovation.

Test Your Soil

Can you tend your lawn organically without a soil test? Absolutely. If you top-dress with compost, water, and mow properly, you can have a decent lawn. But if you're going to spend a lot of money on nutrients, even organic nutrients, you should have a test first. Keep two thoughts in mind before you begin. First, not all soil tests are the same. As you've seen from the rest of this chapter, soil is a complex system that can't be completely measured in levels of N-P-K and pH. Like most things, you get what you pay for. Second, moisture levels and extreme high or low temperatures can skew pH readings. For the best average reading, test soil in mid- to late spring or early fall.

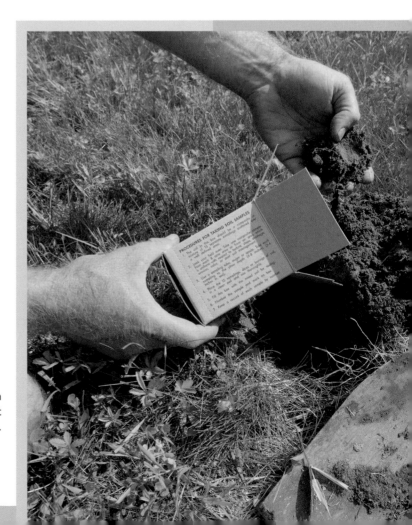

Soil samples should be taken from the root zone of the lawn about 4 inches deep.

pH and Nutrient Tests

These are available through the Cooperative Extension Service at most state universities in the United States, along with several private soil labs. These tests usually give you a good measure of the soil's pH and the available macronutrients potassium and phosphorus, as well as the percentage of organic matter. Most of these tests will also measure the micronutrients sulfur, calcium, magnesium, zinc, iron, and manganese. Some tests also measure nitrogen levels.

The tests come with easy-to-read instructions that generally tell you to dig down to the root zone of your turf —

```
SOIL ANALYSIS REPORT FOR TURFGRASS

SOIL AND PLANT TISSUE TESTING LAB          LAB NUMBER: S060920-138
WEST EXPERIMENT STATION                    BAG NUMBER:  68763
UNIVERSITY OF MASSACHUSETTS
AMHERST, MA 01003

                                           SOIL WEIGHT:  6.43 g/5cc
                                           CROP: ORGANIC LAWN

        SAMPLE SOIL TEST                 COMMENTS:
        WEST EXPERIMENT STATION UMASS
        AMHERST MA  01003

SAMPLE ID: QC 4
- - - - - - - - - - - - - - - - - - - - - - - - - - - - - - - - - - - - - - - - -
    RECOMMENDATIONS FOR ESTABLISHED LAWNS

  Apply  50 lb of calcitic limestone/1000 sq ft.
  Lime may be applied at any time, but mid-autumn or early spring is best.

  Recommendation:  0 lb/1000 sq ft P2O5, and  1 lb/1000 sq ft K2O.

  Many fertilizer sources and rates may provide an acceptable response.
  If you wish to use one or more of the "natural" or "organic" fertilizer
  products available please contact this lab to discuss the use
  of specific materials on turfgrass.




  MICRONUTRIENT    PPM   SOIL_RANGE      MICRONUTRIENT    PPM   SOIL_RANGE
  Boron       (B)  0.2    0.1-2.0        Copper      (Cu)  0.5   0.3-8.0
  Manganese  (Mn) 18.4    3 - 20         Iron        (Fe)  1.7   1.0- 40
  Zinc       (Zn)  1.1    0.1- 70

- - - - - - - - - - - - - - - - - - - - - - - - - - - - - - - - - - - - - - - - -
  SOIL pH    6.0        NITROGEN: NO3-N =   27 ppm
  BUFFER pH  6.7        ORGANIC MATTER:  3.4 % (Desirable range  4-10%)

NUTRIENT_LEVELS:_PPM_|    Low   Medium              High_____   Very High
Phosphorus  (P)   19 |XXXXXXXXXXXXXXXXXXXXXXXXXXXXXXXXX
Potassium   (K)  109 |XXXXXXXXXXXXXXXXXXXXXXXXXXX
Calcium     (Ca) 993 |XXXXXXXXXXXXXXXXXXXXXXXXXXXXXXXX
Magnesium   (Mg) 124 |XXXXXXXXXXXXXXXXXXXXXXXXXXXXXX

CATION EXCH CAP       PERCENT BASE SATURATION       MICRONUTRIENT LEVELS
   7.2 Meq/100g          K= 3.1 Mg=11.0 Ca=53.7        ALL NORMAL

EXTRACTABLE ALUMINUM:   23 ppm  (Soil range: 10-250 ppm)

The lead level in this soil is low.
```

A soil test from your local Cooperative Extension branch will give you an overview of your soil's nutrient content.

about 4 inches deep — in 6 to 10 locations on your average, third-acre lawn. You then blend the soil together in the box or non-airtight bag and mail it off to the lab. If you already know you have multiple soil types on your property, you may need to take multiple tests. In a few weeks you'll receive a computer printout that tells you a story about your soil. It's a good story, with enough information to make you reasonably successful. You'll learn, for example, how many pounds of lime or wood ash to add to raise the pH level or how much sulfur to add to lower the pH. You may also learn that you have plenty of available N-P-K and that your pH is within the 6 to 7 range that most turf likes . . . and yet you might still be unhappy with your lawn. That's where the other soil tests below come into play.

Frequency: Annually for three years, then once every three years.

Bioassay

This comprehensive test is recommended for anyone planning on a substantial lawn renovation or construction. It's the blood count and CAT scan of the soil world, and assesses the amounts and activity of bacteria and fungi in your soil or compost and provides professional advice about how to fix any imbalances. It's expensive — about ten times the cost of a Cooperative Extension test — but it tells you everything you need to know about the nutrition and life of your soil.

Frequency: Optional.

Soil Life Test

Originally developed by scientists at the Woods End Research Laboratory in Maine, this type of test measures the life of your soil or compost. The most basic soil life tests — inexpensive as soil tests go — are simple kits that evaluate the release of carbon dioxide, which indicates the presence of microbial activity. In general, the higher the reading on the test, the better. Soil that produces a low reading can be corrected by adding compost or compost tea. If you're regularly adding compost, you may opt to forgo this test. It can, however, be a good diagnostic tool if you're making the transition to organic lawn care.

Frequency: Optional.

Over-the-Counter Curiosities

Every garden center has them. They range from boxed soil kits filled with plastic jars and pH litmus strips to spike-style gauges that look like the thermometer you stick into your Thanksgiving turkey. In general, I wouldn't bother. If the garden center is charging less than $10 or $15, I can almost guarantee you the gadget has no real usefulness. If the cost is more, the kit may work, but you're better off spending your money on one of these other tests listed below.

Frequency: Not recommended.

4 Grass Is Grass Is Grass?

You probably have about 12½ million of them, but if you're like most us, you rarely give them a thought. They are the foot soldiers of your landscape, guarding your soil against rain, snow, sun, heat, and cold, and yet you may not know a single one of their names. Sure, the occasional Whitman may poetically sing their praises, but most grass plants go through life as the Rodney Dangerfields of gardening. I guess it's hard to respect something that we take so much for granted.

Though I had to give soil top billing, the grass itself comes in a close second on the priority list for a successful natural lawn program. You might think all grass is created equal, until you hear about research programs around the world that spend tens of millions of dollars each year to develop the latest and greatest varieties of lawn grasses. In recent years scientists from both the public and private sectors have acknowledged that our planet can no longer sustain lawns as usual. The pace has quickened dramatically on the selection of grasses for drought tolerance, disease and pest resistance, and growth regulation (in the pursuit of grasses that don't grow as quickly or as tall). Some of the research gives us what we want: Bermuda grasses from Florida that can grow as far north as Virginia and fescues from New Jersey that will make it in Texas. Much of the research is trying to give us what we need: tools to care for our lawns naturally, without wasting water, resources, and effort.

Choosing the Right Grass

1. Assess sunlight, remembering that full sun is at least 6 hours per day and that no lawn grasses like full shade.

2. Investigate water availability, including any water restrictions and normal seasonal rainfall variances in your area.

3. Consider lawn usage, such as sports and other lawn games, social events, and walking patterns.

4. Understand your zone and climate, including temperature highs and lows and frequency of droughts.

5. Gauge your expectations for the lawn's appearance, including bare patches and, especially, summer and winter dormancy.

6. Factor in the maintenance needs, such as mowing, watering, fertilizing, aerating, dethatching, and insect and disease pressure.

7. Check availability in your area, of sod, plugs, sprigs, and seed and shop for the best pricing.

8. Determine if salt is a factor in water or from roadsides and if so, be sure to select only salt-tolerant varieties of grass.

9. Match the right grass with the right soil type and make any necessary modifications in advance of planting.

10. Educate yourself about prevalent insects and diseases in your area and where applicable, pick tolerant varieties of grass.

The Categories

Grass is no different from the rest of the plants in the world of horticulture; some like it hot and some don't. Some can make it where it's dry and some can't. Since the weather varies from one season to another everywhere except for a few subtropical areas of the Deep South and the West, most grasses go through major changes in appearance, health, and overall vitality throughout the year. It's unreasonable to expect a lawn to look great every day, or for a single lawn grass to be all things to all people.

A good start to a healthy lawn is choosing grasses that are suited to your region. Lawn grasses are typically divided into three categories based on geography (see map at right): cool-season grasses for northern areas, warm-season grasses for southern areas, and transition-area grasses for the region in between.

Cool-Season Grasses

If you painted a swath across the top half of the United States and the southern part of Canada, you'd encompass most of the areas where cool-season grasses are naturally suited. They thrive in temperatures from 50° to 80°F and may go into a sleeplike stage known as dormancy in periods of extended heat in summer or in the cold of winter. Their color typically changes to brown during summer dormancy but only to lighter green during winter dormancy — unless the winter is "open" with no snow cover, in which case the grasses will likely brown as well. These grasses usually break dormancy easily when more moderate conditions occur.

Some cool-season grasses are grown in the South where property owners afford themselves of regular irrigation. Tall fescues are the most common type grown in the South. Cool-season grasses are also often overseeded into warm-season grasses in winter by homeowners who don't like the brown appearance of southern lawns in winter. Have you ever watched the Masters Tournament on television and marveled at the green fairways? Well, the greenskeepers at the famed Augusta National Golf Club overseed the fairways with cool-season ryegrass just to be sure their grass looks as near to perfect as possible.

When purchasing cool-season grasses, you'll rarely find 100 percent of any one species in a package. Kentucky bluegrass, perennial ryegrass, and perennial fescues are typically sold in some combination based on site-specific needs. A "park

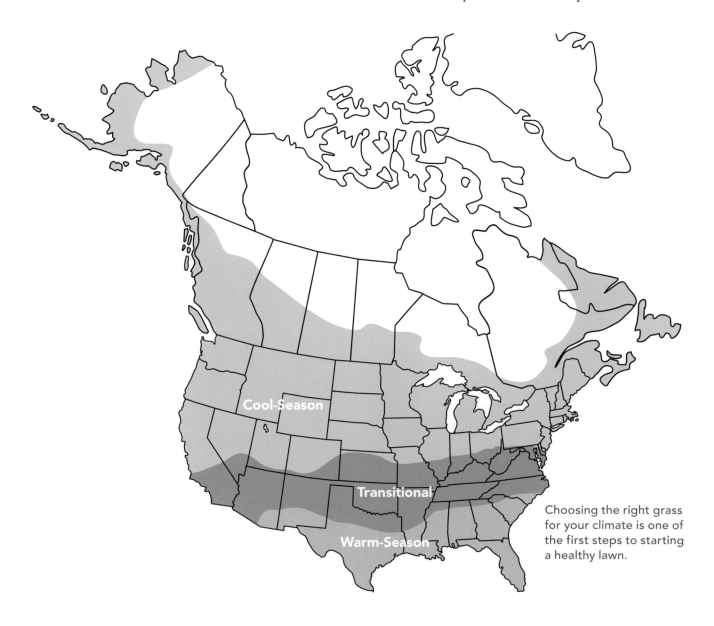

Choosing the right grass for your climate is one of the first steps to starting a healthy lawn.

mix" designed for high foot traffic will often have a high percentage of perennial ryegrass, since it stands up well. A "shade mix" will have higher percentages of fescues, which tolerate shade far better than bluegrass. Bluegrass, ryegrass, and fescue get along remarkably well, as they are all relatively similar in appearance. In fact, planting just one grass species, or a monoculture, is not recommended because it makes the lawn more prone to disease and insect infestation.

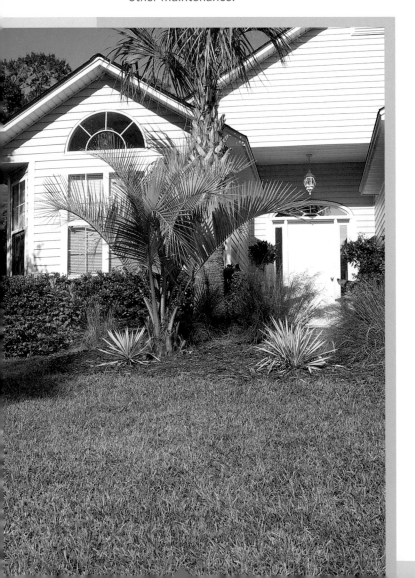

This centipede grass lawn in South Carolina requires little mowing and virtually no other maintenance.

Warm-Season Grasses

If you took that same paintbrush from above and dragged it across the southern third of the United States — with plenty of dips and valleys to accommodate mountains and other microclimates — you'd cover the areas where warm-season grasses dominate. They love it when it's hot, unless it's also dreadfully dry. They usually go brown when it's too cold, but will bounce right back when the weather warms.

Long dominated by two warm-season species, Bermuda grass and St. Augustine grass, the southern lawn care industry has opened its arms at least partway to five other grasses (see chart, page 68) that may all thrive on less maintenance, fertilizer, and water than the Big Two. To varying degrees, these other grasses — Bahia, carpet, centipede, seashore paspalum, and zoysia — are gaining footholds, and in the right situation, can all make excellent lawns. If your lawn care professional tells you otherwise, ask yourself how he or she makes money. By mowing and fertilizing? Probably. If less mowing and fertilizer is required, that may be bad for the lawn care company, but it's great for you and the environment.

Warm-season grasses, with a few exceptions (see box on page 61), generally are not mixed. Appearances and growth habits are often so different that combinations don't work; one usually outcompetes the other. Within most species of warm-season grasses, however, you can find numerous varieties, also known as cultivars, that have been bred for certain characteristics. It is a good idea to plant multiple varieties of each grass within one lawn to increase stress and disease resistance. Endophytes (see below) are not yet available in warm-season grasses.

Transition-Area Grasses

Some areas defy the general categorization of warm-season and cool-season (you probably know them if you live there). States like Kentucky, which averages 87°F in July and 23°F in January, can make it tough on either warm- or cool-season grasses. Colorado can hit –40°F at high elevations and 120°F at low elevations. In those cases, be sure to contact your local Extension agent or lawn care professional to determine the best grasses for your community. When in doubt, it's usually safe to go with a combination of fescues, or to rely on a couple of native grasses that can stand both extreme highs and lows. Buffalo grass and little bluestem are both conditioned to take wide climate and rainfall variances, and may be good alternatives.

Endophytes: The Answer or a Question?

ON THE ONE HAND, beneficial fungi in grasses known as endophytes appear to be the answer to natural lawn care's prayers. After certain ryegrasses and fescues are inoculated with these fungi, they generally have a far greater resistance to diseases and leaf-feeding insects and a better overall vitality, especially in unfertilized soils or drought situations. These grasses have been good sellers since entering the marketplace in the 1990s.

On the downside, though, not everyone agrees that putting endophytes in grasses is a good idea. Among the potential side effects of grasses with endophytes are the following: possible adverse reactions from cattle, horses, and other livestock, as well as birds and rodents, after eating these grasses; the grasses don't biodegrade as quickly as nonendophytic grasses; and endophytes degrade in the grass seed if the seed is not stored at the proper temperature and humidity.

"We are only just beginning to understand how endophytes function in natural communities where endophytic plants and herbivores [plant-eating animals including insects, birds, mammals] coevolve over long periods of time," says David Patriquin, professor of biology at Dalhousie University in Halifax, Nova Scotia. "Endophytic grasses for turf have become widely available only in the last few years, but are already included in many general-use mixes. In my view, not enough consideration has been given to possible deleterious effects of widespread planting of endophytic grasses in turf."

So what should a homeowner do? You could avoid them, at least for now. Plenty of grasses on the market have not been enhanced by endophytes; people have grown lawns for generations without this technology. Or you could proceed with caution. Professor Patriquin is in the minority opinion, but he is correct that endophytically enhanced grasses have become widespread in the marketplace. The benefits are many. All you can really do is learn more about the subject and make your best decision. If you do have farm animals grazing on your property, however, you should definitely *not* grow endophytically enhanced grasses. I could not find any information about the effects of endophytes on dogs and cats while researching this book.

The Choices

What follows is a general overview of the most common lawn grasses for North America. Many of these grasses have had entire books dedicated to their every nuance. Space limitations make it impossible to get all those sorts of details into a book of this size. If you're planning on a major lawn renovation or installation, I strongly encourage you to seek out all possible sources of information in the beginning. That will save you a lot of time and expense in the end.

Cool-Season Grasses
Kentucky bluegrass

Poa pratensis

Part of the American landscape since the earliest European settlers loaded seed on ships and planted it here to feed their livestock, Kentucky bluegrass is still the king of all lawn grasses. Lawn historians tell us the first triumphant scientific evaluation of grass improvements came when 'Merion' Kentucky bluegrass was discovered on the 17th green of the famous Merion Golf Club in Ardmore, Pennsylvania, around 1950, the year Ben Hogan won the U.S. Open Championship at the course. Coincidence? Not likely. Sociologists have long pointed to a connection between the rising popularity of golf and our obsession with the lawn.

When this new cultivar came to market, with its fine, soft foliage and deep blue-green color (which was only enhanced by the addition of the newly emerging synthetic lawn fertilizers), it helped spawn the new American dream: a fairway front yard . . . and backyard, side yard, and median strip.

Kentucky bluegrass is such a nice grass, most homeowners seem to want it to look even better; they don't know when to stop applying fertilizers, weed killers, and other pesticides. Because

Species vs. Cultivar

YOU MAY RECALL high school taxonomy, which is the classification of all living things in descending level of detail from kingdom to phylum to class and finally down to order, family, and genus. As is true with both plants and animals, most things within the same genus have a lot in common but still look quite different. Underneath genus is the classification of species; as it relates to grass, everything within a species appears quite similar, but not always identical. The species Kentucky bluegrass looks visibly different from another grass such as the species Bermuda grass.

For even more clarification, however, botanists refer to cultivars. These are varieties within a species that have subtle differences from each other. 'Zenith' zoysia grass is slightly more drought tolerant than 'Meyer' zoysia grass, for example, but otherwise it's difficult to tell them apart.

Studying cultivar differences can lead to greater success in natural lawn care. If you insist on growing Kentucky bluegrass, a species that generally uses far more water and nitrogen than most other grass species, you can look for the most drought-tolerant bluegrass cultivar, or a bluegrass that grows better on infertile soils. Seed companies will provide listings that make those distinctions.

older Kentucky bluegrass varieties are not deeply rooted compared with other grasses, they don't hold nutrients and water well and need a high level of maintenance to keep up their appearance.

Ongoing breeding efforts at Rutgers University and elsewhere have improved bluegrass's ability to sustain its appearance without as much water and fertilizer. Be sure to study the traits of available bluegrass cultivars from your seed source, and match them against recommendations from your Extension agent or lawn care professional. In most situations, bluegrass is now mixed with perennial ryegrass and fescues to create a diverse lawn capable of withstanding various conditions throughout the year.

In many regions, after all these years, bluegrass is taking a backseat to those ryegrasses and especially fescues, which don't require as much water and fertilizer to look their best.

Other bluegrasses. You may occasionally encounter bluegrasses other than Kentucky in seed mixes and in lawn literature. Rough bluegrass, *Poa trivialis*, has some use in moist, shady areas, but is so thinly rooted that it doesn't work well in most lawn situations. Canada bluegrass, *Poa compressa*, survives poor soils and may be used in low-traffic areas or to hold banks, but it also suffers from an inadequate root system. Annual bluegrass, *Poa annua,* is a weed with no practical application for lawns.

One emerging potential cool-season lawn grass is the ultra-shade-tolerant *Poa supina* 'Supernova', according to tests at Michigan State University. It reportedly needs cool temperatures and plenty of moisture to thrive, and I'm excited to try it at my home in Maine, where it's likely to fit our weather to a tee.

Perennial ryegrass
Lolium perenne

Often combined with Kentucky bluegrass and the various fescues in seed mixes for northern areas, this is a nice, wear-tolerant grass variety. Southerners also use this grass as an off-season green-up when their grasses go brown due to cold. Perennial rye, like annual rye, germinates incredibly quickly even without a whole lot of effort to prepare the soil. If you need to hold an embankment around your home, plant perennial rye.

This grass could replace Kentucky blue at the top of the turf charts, except that it's a bit too well behaved. As a clump-forming grass, it doesn't knit together to form sod, and it won't self-repair an open area of the lawn because it has no rhizomes or stolons to help it creep. It will also struggle outside of full-sun areas; in shade, it may green up quickly in spring before the trees leaf out and then languish until autumn.

Perennial ryegrass should not be confused with annual ryegrass, *Lolium multiflorum*, which can make us all feel like amazing gardeners when it grows quickly and greens up. It will die back, though, during the first real prolonged heat or cold. Beware: Annual ryegrass is far less expensive than its perennial cousin and still often shows up in cheap seed mixes; it's a nice coup for the seed company if it can get you to buy new seed every year.

Note: If you're a southern homeowner with a centipede grass lawn, you should overseed with *annual* ryegrass, not perennial ryegrass, for your winter green-up. The root systems of perennial rye and centipede don't get along.

Fescues

Festuca spp.

By far the most versatile grasses across the widest area, fescues will be the primary component of natural lawns of the future. Once derided as pasture grass that was brought here with bluegrass by the European settlers, fescues have gained favor in the past two generations for their shade tolerance, drought resistance, and evergreen nature. Though still usually referred to as cool-season grasses, even by most professionals, many fescues double as ideal grasses for the transitional zones in the Mid-Atlantic, the Midwest, and the West because of their reasonable heat tolerance.

Any remaining confusion about fescues probably stems from the myriad subcategories within the species. Fescues covered in this book are typically known as either "tall," "chewings," "red," or "hard." For further complication, red fescue is also commonly known as creeping fescue. You might find as many as a half dozen different fescues in a single seed mix, which simply gives the lawn more resilience to multiple situations.

Here's a breakdown of the primary lawn fescues:

Turf-type tall fescue, *Festuca arundinacea.* Simply known as tall fescue in many classifications, the phrase "turf type" has been added in recent years to differentiate the new cultivars from pasture grass. Tall fescues have been used on lawns since 'Kentucky-31' was plucked from a Kentucky farm in 1931. People, especially in the North, weren't all that happy with K-31's weak performance and coarse blades and might have written off tall fescues as an option.

With the arrival of 'Rebel', 'Olympic', 'Houndog', and other cultivars in the 1970s, turf-type tall fescues began their migration toward popularity. Finer textured and denser than their predecessors, turf-type tall fescues offer great year-round color. They may tend to thin out during really hot, dry summers and will usually benefit from a late-summer overseeding. They may also winter-kill slightly in some of the coldest climates, but will usually bounce back when the weather warms.

Tall fescues wear slightly better and are more tolerant of a wider range of soil conditions than other fescues. 'Endeavor', the cultivar indicated on the chart (see page 67), gets high marks for tolerating heat and humidity, and for its dark green color.

'RTF' tall fescue, *F. arundinacea.* For years, the primary complaint about tall fescues as lawn grasses was that the individual plants were clump forming and never weaved together. In the worst-case scenario, tall fescue lawns looked like a series of misfit strangers keeping their distance at a party. That is all changing quickly. A recent introduction, rhizomatous tall fescue ('RTF') sends off rhizomes that knit together to form an even-textured lawn. A tall fescue with rhizomes takes care of the final argument about bluegrass versus fescue, and this new hybrid is a significant development in lawn-grass breeding that scientists will only try to further improve in the years ahead.

Creeping red fescue, *F. rubra.* As the "creeping" in the name suggests, this fescue differentiates itself with short rhizomes that allow it to fill in open spaces in the soil. Any all-fescue lawn will typically have some creeping red in the seed mix to help give the lawn that lush sod appearance. Creeping fescue is also included in many bluegrass mixes.

One of the so-called fine fescues — as opposed to turf-type fescues — creeping red has a lower growth habit than tall fescue and is slightly more shade tolerant. It may not fare quite as well in the stifling heat of some of the transition areas, but it will bounce back when the weather cools. The cultivar 'Flyer I' improves on both the shade and the heat tolerance of creeping fescue, and some people use it as their only grass.

Chewings fescue, *F. rubra var. commutata.* Another fine fescue really similar to creeping red fescue, this is the only grass that truly tolerates shade. Planted in a light, airy loam with plenty of organic matter, chewings fescue can get by on just two hours of sun a day. It is clump forming and doesn't tolerate a lot of foot traffic, just like creeping fescue, but if it's willing to put up with such little sunlight, you can't ask it to do too much more. Grown in sunlight, it will fill

in better and won't require much in the way of fertilizer.

The cultivar 'Shadow II' has dominated the national chewings fescue trials because of its tolerance of drought, shade, and full sun, as well as a leaf texture and color that rival the best of the bluegrasses.

Rhizomes vs. Stolons

ALL GRASSES HAVE ROOTS THAT ANCHOR and nurture the plants. Some species are clump forming, meaning their roots generally expand outward in a circle in the soil as a plant matures, but the plant stays put. Other species have the ability to wander, which allows them to send up new shoots and knit together with other plants nearby into what we commonly refer to as turf sod. The ability of a grass to move about the soil is made possible by the presence of stem runners known as either rhizomes, which are belowground, or stolons, which grow aboveground.

The most popular grass in the South combines both properties within the same species. Bermuda grass sends out stolons *and* rhizomes, which makes it highly aggressive. Common Bermuda grass, which has not been improved through breeding into new cultivars, is in fact quite weedy because it can easily escape from the lawn and into gardens and pathways. Never buy grass seed containing only common Bermuda grass; be sure your selection is a named cultivar.

Bluegrass similarly spreads by rhizomes to create a full, lush carpet. Landscape contractors love it because it forms such a nice, uniform sod that can be harvested and reinstalled in customers' yards. Until recent breeding breakthroughs, fescues were only clump forming, which means they didn't lend themselves well to sodding. A new hybrid cultivar known as rhizomatous tall fescue, or 'RTF', will have wide application and lead to even more breeding improvements in the years ahead.

Hard fescue, *F. longifolia*. The toughest of all the fine fescues in terms of cold and heat tolerance, this is a great grass for a low-maintenance lawn. A bit slower growing than the others, it is a true minimalist that doesn't need a lot of TLC.

The cultivar 'Discovery' has earned raves from national judges for drought and shade tolerance. Because it contains endophytes (see page 53), it also offers resistance to many common lawn-grass diseases.

Fairway wheatgrass

Agropyron cristatum

Primarily grown as a forage crop on the Great Plains, this species gives natural lawn growers a truly low-maintenance option for cold climates. Imported from Russia and introduced in the United States via Canada, it can handle the extremes of summer and winter temperatures in the mountains, provided the heat isn't too prolonged. Shorter and more finely textured than most wheatgrasses, this species, also known as crested wheatgrass, tolerates drought and grows vigorously without being fertilized.

The cultivar 'Ephraim', with a low and slow growth habit, is ideal for lawns where you only want to mow four or five times a year.

Bent grass

Agrostis palustris

Some readers may be surprised that I'm not including bent grass on the chart on pages 66–67. While it's true this grass is luxuriantly fine textured and low growing, it really has no place in a natural home lawn, with the possible exception of the Pacific Northwest. The maintenance required in mowing and fertilizing is just too much. This grass is also one of the most disease and insect prone of all the cool-season lawn grasses.

Warm-Season Grasses
Bermuda Grass

Cynodon spp.

Called the sports turf of the South, Bermuda grass is the Kentucky bluegrass of Dixieland. When the PGA golfers make their spring swing through Florida, while the rest of the country is still frigid, they're usually playing on Bermuda fairways. This deep green grass just loves the sun; in fact, it won't tolerate shade and cool temperatures below 50° or 60°F. Bermuda grass is typically mowed quite low, to an inch or less, which is an appearance that draws us all in.

Common Names vs. Botanical Names

WHERE APPLICABLE, both common and botanical names appear in this book. People in different regions often have different common names for grasses. For example, in South Carolina they call St. Augustine grass "Charleston grass" and folks I met in Georgia had me scratching my head when they called perennial ryegrass "feathergrass," but the botanical names are the same everywhere. The botanical Latin names are listed in italics.

On the face of it, Bermuda lawns do have much to offer. They fill in quickly; lawns started from seed can be fairly lush within three months. They tolerate salt and heavy foot traffic, and if your family plays a lot of games on the lawn, this is probably the grass for you if your climate is suitable.

On the downside, Bermuda grass requires the most nitrogen of any of the warm-season species to stay dark green, and the nitrogen also tends to attract insects, such as sod webworms, and promotes heavy thatch buildup. The key to success is to promote good soil fertility and natural nitrogen cycling (see page 42), so that quick bursts of nitrogen through synthetic means are not necessary.

Bahia grass

Paspalum notatum

Used for lawns in the South from Florida north to the Carolinas and west to California, this is among the most environmentally friendly lawn grasses on the planet. Highly drought tolerant, Bahia establishes easily from seed, requires little fertilizer, and has great natural disease and insect resistance. You want more reasons to grow it? Well, it also survives in a variety of soils from sandy to clay, and can even take low mowing and foot traffic.

So why isn't Bahia grass growing at three out of four South Florida homes instead of St. Augustine grass? Probably it's the seed heads, and an old reputation for putting out a scanty turf cover. During the peak growing season of July through September, Bahia will begin to send out seed from the top of its stems unless you mow frequently. I don't mind the appearance; some folks apparently do. And while it's true that some of the older Bahia grasses were relegated to the ditch as bank covers, improved breeding efforts have resulted in Bahia 'Argentine' for the hottest regions of the South and 'Pensacola' for cooler regions. They make really great lawns, but many traditional

Lawn Wear vs. Leaf Texture

WE'VE PROBABLY all been seduced at one time or another by the soft, fine blades of Kentucky bluegrass. That wonderful sensation when walking through it barefoot is caused by a leaf texture that is perky but not pointed, supple but not stout. I was shocked the first time I got off a plane in Florida and felt St. Augustine underfoot; I doubt Walt Whitman ever would have written *Leaves of Grass* had he lived at my father's winter home, where sandals are required for a comfortable walk on the lawn.

Oddly enough, there is no correlation between leaf texture and lawn wear. Fine fescues and bluegrass hold up far better to foot traffic and field sports than coarse-leaved grasses like St. Augustine and centipede.

lawn care companies still turn up their noses because of one other attribute: Bahia grass will begin to suffer after applications of synthetic weed killers. In a natural lawn care system, of course, that doesn't matter.

Centipede grass
Eremochloa ophiuroides

I had a really interesting conversation with one lawn care professional about this grass. "If someone is growing centipede on his lawn, I won't even bother going back," he said. "He doesn't need me. You hardly ever have to mow it and it doesn't need any nitrogen. There's no business in centipede." And he thought that was a bad thing.

Called the lazy man's grass, centipede is the answer to natural lawn care's prayers. I spent a lovely September day with Robert Houser, an organic lawn care professional from Charleston, South Carolina, who showed me all sorts of centipede lawns that appeared lush and green even after a long season of drought. He was treating them with a couple of annual applications of compost tea (see chapter 7), and that was about it.

"I often go two or more weeks without having to mow," he said. "You probably only get about three inches of growth in an average year, but the grass always looks good."

You can't have everything, though. Centipede is not a good sports turf and won't take heavy foot traffic.

In 2001 the first new cultivar of centipede grass, 'TifBlair', was introduced by Dr. Wayne Hanna at the USDA

Breeding vs. Genetic Engineering

THIS IS AS GOOD A PLACE in the book as any to touch on the sensitive subject of genetic engineering and how it's different from simple breeding. In horticulture and in this book, *breeding* refers to taking pollen from one plant and dabbing it on another in hopes of creating offspring that combine the traits of the two parent plants. In other words, human bumblebees are trying to get a leg up on Mother Nature by speeding up the process of natural selection. In breeding, only plants within the same species are involved; it's impossible to naturally breed a bluegrass plant with a Bermuda grass plant.

In genetic engineering, scientists insert genetic material from unrelated species — of plants, animals, or bacteria — into parent plants. At least one major company is testing genetically altered lawn grasses that resist weed killers. That means lawnkeepers could spray the weed killer but the grass would live.

Though this book is not the place for a full-blown argument about genetic engineering, the practice is not accepted as part of a natural lawn care program, or by nationally recognized organic standards. It's best to learn more about the process to help you make an informed decision.

Experiment Station in Tifton, Georgia. By exposing seeds of common centipede grass to radiation, which caused a genetic mutation, he developed a strain of centipede grass that is far more cold hardy and tolerant of acid soils. Organic purists may object to this cultivar due to the radiation; it is a choice you should make for yourself.

Zoysia

Zoysia spp.

Talk about wild marketing claims. When this grass hit the lawn care scene with a vengeance, back in the '70s and '80s, it sounded as if you could just plop a few plugs in the ground and get out of the way. Most of us in the North who had never heard of "plugging" lawns (see page 84) were bemused, but those of us who tried the grass were less than impressed.

It's not that zoysia isn't a fine grass. From Florida north to Maryland, zoysia is one of the better grasses on the market, far more attractive than St. Augustine, carpet, or centipede grass. North of Maryland, however, the grass turns brown for about six months of the year; we're spoiled in that regard up north. When there's no snow on the ground, we expect our lawns to be green except between January and March.

The good news is that zoysia lawns are now possible from seed. The cultivar 'Companion' germinates readily and then spreads by rhizomes and stolons to fill in nicely, much more quickly than some early zoysia cultivars. Seeding brings the cost of a zoysia lawn more in line with

Bermuda grass and makes it less expensive than a sodded or plugged St. Augustine lawn, so zoysia should become more common in the next decade.

It's fairly disease and insect resistant, and its growth habit helps it outcompete many weeds. Zoysia is often grown in a mix with tall fescue in transition areas; the zoysia thrives in the summer, and the fescue takes over the rest of the year.

St. Augustine grass

Stenotaphrum secundatum

When my father retired and moved to a new Florida development, the local

Blends vs. Mixtures

ALMOST ALL GRASS SEED in garden centers is packaged as either a "mixture" or a "blend." Even though the words are occasionally used interchangeably, they often mean something quite different. A mixture contains more than one type of grass species, maybe carpet grass and centipede grass, or zoysia with tall fescue. The package label will indicate the percentage by weight of each type, along with a cultivar or hybrid name and the expected germination rate of the seed.

A blend contains only one species of grass, with multiple named cultivars of the same species. For instance, one company offers a blend of 'Princess 77' and 'Sultan', two hybrid Bermuda grasses. Each variety has certain desirable traits and together can improve the quality of your lawn.

When possible, it is better to go with a mixture to increase the genetic diversity of the lawn, which will generally increase its resiliency. Some grasses mix reasonably well with others, with the notable exceptions of Bermuda, St. Augustine, and paspalum grasses, whose appearance and growth habit are just so different from those of other grasses.

covenants gave him three choices in grass: St. Augustine, St. Augustine, or St. Augustine. The landscapers love it because it does tolerate a little bit of shade, but mostly because it requires frequent mowing and fertilization, so they make a lot of money.

To me, St. Augustine grass has little place in a natural lawn care program. Seed is not commercially available, so you can't combat a weed problem by dethatching and overseeding. When weeds do infiltrate St. Augustine lawns, it usually takes multiple applications of hormone-based weed killer to hold them back; many common synthetic weed killers are not viable for use on St. Augustine. Insects, especially chinch bugs, are a major problem, and diseases can ravage the grass unless conditions are perfect. Furthermore, it doesn't tolerate foot traffic, it has huge problems with thatch, and the stolons are ugly when the grass thins in bare spots.

Enough said. You can find all sorts of other grasses for your natural lawn.

Carpet grass

Axonopus affinis

Creeping along with stolons, even in fairly infertile soil, carpet grass is another low-maintenance alternative to St. Augustine or Bermuda grass. As with Bahia grass, the primary objection is tall seed heads that continually pop up in the growing season. If you keep these mowed regularly, you'll be rewarded the rest of the year with a lawn that doesn't require a lot of attention.

Though carpet grass has not been improved in any breeding programs, it is the only native grass among the seven primary warm-season grass choices. It is ideally suited for moist locations with low soil pH, although it won't tolerate salty sites. It has the best shade tolerance

Dormant vs. Evergreen

ALL GRASSES COMMONLY used for turf have a built-in ability to enter a sleep state known as dormancy, which protects the plants from excess heat, cold, or drought. Some grasses stay green year-round in areas where the climate is appropriate. In areas of South Florida where the temperature rarely goes below 55°F for extended periods, for example,

Bermuda, zoysia, and St. Augustine grasses will remain green through the winter.

In areas farther north, these grasses will go dormant and turn brown in the coldest months. Some cool-season grasses, like Kentucky bluegrass, perennial ryegrass, and the fescues, are green throughout the winter, even under the snow. The only time they'll go dormant

and turn brown is during extreme dry periods of summer or during cold periods of an open winter with no snow cover.

In the South, homeowners can overcome the brown appearance of winter dormancy by overseeding cool-season varieties into their lawns (see page 181). To learn more about how watering relates to dormancy, see chapter 8.

of the warm-season grasses and will tolerate reasonable foot traffic.

For a well-rounded turf mix that includes carpet grass and centipede grass, look for 'Pennspeed' at your local seed supplier.

Seashore paspalum

Paspalum vaginatum

This truly is the grass of the new millennium. Few people beyond some southern universities had even heard of seashore paspalum until about 1999. When word began to spread, certain aspects of the grass's performance were quickly exaggerated. You might have thought the new wonder turf would grow on pavement with no water.

As the truth has been weeded out from myth, what has emerged is a tremendous alternative, especially to Bermuda grass, in low-mowing, low-fertility, and low-water or poor-water-quality situations. Noninvasive and yet robust in growth, seashore paspalum has already been planted on golf courses from Florida to Texas and is beginning to make its way into more and more homeowners' yards, especially now that a seeded variety is readily available.

To fully understand this grass, I got together with the breeder for a question-and-answer session (see page 64). R. R. "Ronny" Duncan spent a long and distinguished career in turf breeding and analysis at Auburn University in Alabama before his career culminated with the introduction of seashore paspalum.

Transition-Area Grasses
Buffalo grass

Buchloe dactyloides

Texas likes to lay claim to this American native, but it also grows naturally in many areas of the West and Midwest. Buffalo grass is showing up in more and more university test trials, and will be one of the primary lawn grasses we turn to in the future when the proverbial water well really does run dry.

Once it's established, buffalo grass can survive on little water and with virtually no extra nitrogen. It actually grows best in areas with less than 25 inches of annual rainfall, which is the major reason why most people don't grow buffalo grass lawns in the East and in the Pacific Northwest.

Uniform and attractive with a green to blue-green color, its mature height is only about 6 inches. Its narrow leaves curl slightly downward, making it appear even shorter. It may not grow in as densely as Bermuda or St. Augustine grass, but the blades are much finer. I find it to be a far more pleasing turf overall in terms of texture.

If you need to remember anything about this grass, it's to leave it alone. You can literally kill it with kindness. Give it too much water or fertilizer and the problems begin. If you mow it too often, you'll only be wasting your electricity or gas; it just doesn't need it.

When you're shopping, look for '609' or 'Stampede', two varieties that have come out of university breeding programs in recent years. Both spread fairly quickly and provide nice, full coverage.

Seashore Paspalum: A Versatile Grass from the South

TO LEARN MORE about an exciting new lawn grass available to homeowners, I went to the man credited with bringing seashore paspalum to the market. R. R. "Ronny" Duncan takes the mystery out of his discovery and sees a bright future for what he calls "the environmental turfgrass."

Q: Mowing heights for seashore paspalum seem unusually low, especially compared with most grasses. Can you give us a good mowing program?

A: Mowing height in home lawns should not be over 1 inch. Heights over 1¼ inches will invite disease problems and should be avoided. This grass is no more difficult to mow than other lawn grasses, but you need to keep the mower blades sharp. I use a mulching mower and try to sharpen the blades monthly. I start at ¾ inch coming out of winter, then raise the height to 1 inch during the heat of the summer.

R. R. "Ronny" Duncan

Q: Some of the literature says this grass actually likes to be watered with ocean water. Is that true?

A: I really discourage that. My greatest fear is that people will load the soil with so much salt that the land becomes sterile. Some common sense must come in here. Yes, the grass has the capability to tolerate poor water quality and very high salts, but environmentally that is not sustainable in the soil.

Excessive irrigation has also led to disease challenges. You must irrigate infrequently but deeply. In essence, you train the roots down deep into the soil profile. If you irrigate every night, the roots will stay shallow and you will have plenty of problems with disease. Paspalum has twice the root volume of Bermuda grasses, which makes it far more drought tolerant.

Q: Is this strictly a shoreline turf?

A: The grass can be grown in zones similar to hybrid Bermuda grass. With the current cultivars on the market, you can draw a line from Virginia Beach to Raleigh to Chattanooga to Little Rock to Dallas to Albuquerque to Las Vegas and on to Sacramento, essentially USDA Zones 7 to 10.

Q: Can you talk about the range of soil conditions seashore paspalum tolerates?

A: I have successfully planted this grass in sands, mucks, silty soils, expanding and contracting clays, and nonexpanding clays. It has an uncanny ability to root if given half a chance. It evolved on sand dunes exposed only to ocean- and rainwater for nutrients and moisture.

Q: Can you provide a good fertilizer program for the grass?

A: On home lawns, you should be applying about 1 or 2 pounds of actual nitrogen per year in a spoon-feeding scenario. The most abused practice on this grass is too much nitrogen fertilizer. This grass has the most efficient uptake of nutrients of all lawn grasses and it generally has low requirements for most nutrients. Maintaining calcium and the micronutrient levels is actually more important than nitrogen. I also use a seaweed product on any weak areas or scalped areas to enhance root development.

Q: Does seashore paspalum have any invasive tendencies?

A: Unlike Bermuda grass, seashore paspalum will not take over surrounding areas if left unattended. It has been in Florida and Hawaii since the early 1950s and with a 365-day growing season has not gone where it is not wanted.

Seashore paspalum creeps through the soil with underground stems known as rhizomes.

Little bluestem

Schizachyrium scoparium

I've seen this prairie grass all across the United Sates and Canada, but only recently thought about its application as a lawn grass. One of the most common grasses on our continent prior to the rapid expansion of our population and rampant naturalization of grasses from Europe, common little bluestem sort of minds its own business as a short, blue-green, clump-forming stalwart.

Some lawn care professionals mix bluestem with hard fescue for a drought-tolerant, low-maintenance lawn seed mix that stays green year-round in most climates other than the Deep South. On its own, little bluestem behaves like a warm-season grass, in that it will brown out in cold weather and be slow to green up in spring. The cool-season fescue will hold the lawn's green appearance in winter, however. Wherever mowing isn't necessary, this type of lawn can look magical in summer by letting the wisps of blue grow out their seed heads. Depending on how you want to manage your own lawn, you could get away with mowing only a few times a year. Think of what you could do with all that extra time.

'Camper' is a cultivar that thrives in colder climates; 'Cimarron' grows well in more southern locales.

Turfgrass: The 24-Point Test

The following chart is intended to give you general comparisons of the most commonly grown lawn grasses in North America. "General" is the key word. Within most of the species are varieties that may offer slightly different characteristics from the ones listed here. Whether you're starting from scratch or planning a lawn renovation, you should match your needs and desires for a lawn against the information in the chart.

Here are a few other points to keep in mind: The chart is based on growing from seed (except for St. Augustine grass); all lawn seeds need moisture while germinating and establishing, even if water requirements are listed as "low"; the chart should be used as a starting point only, and homeowners should contact Extension agents or turf professionals for further recommendations; check area maps, which indicate where a grass is commonly grown; in most cases, "improved cultivar" is just one of many possible choices; the following information comes from hundreds of sources, including universities, seed companies, sod companies, Extension agents, lawn professionals, the National Turfgrass Evaluation Program (NTEP), and personal observation; and the information is geared toward home lawns.

Cool-Season Grasses

	Bluegrass
USDA zones	3–9
Origin	Europe
pH range	5.8–7.0
Germination days	14–30
Establishment	Slow
Seed rate (lb/1,000 sq. ft.)	2–3
Mowing height (in.)	2–4
Growth spread	Rhizomes
Water requirement	High
Wear	Excellent
Nitrogen (lb/1,000 sq. ft.)	4–5
Salt tolerance	Low
Heat tolerance	Low
Cold tolerance	Excellent
Maintenance	High
Ideal soils	Loam-clay
Shade tolerance	Poor
Insect resistance	Low
Disease resistance	Low
Color	Dark
Leaf texture	Fine
Mower	Rotary
Planting time	Aug.–Sept.
Improved cultivar	'Midnight'

Bluegrass

Fescue blend

Perennial rye

	Perennial rye	*Fairway wheat*	*Red fescue*	*Chewings fescue*	*Hard fescue*	*Tall fescue*
	3–9	2–6	4–9	4–9	3–9	4–9
	Europe	Russia	Europe	Europe	Europe	Europe
	5.8–7.2	6.5–8.0	5.3–7.2	5.0–8.0	5.5–8.0	5.5–8.0
	5–10	10–20	6–10	6–10	7–14	10–14
	Fast	Slow	Fast	Fast	Medium	Fast
	8–10	.75	6–7	7–8	8–10	7–8
	3–4	3–4	3–4	2–3	3–4	3–4
	Clumps	Rhizomes	Rhizomes	Clumps	Clumps	Clumps
	Medium	Low	Low	Low	Low	Low
	Excellent	Medium	Medium	Low	Low	Good
	2–3	1–2	2–3	2–3	2–3	2–3
	Medium	Medium	Medium	Medium	High	Medium
	Medium	Low	Low	Medium	Medium	Medium
	Good	Excellent	Good	Good	Good	Good
	Low	Low	Low	Low	Low	Low
	Loam-clay	Sand-loam	Silt-loam	Sand-loam	Silt-loam	All
	Low	Poor	Good	Excellent	Good	Good
	High	High	Good	Good	Good	High
	High	High	Good	Good	Good	Medium
	Medium	Medium	Medium	Medium	Medium	Medium
	Fine	Medium	Fine	Fine	Fine	Medium
	Rotary	Rotary	Rotary	Rotary	Rotary	Rotary
	Aug.–Sept.	Aug.–Sept.	Aug.–Sept.	Aug.–Sept.	Aug.–Sept.	Aug.–Sept.
	'Integra'	'Ephraim'	'Flyer I'	'Shadow II'	'Discovery'	'Endeavor'

Turfgrass: The 24-Point Test

Warm-Season Grasses		
	Bahia	*Bermuda*
USDA zones	8–10	7–10
Origin	South America	Africa
pH range	5.5–7.2	5.8–7.5
Germination days	14–28	7–14
Establishment	Medium	Fast
Seed rate (lb/1,000 sq. ft.)	1	2
Mowing height (in.)	2–3	1–2
Growth spread	Rhizomes	Rhizomes/stolons
Water requirement	Low	Medium
Wear	Good	Good
Nitrogen (lb/1,000 sq. ft.)	1–2	4–5
Salt tolerance	Low	Good
Heat tolerance	Good	Excellent
Cold tolerance	Poor	Medium
Maintenance	Low	High
Ideal soils	All	All
Shade tolerance	High	Low
Insect resistance	High	Medium
Disease resistance	High	Medium
Color	Light	Dark
Leaf texture	Coarse	Medium
Mower	Rotary	Rotary or reel
Planting time	April	April
Improved cultivar	'Argentine'	'Mohawk'

Centipede

St. Augustine

Seashore paspalum

Zoysia

Centipede	St. Augustine	Seashore paspalum	Zoysia	Carpet grass
7–10	9–10	7–10	6–10	7–10
Asia	Africa	South Africa	Asia	North America
4.8–6.5	5.5–7.5	5.5–8.0	6.2–7.2	5.0–7.0
14–21	N/A	7–14	15–30	10–14
Medium	Medium	Fast	Slow	Fast
.5	N/A	1	2	7
2–3	2–3	¾–1	2–3	2–3
Stolons	Stolons	Rhizomes/stolons	Rhizomes/stolons	Stolons
Low	Medium	Low	Low	Medium
Low	Medium	Medium	Medium	Medium
1–2	3–4	1–2	3–4	2–3
Low	Good	Excellent	Good	Low
Good	Good	Excellent	Good	Good
Medium	Poor	Medium	Good	Medium
Low	High	Low	Medium	Low
All	Sand-silt	All	All	Sand
Medium	Medium	Low	Medium	Low
Medium	Low	Low	Medium	Medium
Medium	Low	Medium	Medium	High
Light	Medium	Dark	Dark	Medium
Coarse	Coarse	Medium	Medium	Coarse
Rotary or reel	Rotary	Rotary or reel	Rotary or reel	Rotary or reel
April	April	April	April	April
'TifBlair'	'Floratam'	'Seaspray'	'Companion'	N/A

Turfgrass: The 24-Point Test

Transition-Area Grasses	Bluestem	Buffalo
USDA zones	3–9	5–9
Origin	North America	North America
pH range	4.5–8.0	6.5–8.5
Germination days	21–30	14–30
Establishment	Slow	Slow
Seed rate (lb/1,000 sq. ft.)	2	5
Mowing height (in.)	3–5	3–5
Growth spread	Clumps	Stolons
Water requirement	Low	Low
Wear	Medium	Medium
Nitrogen (lb/1,000 sq. ft.)	0–1	0–1
Salt tolerance	High	Low
Heat tolerance	High	Good
Cold tolerance	Good	Good
Maintenance	Low	Low
Ideal soils	Sandy	Silt-clay
Shade tolerance	Low	Low
Insect resistance	High	High
Disease resistance	High	High
Color	Blue-green	Gray-green
Leaf texture	Fine	Fine
Mower	Rotary	Rotary
Planting time	April	April
Improved cultivar	'Camper'	'Stampede'

Hudson, Quebec

AT THE TIME, scarcely anyone in North America noticed. In May of 1991 the small town of Hudson, Quebec, located just west of Montreal, adopted a bylaw restricting the use of lawn pesticides on all property, privately held or municipally owned, within town limits. The news barely made a ripple a year later when two lawn care companies were hit with a fine of $300 (Canadian) for spraying pesticides in the town.

What happened next, however, set in motion a chain of prescient events.

The lawn companies, angry about losing their share of the few hundred potential customers in Hudson, took the town to local court . . . and lost. The companies appealed to Quebec Superior Court . . . and lost again. Still not willing to let the matter rest, the companies appealed all the way to the Canadian Supreme Court. In a process that took two years and hundreds of thousands of dollars, the little town that could won the case for good on June 28, 2001. The lawn companies even had to pay Hudson's court costs.

"Permitting the town to regulate pesticide use is consistent with international law's 'precautionary principle,' which states it is better to be overly cautious than to create a potential risk to the environment," wrote Justice Claire L'Heureux-Dubé in defending the court's unanimous decision.

Spurred by Hudson's initiative, other Canadian cities and towns took up the fight. As a result, it is now against the law to apply lawn pesticides around homes or public spaces anywhere in the entire province of Quebec. In Hudson, homeowners may petition the town for an exemption in the case of a severe insect infestation, but few people bother.

"In 2006, we granted only eight permits for spraying pesticides," said Nathalie LaVoie, the town's urban planning manager. "It used to be a few more, but these days people have become accepting of a few weeds and insects on their lawns."

Recognition as North America's first town to take such as strong stand on pesticides provides a sense of civic pride for Hudson's 5,600 residents.

"Everyone here is aware of what we accomplished," said retiree Gordon Drewett, who was chairman of the Hudson Environment Committee throughout the court battles. "We still have beautiful gardens and lawns — maybe a few more dandelions than some towns might. You even see people bending over and pulling out weeds by hand. I'm not sure you see that everywhere else, but there's a strong sense here that taking the stand against pesticides was the right thing to do."

5 Starting Off Right

in a perfect lawn world, the 2 feet of fertile soil gardeners in England like to brag about would surround all of our homes. We'd have plenty of sun, with only occasional slow, steady rain. We'd even have willing, able-bodied teenagers in the house who couldn't wait to water, rake, and mow.

And then there's the real world. Many of our homes sit in a sea of gravel, or heavy clay, or whatever excuse for soil the building contractor left behind. Sun varies, rain is unreliable, and as for the teenagers . . . as the old-timers say, they don't make 'em like they used to.

Still, if you've made it this far in the book, you're probably ready to give a lawn a try anyway. This chapter is separated into two sections, one for those of you who have the luxury of starting from scratch and the other for folks who want to refurbish their existing lawn. The processes are substantially distinct, with different costs, timetables, and inherent expectations, yet both can bring your lawn around to the same place — a haven where you can get the most out of your life at home.

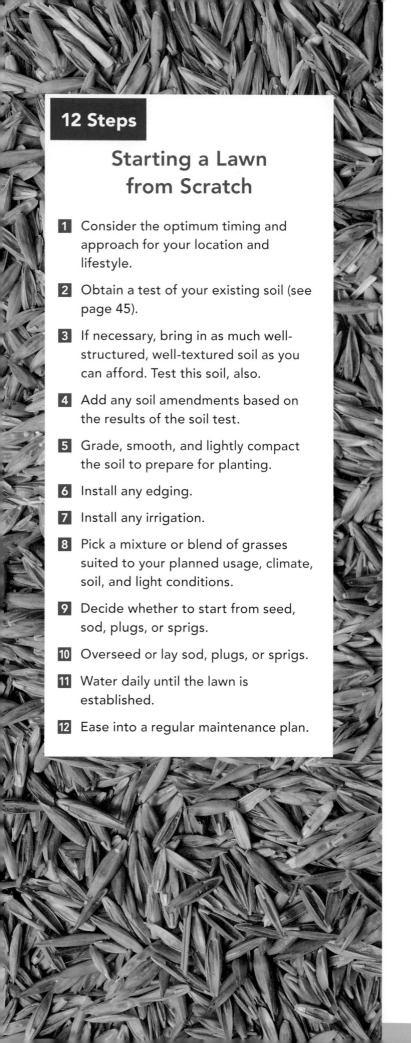

Starting a Lawn from Scratch

1. Consider the optimum timing and approach for your location and lifestyle.

2. Obtain a test of your existing soil (see page 45).

3. If necessary, bring in as much well-structured, well-textured soil as you can afford. Test this soil, also.

4. Add any soil amendments based on the results of the soil test.

5. Grade, smooth, and lightly compact the soil to prepare for planting.

6. Install any edging.

7. Install any irrigation.

8. Pick a mixture or blend of grasses suited to your planned usage, climate, soil, and light conditions.

9. Decide whether to start from seed, sod, plugs, or sprigs.

10. Overseed or lay sod, plugs, or sprigs.

11. Water daily until the lawn is established.

12. Ease into a regular maintenance plan.

Starting from Scratch

Here's a hypothetical choice: You can have home A surrounded by bare ground or you can have the same home on lot B surrounded by green grass. The real estate agents will tell you the choice is obvious. Everyone goes for the grass, even if it's really not great grass.

At our most recent house, which was of fairly new construction, I was excited that there was very little front lawn, other than a lot of scrub weeds growing right up to the front porch. I saw the blank canvas as an opportunity to begin this new lawn the right way. I was able to plant only the amount of grass I wanted, not a preexisting patch that I felt obligated to mow. I was able to select the species of grass I wanted to live with for many years, not something I needed to tolerate in the meantime. I was also able to select the best materials, from the soil to the seed, sod, and fertilizer. I didn't have to guess what was underneath the grass, because I had put it there myself.

Before I got started with my lawn makeover, the ground in front of our new home was covered in weeds and scrub grasses.

Timing the Installation

First off, you should take the time to check building codes in your city or town. You may need a permit to begin moving around substantial quantities of soil or to bring heavy equipment onto your property to begin the digging process. Most towns are fairly lenient when it comes to lawn construction, but you don't want to be bogged down later by a fine or by having to explain yourself to a code enforcement officer.

You should also call your local electricity supplier to determine the location of any underground power lines. A copy of your plot plan showing the location of any wells, sewage pipes, and underground utilities would also be useful. Mark any known lines for your cable, phone, gas, and electricity before you begin. In the Northeast, an organization known as Dig Safe should be called prior to any underground excavation. They come in and mark the location of any utility lines prior to excavation work. Similar organizations exist across North America.

Time of year and time of life come into play in the decision of when to put in the lawn. Contractors will install lawns almost any time of year. Even in northern New England, I've seen sod go down as late as December and as early as March. If you're doing it yourself in the North, go for late August through early October. Lawns installed in autumn will have a chance to establish their roots through the late fall, winter, and spring prior to the stress of summer. Lawns put down in spring barely have time to become established before the threat of heat, drought, and insect infestation. Far more weed seeds are moving around in spring than autumn, too, a major factor if you're starting from seed. In the South you can also install the lawn in August to give it time to establish prior to winter dormancy, but most folks begin their lawns in April and May, after dormancy ends and prior to the heat of summer.

The other time-related consideration centers on aftercare. Establishing a new lawn is like caring for a newborn child;

Anticipating Irrigation

IN-GROUND WATERING SYSTEMS can be installed at any time, even in existing landscapes, but they are far less invasive if you put them in during lawn construction. That way, you won't have to tear up any turf.

This is also a good time to think about the lawn design as it relates to your watering needs. Are you planting turf outside the reach of an irrigation system, or in areas that are difficult to reach by hose? If so, ask yourself if that grass is really necessary; consider a lawn alternative instead.

it needs us around in the early days for plenty of nurturing. If your new lawn goes completely dry, it can easily die and therefore waste some, although not all, of your effort. In general, you should plan on a month or two of constant babying a lawn started from seed or sprigs and two or three weeks for a sodded or plugged lawn.

Preparing the Soil

If you're making the investment to start from scratch and are intent on a natural lawn care system, start with a soil test from your local soil-testing service (see chapter 3 for more information) to get an overall view of the nutrient needs, pH, and organic content of your soil.

Be wary of contractors who leave behind only a scant coating of soil under sod after new construction.

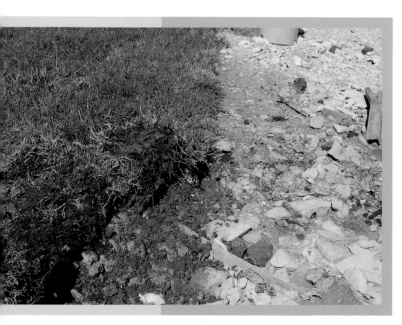

From what I've seen firsthand from East Coast residential construction in the past 20 years, the amount of top-soil left behind by building contractors is usually woefully inadequate. Mother Nature isn't typically all that generous either, unless you live in a known fertile agricultural area. The ideal soil depth for a lawn is a minimum of 6 inches, and you should go for deeper if you can afford it. Anything less will cost you far more in watering, disease and weed pressure, and poor appearance.

It's a good idea to test any new soil you bring in, too, and consider blending it with a bulk load of healthy compost in a ratio of 2 parts soil to 1 part compost, or even a 1 to 1 ratio. Finding a local contractor with a soil mixer is ideal, but soil and compost can also be blended reasonably well on the ground with the one-time use of a rototiller. Just don't go gung-ho with the rototiller, because it can damage soil structure (see page 177.)

Don't skimp on soil. Just don't. Preparing the soil is the single most important factor in new lawn construction. If you don't have the money for soil, delay construction of the lawn until you do. Check the table on page 77 to determine how much soil and compost you'll need. You'll see that adding 4 inches of soil to a 5,000-square-foot lawn requires about 62 cubic yards, costing more than $1,000. Believe it or not, that will be paid back in time through increased vigor of your grass, reduced watering and fertilizing, and a dramatically improved appearance.

Good Grading

Depending on the scale of the job, you may want to consider renting a small tractor with a bucket loader, a small bulldozer, or an attachment known as a grader blade or power rake. If you have the time and are physically able, try doing the job manually with a landscape rake, a wide, metal-tined device about 30 to 48 inches across. Don't rely on the standard metal rake you probably have in your garage; it's not wide enough to give you a nice, even grade.

The goal is to spread the soil evenly, without dips or divots, out away from the home's foundation. It is always a good idea to start closest to any buildings and work outward, making sure the finished grade will never force water back toward the foundation.

A wide landscape rake makes easy work of smooth grading during preparation for sodding, plugging, sprigging, or seeding.

How Much Compost or Soil Do I Need?

Amount of Compost or Soil (in cubic yards)

Area	Depth (in inches)							
	½	1	1½	2	2½	3	3½	4
100 sq. ft.	⅙	⅓	½	⅔	¾	1	1⅙	1¼
500 sq. ft.	¾	1½	2¼	3	3¾	4⅔	5½	6¼
1,000 sq. ft.	1½	3	4⅔	6	7¾	9¼	10¾	12⅓
2,500 sq. ft.	3¾	7¾	11½	15½	19⅓	23¼	27	31
5,000 sq. ft.	7¾	15½	23	31	38½	46⅓	54	61¾

The rough grade. You'll start with a "rough" grade, which consists of getting all the soil into its approximate final position. At this point, you should also add any other soil amendments (see below). To begin with, the rough grade should take into account how you want to use the lawn: whether to keep it flat for picnics and sports or to contour it for a more aesthetic appearance. You'll also need to consider the location of existing trees, driveways, walkways, or a pool and to take care never to create a grade that traps excess rainwater or irrigation in any one spot. In the case of existing trees, you should also be careful not to increase the soil's depth over the tree roots; mulch this area instead and think about using an edging around the base of the tree to keep the lawn and tree areas separate (see page 80).

If your property appears to be boxed in, with nowhere for excess water to travel, review the sections in chapter 3 on French drains and underground reservoirs. You may also want to jump ahead to the section in chapter 12 on rain gardens, a method of dealing with low areas and rainfall on your property.

Keep in mind that your neighbor's yard is not a drainage area! If your excess water suddenly winds up harming an abutting landscape, the property owner has every right to ask you to correct the situation, though preferably not in court.

The ideal situation is a grade that slopes away from the house at about 1 foot for every 50 feet of distance. Professionals use a telescoping device known as a transom for exact readings, but you can determine the slope with a simple string: attach one end to the foundation of the house and the other end to a shovel or stick you push into the ground 50 feet away. Use a level to find the spot on the stick that is level with

Adding Soil Amendments

BY MIXING COMPOST with your soil before starting a new lawn, you've already added the biggest amendment of all. If, after a soil test, you still need to add more fertility or adjust the pH, now is the time. Say your soil is still deficient in nitrogen and the test tells you to add 2 pounds of nitrogen per 1,000 square feet. Pick a readily available amendment from the list of natural sources in chapter 7 (such as blood meal, which contains 7 to 15 percent nitrogen on average). You would need approximately 15 to 30 pounds of blood meal per 1,000 square feet to get the 2 pounds of necessary nitrogen.

By raking the amendment into the soil before planting, the nutrients will be available to the young grass plants far more quickly than if you top-dress with amendments later. And don't worry: natural amendments won't burn seed or young roots the way a synthetic chemical fertilizer might.

the foundation and then drop the string down 1 foot. Keeping the string taut, grade the soil to match the level of the string.

If your lawn naturally slopes more steeply, you may want to consider creating a series of terraces, which are exaggerated landscape steps. The individual terraces can be held in place by stones, prefabricated pavers, or stout pieces of wood known as landscape ties. Consult an expert or a good how-to guide prior to constructing your own lawn terraces.

Making the final grade. With the rough grade and any amendments in place, it's time to take the final step before planting. You'll need some mechanism to lightly compact the soil; the most common tool is a drum roller that is filled about a third to a half full with water. By rolling the drum across the soil, you'll close any large air pockets and reveal any differences in soil density.

This phase requires some finesse and patience. After the first roll of the drum, you may look across the lawn and see several uneven areas. You'll need to have additional topsoil on hand for just such an occurrence, and you may have to fill in any low areas. The drum roller may also reveal stones that should be pulled up now; fill in these holes with topsoil as well.

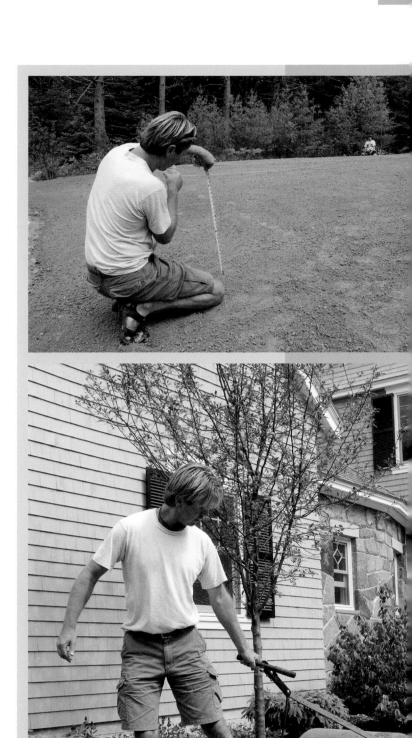

Top: An ideal lawn grade slopes 1 foot for every 50 feet of lawn.

Bottom: Push the roller across the soil on the first pass and pull it on the final pass.

After a final raking, roll the lawn one last time with the drum only about a quarter to a third full of water. If everything looks smooth, you are now ready to plant the grass.

Note: If the soil feels overly dry or if it hasn't rained for a long period, soak the top few inches of the soil and let it dry for a day before rolling it the final time. How do you tell if it's dry enough to need watering? If you pick up a handful of soil and it immediately crumbles, it should be watered.

Permanent Edging

Defining your lawn, right from the beginning, is one of the primary benefits of starting from scratch. Lawns and gardens, by nature, are not ideal neighbors. Many grass plants like to spread; flower-

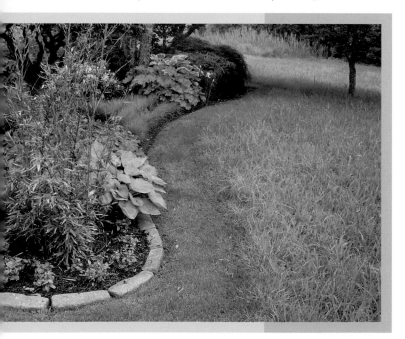

As lawn edging, granite cobblestone pavers lend an air of permanence and sophistication to a landscape design.

ing or foliage plants will generally roam, too. That's where edging comes in: It creates either a natural or a permanent barrier to keep grass apart from the rest of the landscape.

Putting down a permanent edge does save labor. Especially in highly formal or refined landscapes, edging adds to the appearance. In free-flowing landscapes with curved beds, some of the new plastic, copper, and aluminum edging materials allow for creative flexibility; since these materials are solid construction, it prevents "weed creep" into flower beds by underground roots. These edging materials can be installed at or just above the soil surface so they become nearly invisible in the overall landscape. A lawn mower can mow over them without catching the blade.

In some landscapes, edging is a major design element. With concrete or granite pavers (also known as cobblestones), along with the old standby of bricks or wood, the edging can accent a garden or patio. Stone lends elegance; wood often conveys warmth and a more relaxed atmosphere. These materials are typically installed above the soil surface and, therefore, the lawn mower should avoid them. That means you'll have to trim back the grass and any weeds by hand with shears or a string trimmer. Beware: String trimmers can do significant damage to just about every kind of edging except granite pavers.

If you purchase plastic, copper, or

another flexible edging material, look for types with anchoring stakes to hold the edging in the ground. Without the stakes, the edging will heave in frosts and through frequent expansion and contraction of the surface soil.

With brick, stone, concrete pavers, or wood, you'll need to properly prepare the subsurface as if you were laying a walkway. That means digging down to a depth of 18 inches, backfilling with stone dust, and compacting every few inches as you backfill. A properly prepared base will keep the edging from heaving and becoming uneven in time.

Note: Edging around trees and shrubs can be especially challenging, more so if the trees are shallow-rooted species like maple, ash, sweetgum, poplar, willow, and elm. Cutting down into the roots damages the plants, and covering the roots too deeply with soil will suffocate the plants.

The alternative to permanent edging is to simply edge the lawn by hand. I've worked on plenty of properties where the owners wanted me to use a power edger at least every other time I showed up to mow; this is highly labor intensive, but certainly creates a refined appearance with a clean, beveled edge. A power edger (see page 229), available at most lawn equipment dealers and home improvement stores, will do the job quite nicely but is yet another power tool that consumes fuel, needs repairs, and must be stored. A far more environmentally friendly solution is to use a flat-bladed spade for your edging, or one of the dedicated edging tools that require some measure of foot power and bull work. Many companies produce manual utensils that make quick work of edging in small areas. See page 82 for more information on edging by hand.

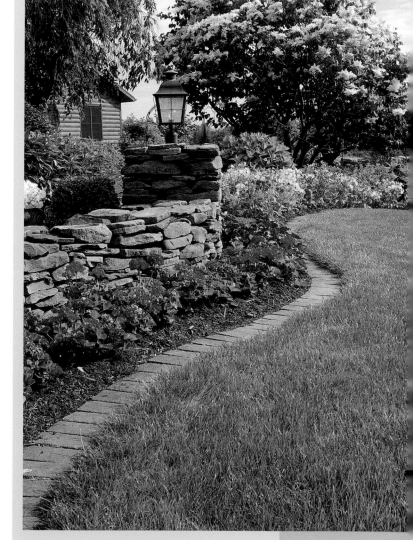

Brick edging decreases the need for string trimming around the lawn; you can run the wheel of the mower right over it.

Installing Permanent Edging:
A Step-by-Step Guide

FOR AREAS WHERE lawns and gardens meet, homeowners often prefer to keep the grass and the garden plants apart through a process or a set of materials that are both known as edging. As a lawn care verb, *edging* is defined as the act of cutting down into the lawn with a shovel or machine to create a definable line, or edge, that marks the lawn's outer limits. As a lawn care noun, *edging* is any wood, stone, plastic, or metal material used as a blockade between lawn and garden. As the chart below details, different forms of edging materials have varying pros and cons based on price, attractiveness, longevity, difficulty of installation, and whether or not they really keep the grass and garden apart.

Many forms of edging, especially brick and stone, are laborious to install properly. Digging to a depth of 18 inches or more is required, along with backfilling with granite dust or fine gravel, to ensure that the edging will not heave in frosts. For a simple project around our strawberry patch, my wife, Katie, installed flexible aluminum edging that is lightweight and relatively easy to install.

Tools of the Trade

- Straight-bladed spade
- Hammer
- Stakes
- Edging

Edging Materials: The Pros and Cons

Material	Pro	Con
Plastic	Inexpensive, durable, flexible, easy to install, may be invisible	Heaves easily, nonrepairable
Brick	Inexpensive, attractive	Crack prone, weed creep, attracts moss
Granite pavers	Permanent, attractive, resist heaving	Expensive, heavy, weed creep
Concrete pavers	Inexpensive, attractive, color variation, durable	May crack, heavy, weed creep
Aluminum	Attractive, permanent, flexible, resists heaving, color variation	Often expensive, may corrode
Copper	May be invisible, permanent, flexible, resists slugs	Expensive, corrodes
Wood	Inexpensive, natural appearance, easy install	Rots, weed creep, resists curving, color changes

1 **Cut an edge.** Using a straight-bladed spade or other edging tool, cut down into the soil about 6 inches to accommodate the depth of the aluminum edging. Use the shovel as a pry bar by pushing forward and backward to make room for the edging to slide down into the V-shaped crevice.

2 **Set the edging.** Place the aluminum edging into the ground, with about 1 inch of the aluminum above grade.

3 **Set the stakes.** Align the metal stakes into grooves in the back of the aluminum edging and pound downward with a hammer until the tops of the stakes are flush with the top of the edging. These stakes should anchor the edging sufficiently that the edging will not be affected by frosts.

Selecting Grass

Chapter 4 spends a great deal of time detailing the attributes of 16 different lawn grasses. Several factors go into proper selection, from the obvious ones like geography, sunlight, and appearance to characteristics like drought tolerance, salt tolerance, growth rate, and fertilizer needs. Be sure to spend plenty of time with the charts on pages 66–70 before making your purchase, and always remember to combine at least three or four different cultivars of each grass into your selection. In the North especially, most homeowners grow more than one species in the same lawn as well, maybe a mixture of ryegrasses and fescues. Growing just one cultivar of a species creates a monoculture that may be overly susceptible to insects and disease.

Warm-season grasses like seashore paspalum are often sold as 3-by-3-inch plugs; they can also be cut from one section of a healthy lawn and used to repair another part of the same lawn.

Seed, sprigs, plugs, and sod.

Depending on the grasses selected, you will need to choose a method to get the lawn started. For most grass species, with the notable exception of St. Augustine grass, seeding is still the most common technique for starting a lawn. This time-honored task is labor intensive and can take a year or more to fully establish the lawn, but it's by far the most cost-effective (see page 90). Planting a full-grown lawn from sod has become more and more popular in recent years, though few species of grass will likely be available as sod in your area. Sodding gives you a lawn almost instantly, but it is by far the most expensive in the short term. A technique known as sprigging is also popular in the South and West, especially for St. Augustine grass, the predominant turf in Florida and other parts of the South and West. Sprigging falls between seeding and sodding in terms of both time and cash outlay.

Sprigs are small snippets of grass with a few roots and little top growth.

One other method, known as plugging, is also sometimes used, especially with zoysia lawns. Whereas sprigs are individual snippets of grass, with a few roots and a little bit of top growth, plugs come in 3-by-3-inch squares or 2-by-3-inch rectangles, with a mass of roots and grass intact. Plugs are mini pieces of sod, which are placed about 6 inches apart in all directions when planted. In warm-season climates, the plugs will grow together to form a dense lawn a few weeks faster than seeding or sprigging.

Spend some time on this decision. After thinking about your budget and time frame, begin your search for seed or sod sources (sod sources may also offer sprigs and plugs). If you go to the local garden center and purchase whatever it has in stock, you may not be getting the best product for your situation.

The initial cost of a sodded lawn is generally 10 to 20 times more than that of a seeded lawn, but this varies depending on the type of sod (warm-season sod is usually less expensive) and whether or not you cover the seed with straw or commercially available mulch, which can be $7 or more per bale or several dollars per bag. The least expensive seeding method is to rake the seed directly into the soil and compost mixture, then mulch with a thin layer of compost to help keep the seed moist and to keep it from being eaten by the birds. Post-application watering should also be factored in; seeded lawns typically take up to three times more water than sodded lawns.

One big tip is to buy direct. Don't be afraid to call a local wholesale sod or seed supplier if you have a big area to cover. Many growers will sell sod at wholesale prices to consumers who purchase a certain minimum amount, whereas local garden centers will mark up the cost of that same sod.

Top: My lawn, just after the rough grade, still looked like a mud field.

Bottom: Within weeks of laying sod over part of the property, the lawn seemed like it had been in place for years.

Watering in the Initial Phase

Seed, sod, or sprigs should not be allowed to dry out. Period. As you'll see in chapter 8, this is the only time you should water your lawn frequently and shallowly, to keep the surface constantly moist. Failure to water properly will almost certainly result in disappointment unless you get lucky and it rains for three weeks after you plant the lawn. Believe it or not, that's what happened to me when I put down the sod at our most recent home. I had to water only once in the second week, and then not again until the fourth week.

When you can tell the roots of the sod are established — you'll know by gently tugging upward on the turf — or if the seed has fully germinated, you can cut back watering to every other day or so. You'll need to gauge heat, humidity, wind, and sunshine to see how quickly the surface dries out and water accordingly. When in doubt, water.

By the sixth week after planting sod, or the second or third month after planting seed, you should be able to reduce water to the same pattern as an established lawn (see page 148). Even this isn't a hard-and-fast rule, though. You'll have to watch closely. Remember, your lawn is like a newborn child.

Beginning Maintenance

Your seeded, sodded, or sprigged lawn will likely grow unevenly at first. Some blades will shoot up to 6 inches high in a heartbeat and others will struggle to get to 1 or 2 inches, especially if you use more than one species or cultivar in your

Seed vs. Sod: The Debate

ISSUE	Seed	Sod
Initial cost	Low	High
Establishment time	Long	Short
Prep work	Identical	Identical
Installation labor	Low	High
Grass choices	Many	Few
Best timing	Spring (South); fall (North)	More flexible
Post-planting work	High	Low
Risk of failure	High	Low
Weed pressure	High	Low
Erosion pressure	High	Low

turf. A good rule of thumb is to set your mower on its highest setting and cut the grass frequently, up to twice a week, after the sod has been on the ground for at least one week. You probably won't be mowing a seeded lawn for about three to six weeks, depending on its growth rate. Be absolutely certain the mower blade is sharp; a dull blade will yank young grass seedlings right out of the soil or overly stress sod plantings.

When you feel the lawn is filling in toward full establishment, gradually lower the blade to the desired height while never removing more than a third of the grass plant's total height during any one mowing.

Since you started off with a soil test and, I hope, made any adjustments by incorporating the proper amendments, your newly established lawn should not require any additional fertilizer for the first six to eight weeks. Though phosphorus rarely needs to be added in large quantities on established lawns, supplementing with a phosphorus-rich material may benefit the root system of a new lawn. If the roots of your sod are not firmly established within a few weeks, or if the roots of your seeded lawn have not reached down 2 inches into the soil, look for a good source of phosphorus, such as bonemeal (see the chart on page 144).

In addition, it's a good idea to minimize foot traffic over newly seeded areas until the grass is fully established. This may mean roping off the lawn to keep children and visitors from trampling the young seedlings.

Depending on rainfall, sprinklers may have to run frequently in the days and weeks after a lawn is started from seed.

Starting from Sod: A Step-by-Step Guide

ONCE YOU HAVE FINISHED THE FINAL GRADE (see page 79), your sod lawn is ready to plant. Order the sod from a reliable supplier; most wholesale growers will sell directly to consumers if the area is large enough (2,500 square feet or more). Sod typically arrives in rolls. *Important:* Any sod that is not installed during the first day should be unrolled and placed in a shaded area if possible. If left rolled, the sod is likely to be damaged or killed from overheating.

Tools of the Trade

- Sod
- Hose with spray nozzle
- Strings and stakes
- Utility knife
- Drum roller

1 **Soak each strip of sod.** Spray the top and bottom of each strip with a spray nozzle. Soak the surface of the soil in the area where the sod will be laid.

2 **Lay the sod.** Run a straight line with a string as a starting point in the middle of the lawn. Lay the first "course" of sod along the string line; be certain to tightly butt together the ends of the sod strips. Repeat the same procedure for the second course, but stagger the strips so the ends are arranged in a checkerboard pattern.

3 **Tightly fit the edges.** Sod strips will shrink by approximately 3 percent as they begin to dry; cramming together the edges and ends should be your goal. This is not quite as imperative with warm-season grasses, which grow together more aggressively.

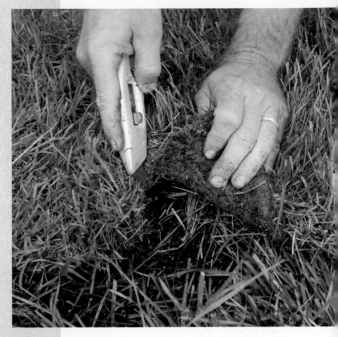

4 **Cut to fit.** As you approach obstacles such as trees, lampposts, walkways, and flower beds, use a utility knife (a razor blade or box cutter will work fine) to cut the sod strips to fit around the obstacles.

5 **Roll it.** Avoid walking on newly laid sod until you are finished laying all of it and can roll the entire lawn with a drum roller about one-third full of water. Have on hand a rake and extra soil for any potholes or footmarks that develop while you're working. It is best to push the roller on the first pass and pull it in a perpendicular direction on the second pass.

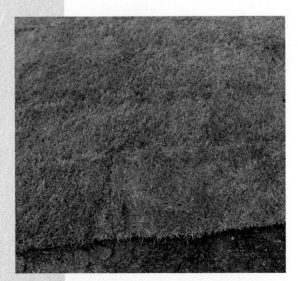

6 **Fill the cracks with soil.** Water the sod thoroughly, but check to be sure no soil erosion occurs. A properly installed sod lawn, like this one, won't have many visible cracks.

Starting from Seed: A Step-by-Step Guide

ONCE YOU HAVE FINISHED the final grade (see page 79), your seeded lawn is ready to plant. Order the seed from a reliable supplier; most wholesale suppliers will sell directly to consumers if enough seed is required (50 pounds or more). When you bring the seed home in a bag, keep it in a cool, dry area until planting. In a small area, seed can be spread by hand or with a hand-operated spreader. A broadcast spreader is recommended for a larger area.

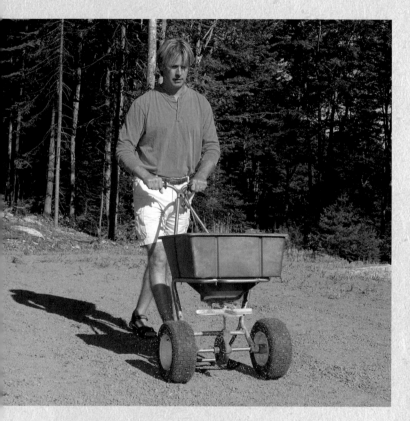

Tools of the Trade

- Seed spreader
- Grass seed
- Drum roller
- Compost
- Shovel or spade
- Hose with spray nozzle

1 **Spread the seed.** Set the dial at a low rate, so the spreader doesn't drop the seed too quickly, and fill the hopper with about a third of the required amount of seed for the area (anywhere from 1 to 8 pounds per 1,000 square feet). Spread it on the first pass over the lawn, then make two more passes in different directions with the remaining seed to ensure an even distribution.
Note: *Mix small seed varieties with sand before planting to keep seed from passing through the spreader too quickly.*

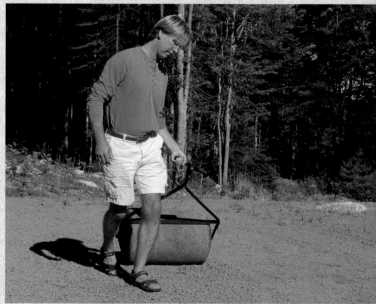

2 **Roll the lawn with a drum roller.** Fill the roller with water to one-third capacity and roll it evenly across the soil to ensure seed contact.

3 **Cover the seed.** Homeowners often use hay or straw, but both of these tend to blow away. Hay also leaves behind weed seeds that will compete with lawn grasses. A fine layer of compost works well as a seed covering. Check with your seed supplier on germination requirements for your seed; a few warm-season species — notably zoysia — require light to germinate and can take only a slight covering of soil or compost or they won't germinate. Straw, hay, and heavy mulches are not recommended for warm-season seeds.

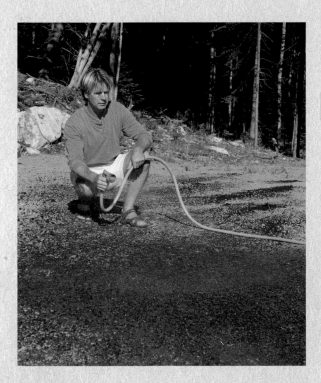

4 **Water the lawn heavily.** Water the lawn frequently after planting — up to three times a day — to keep the soil surface moist, but not in standing water, and not so heavily that the soil erodes. Use a gentle spray if watering by hand and be wary of aggressive pulsating sprinklers which can push grass seed in an outward pattern away from the sprinkler.

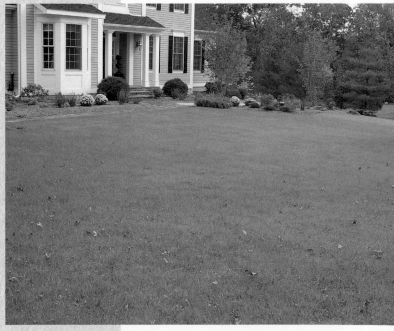

5 **Reseed.** After several weeks, consider reseeding areas that are coming in too thin. Reevaluate the sunlight; poor seed germination is often due to a lack of sunlight, and seeds in shady areas may take longer to grow. Be sure you have the right seed for a shaded area.

Sprigs and Plugs: The Next Best Thing to Sod

In areas where warm-season grasses are grown, many folks start lawns through a process known as sprigging, and occasionally through one called plugging. Sprigs are rooted grass cuttings; plugs are 2- to 3-inch sections of sod. More expensive than seeding a lawn, these techniques are less expensive than sodding and generally establish a lawn more quickly than seed. In the case of St. Augustine grass, which cannot be started from seed, sprigging or plugging is the most common option for establishing a lawn.

For either sprigging or plugging, prepare the soil as you would for sodding or seeding. Measure your lawn area before you order the grass, so that the garden center or grass grower can prepare the correct number of bushels of sprigs or trays of plugs. You'll want to plant the sprigs and plugs as soon as possible after they arrive, or store them in the shade until you do. Keep the material moist and as cool as possible.

Make a planting grid by marking out rows with stakes and string; plugs should be planted 6 to 12 inches apart

Left: Planting plugs in a checkerboard pattern about 6 inches apart is a common method of starting a southern lawn.

Center: My old-fashioned wooden dibble works great for sticking sprigs of turf . . .

Right: . . . but you can also use your bare hands if the soil is loose and well prepared.

(depending on the size of the plug), and sprigs about 4 inches apart in 2-inch-deep furrows hoed out as in a vegetable garden. A bulb planter is an ideal tool to make planting holes about 2 inches deep; a trowel or a dibble will also work. It's a good idea to create a checkerboard pattern of the young sprigs or plugs. You can slightly "hill" up the soil around the plants before firming them into the ground with a drum roller. These plants are not as tender as they may appear; some folks simply tamp the plants with their feet to be sure the roots and soil are firmly in contact. Some manufacturers do make plug cutters, which can be used either to cut a plug of grass out of an existing lawn for a repair somewhere else on the lawn or to cut a planting hole for a new lawn.

After planting, keep the area moist, just as you would for a lawn started from seed. Sprigged and plugged lawns should be ready for mowing in six to eight weeks (plug lawns may be ready sooner); the blade should be on a high setting of 2 to 3 inches, unless you're planting Bermuda or paspalum. In those cases, lower the mower blade to 1.5 inches.

Note: A sprigged lawn will usually fill in within six to nine months and a plugged lawn may grown slightly faster. With slower-growing species like zoysia grass, you may want to plant the sprigs or plugs closer together.

Al Lappin, a professional landscaper, always begins his lawns by hydroseeding — with a blend of seed and paper mulch.

Hydroseeding: The Spray-On Option

I have a landscaping friend, Al Lappin of Scarborough, Maine, who says he'll never seed a lawn the conventional way ever again . . . now that he has discovered hydroseeding.

"Let's face it, seeding a lawn the old way is fairly labor intensive," he says. "The cost of the materials in hydroseeding may be slightly more, but those costs are offset by labor savings. It's also a far better product for the customer, because the lawn immediately looks good when the hydroseed goes down, and the seed germinates faster and more evenly."

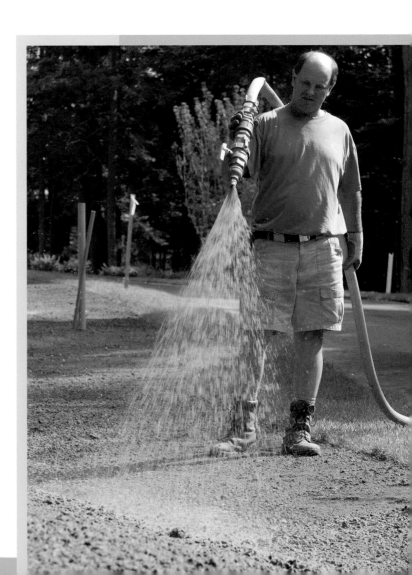

If you're going to attempt this without the assistance of a landscape contractor, you can sometimes rent a hydroseeding tank at an equipment rental facility. You'll also need grass seed, along with mulch — which is typically made of paper or a wood material that comes in 50-pound bags—and a sticking agent known as a tackifier. Many lawn care professionals also include fertilizer and lime or sulfur in the tank, which is unnecessary if you have prepared your soil just as you would for conventional seeding or sodding. If you hire a professional to hydroseed your lawn, be sure to ask about fertilizer and lime or sulfur; what's in his tank could be harmful to the soil's health if your soil test indicates you don't need any fertilizer or that your pH is already adequate.

Applying the hydroseed mix is generally easy; it's like watering your lawn with a thick, green slurry or papier-mâché. A dye in the mulch provides the green color, but that's simply for aesthetics. It's the mulch itself that's the key component of hydroseeding, because it helps keep the seed consistently moist until germination. The hotter the temperature outside, the higher you'll want the ratio of mulch to seed in the tank. This is only if you're not seeding warm-season grasses; they can't tolerate a thick covering of mulch.

Be sure to read the directions carefully at the rental store. The applicator itself may be simple to use; applying the seed and mulch in the proper ratio takes patience and experience. You might be better off hiring a professional.

The Lawn Makeover

As much as new lawn construction removes much of the mystery from the process, a renovation is the ultimate horticultural puzzle. Finding the solution begins with a big multipronged question: What is it about your current lawn that you don't like and what is causing the deficiencies?

Somewhere along the way, you might have read Albert Einstein's definition of insanity: doing the same thing over and over again and expecting different results. In other words, simply putting down new grass seed over your existing soil will likely result in the same poor lawn you've had all along. If you don't fix the underlying problem, the appearance on the surface is doomed to be poor or, at best, mediocre.

With this many dandelions on their lawn, some homeowners might want to tear out their entire lawn. Renovations, however, may be a more practical solution.

Assuming you don't have the money, desire, or time to tear out the lawn and start over, let's review the main considerations in lawn renovation.

Evaluating

Just as your doctor asks you to rate your pain on a scale of 1 to 10, you should rate your level of dissatisfaction with your lawn. Do you really hate it (10) or is it mostly livable (5 or 6)? Then talk to your accountant (or spouse) and rate your ability to pay for a renovation on the same scale of 1 to 10, with 10 meaning money is no object. The final consultant is the daily time manager. On this scale, 10 means you have all the time in the world. If you add up the points on all the scales and score 30, you're a perfect candidate to go back to the beginning of this chapter and start from scratch. If you fall on the other end of the continuum with only three points (no money, no time, and you don't hate your lawn that much), then don't bother making any changes.

Most of us fall somewhere in the middle. At this point, we still have plenty of questions to ask ourselves. What bothers us? Weeds . . . well, what about the soil is causing the weeds? Poor grass color or quality . . . well, why can't the soil grow better grass? Uneven appearance . . . what is causing the imbalance? Uneven surface . . . do we have the time and money to fix the problem?

You get the idea. Every lawn has its unique set of problems, and every homeowner has an equally unique set of desires. Matching those with solutions is the ultimate challenge.

12 Steps

Renovating a Lawn

1. Evaluate your ultimate goal for the lawn's appearance.

2. Obtain a test of your existing soil (see page 45).

3. Mow the lawn low, to about 1 to 2 inches high.

4. Remove as many weeds and as much debris as is practical.

5. Thoroughly rake or dethatch the lawn.

6. Consider aerating the soil.

7. Add any soil amendments based on the soil test, and regrade any low areas.

8. Pick a blend or mixture of grasses suited to your planned usage, climate, and soil and light conditions, as well as compatibility with existing grass.

9. Decide whether to start from seed, sod, sprigs, or plugs.

10. Apply the seed, sod, sprigs, or plugs.

11. Water daily until the new plantings are established.

12. Ease into a regular maintenance plan.

Testing the Soil

In addition to having soil professionally tested (see chapter 3), give it a simple visual test by digging down and looking at what you find. What is the quality of the soil structure and texture? Does it appear to be nice topsoil to a depth of at least 6 inches, or do you quickly hit hard-packed clay or porous sand and gravel? For so many homeowners, that is the first big clue. The soil may simply not be deep enough, and the lawn will always struggle until more healthy, organic-rich soil is added.

If, in fact, you're going to add a substantial amount of new soil, go back to the early part of this chapter and treat your renovation as new lawn construction. The steps are the same.

Preparing to Replant

After you define the area to be renovated, and if you're not going to add more than an inch of new soil, you'll want to prepare the existing soil for a tune-up. Begin by mowing the existing lawn quite low, to 2 inches high at the most. Rake and compost the grass clippings.

Then evaluate your weed population. If your lawn is mostly weeds, you may decide to spray with a nonselective natural herbicide (see Resources, page 262). You can also blanket your lawn with a flexible rubber material that will kill all vegetation (see page 176).

Pulling or digging weeds, of course, is always an option. When you're preparing for a renovation anyway, you don't have to be gentle to the surrounding grass. One option is to dig right in with a grub or grape hoe, which works like a pickax with a hoe blade on the end, and you can eradicate weeds from a large area in no time. If you pull weeds, take the time to yank out as many of the roots as possible and add these to the compost pile, too. Even if you feel it's not practical to remove all the weeds, clipping them back to the soil surface will weaken the plants and give new grass seed a chance to compete favorably.

This sad scenario is all too common: The contractor layered only 3 inches of soil over straight sand.

Dethatching and Aerating

Two other steps may be useful to prepare the soil for amendments and overseeding: dethatching and aerating. Dethatching removes any dead, undecayed material from the grass and also scratches the soil's surface as you go along. Thatch will block fertilizer from getting through to the soil, and serves as a host site for insects and fungal diseases. The good news is that lawns treated organically rarely, if ever, get much in the way of thatch buildup. The soil microorganisms are constantly devouring the thatch as a food source.

Thatch can be removed with a mechanical dethatching machine, sometimes called a power rake, which has wiry tines rotating on a cylinder. The tines scratch the soil surface and rake the thatch to the surface of the lawn, where the mat of dead grass can be easily collected and added to the compost pile. It's also possible to dethatch a lawn manually with a rake: I prefer a bamboo rake, because it grabs the soil surface more efficiently than a plastic rake. Whether you dethatch by hand or mechanically, be sure to scratch the soil in at least two directions to achieve a thorough loosening

Top: A core aerator cuts finger-sized plugs of soil and turf out of the lawn, so air, water, and fertilizer can reach down into the roots.

Center: A mechanical dethatcher, also known as a power rake, quickly lifts thatch and dead grass to the lawn's surface.

Bottom: Katie still dethatches every spring and fall with her bamboo rake.

of the soil surface. The goal is to provide good seed-to-soil contact when you overseed.

Aerating, meanwhile, allows air and water to get to the roots of the grass more readily by opening air holes into the lawn's soil. Many companies still sell spiked devices for aeration, even sandals with spikes on the bottom, but you should avoid these. The spikes do open air holes, but they also compact the soil on either side of the holes.

True aeration occurs when a small plug of grass and soil is cut out of the lawn. Mechanical aerators have fingerlike knives on cylinders that continually cut the plugs out of your lawn and deposit them on top of the lawn's surface. When you're done, your lawn may look like it has millions of bullet holes, with animal

droppings on top. In other words, the lawn looks worse before it looks better when you're using a mechanical aerator. Don't worry about the plugs of grass and soil, though. They'll quickly break down after a few rains and passes with the mower. In the meantime, the holes allow water, fertilizer, and air down to the roots. Just after aerating is a good time to apply a top-dressing of compost, or to overseed with new grass seed.

One note: A mechanical dethatching machine is no more difficult to use than a power rotary lawn mower. A mechanical aerator should be used only by someone in good physical condition who possesses a high level of strength. Aerating machines are not easy to use, and are often best left to hired contractors.

Amending the Soil

Armed with the results of a soil test, you're now ready to take the final steps before putting down new grass seed, sod, or sprigs. Top-dressing with compost is always recommended, no matter what the results of the test may say. Compost is typically fairly low in the macronutrients nitrogen, phosphorus, and potassium — having the compost tested is a good idea — so you may need to add other materials to increase fertility. Take an especially close look at the levels of calcium, sulfur, and magnesium, which in many cases grass plants actually use in higher percentages than they do phosphorus. Chapter 7 details organic sources for many nutrients, and now is the time to work them into your soil.

I always begin a renovation by spreading a half-inch layer of compost across the entire lawn area.

Selecting Replacement Grasses

With the soil prepped, you're ready to begin the process of planting new grass. Choosing the grass is the first step; begin by identifying the primary turf you already have in place. Some grasses mix together well but others won't. Revisit chapter 4 for this information.

You also need to decide whether to overseed your newly prepped area or to put down sod. For small renovations, putting down sod, sprigs, or plugs can be a great way to "patch" the lawn and have it appear — from a distance, at least — as if you were never there. It's rare, though, to find a really good match between sod and an existing lawn.

That's why most lawn renovations are accomplished with overseeding. Once you have identified the primary turf varieties growing in your lawn, you'll usually be able to find seed that blends reasonably well. If you're not sure what's growing in your lawn and can't tell from the descriptions in chapter 4, cut out a small piece of the lawn and take it to your local garden center, lawn care professional, or Extension agent for a positive identification. Otherwise, you might be disappointed if you plant coarse tall fescue in with your Kentucky bluegrass or centipede in with your St. Augustine.

Once you have a seed blend or mix that works well for your lawn, keep some extra seed on hand in a cool, dry area, or at least be sure to write down what you purchased. You never know when reseeding will be necessary again. Overseeding every spring or autumn as a matter of course can be part of a good lawn maintenance program.

Planting

Establishing grass seed, sod, sprigs, or plugs in a renovation is no different from planting a lawn from scratch. Because the areas involved are often smaller, spreading seed can be done by hand. Sodding may be done in a far more random pattern, too. Or the renovated areas might be larger, in which case you will employ many of the same techniques and tools that are on page 88.

If you purchase sod from a garden center or sod farm, try to obtain some of the same kind of turf in a seed mix. By planting the seed next to where the sod ends, it will allow you to "feather" the transition between the new sod and the established turf.

Watering and Maintenance

In a renovation, the issues of watering and mowing are the same as outlined on page 86. These tasks will require patience on your part, including mowing the whole lawn higher than usual if you want to achieve a uniform appearance while the newly renovated areas fill in. That's part of the reason sod is so popular in lawn patching; you can treat it just like your established lawn much sooner than a seeded area.

Patching a Lawn with Seed:
A Step-by-Step Guide

NO LAWN, NO MATTER how well maintained, grows without blemishes forever. Divots, dead spots, and entire brown patches will pop up, seemingly out of nowhere, from all sorts of causes. Southern lawns have a built-in ability to repair themselves through creeping stems and roots known as stolons and rhizomes. Bluegrasses and some of the fescues in northern lawns also have this ability. Even in lawns that can fill in their own bare spots, however, we often feel motivated to speed up the process. When that happens, the most common repair mechanism involves patching with grass seed.

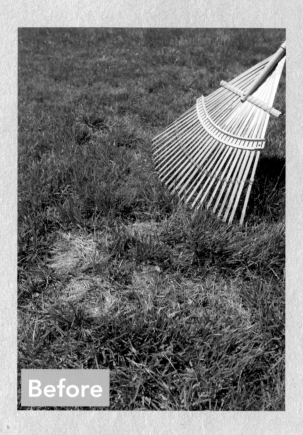

Before

Tools of the Trade

- Lawn rake
- Landscape rake
- Compost
- Grass seed
- Hose with spray nozzle

1 **Rake away the dead grass.**
Establishing good seed-to-soil contact is essential, so the first step should always be to rake away any dead grass or thatch layer. A bamboo rake works best for this task.

2 **Add compost.** A layer of fully decomposed compost spread over the affected area will give the grass seed a head start and will also help maintain moisture around the seed while it germinates.

3 **Spread the seed.** In smaller areas, grass seed may be spread by hand; for larger repair jobs, you should use a broadcast spreader (see page 232).

4 **Cover seed and tamp down.** After covering the seed with a light layer of compost (except for zoysia seed, which requires light for germination), tamping down the area with your feet will further ensure that the seed and compost are in contact. Keep the patched area consistently moist until the grass seed has germinated and the plants are a few inches high.

After

Patching a Lawn with Sod:
A Step-by-Step Guide

SOMETIMES, WHEN YOU'VE decided a lawn repair is necessary, time is of the essence. Maybe a wedding is planned, or you're getting your home ready for a quick sale. In those cases, patching a dead area with sod can make your lawn look as good as new after just a few minutes of work.

1 **Dig in.** Using a straight-bladed spade, cut out the affected area of the lawn, in the shape of a square or rectangle, to a depth of about 2 inches.

Tools of the Trade

- Straight-bladed spade
- Utility knife
- Trowel
- Compost
- Sod

2 **Remove the affected grass.** Add it to your compost pile, being careful to shake off any soil from the base of the roots.

3 **Add compost.** Fill in the base of the hole with compost, healthy soil or a blend of compost and soil, to give the roots of the new sod the best environment for quick establishment.

4 **Cut to fit.** Using a utility knife, cut a piece of sod to fit the affected area.

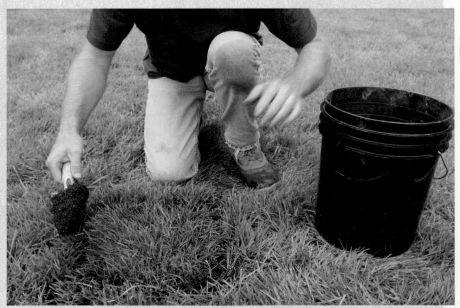

5 **Fill the gaps.** If the fit isn't exact, fill in any spaces with some of the compost mix from your bucket. Lacking regular rainfall, you may need to water the sod patch daily for a couple of weeks until the roots are fully established.

6 Get Your Lawn Off Drugs

PESTICIDE FREE · ZONE

i was keenly reminded about the pain of dietary change recently when my then wife-to-be launched a pre-wedding diet. It removed all bread and processed sugar from the menu, which meant all pastries, candy, and, in her case, the often twice-daily coffee with two creams and two sugars. She went cold turkey on a Sunday, and by the first Tuesday she felt as if she'd already been on the diet for a month.

It wasn't long, though, before some highly visible and subtle changes occurred. Improved appearance aside — let it be noted that she looked good already — she had more energy throughout the day, felt far less fatigued in the evening, and even slept better at night. She still craved the sandwiches and my mother's homemade cookies I was yet eating, but her high-protein meals with high-fiber salads definitely put an extra bounce in her step.

Our lawns are not so different from our bodies. Applying synthetic fertilizers to our lawns is essentially the same thing as drinking a sugary carbonated beverage or eating a chocolate bar for breakfast. We get a rush, a "sugar buzz" if you will, but it's not a meal that will sustain us all day. In the traditional lawn program, the more fertilizer you apply, the more you'll have to continue to apply in the months and years ahead. Lawns, dependent on their next rush of fertilizer,

12 Steps

Making the Transition

TO TAKE YOUR LAWN from a diet of synthetic fertilizers and pesticides to a natural lawn system, here are the steps to follow in the first year. Some of these steps will be repeated in subsequent years until the lawn becomes largely self-sufficient.

1. Have your soil tested by a professional soil-testing laboratory.

2. Aerate and dethatch to allow penetration of water and soil amendments.

3. Evaluate weed population and apply appropriate amendments to alter soil conditions as needed.

4. Top-dress with a fine layer of compost at least once a year.

5. Spray with compost tea at least three times a year.

6. Mow high, with a sharp blade, and never remove more than one-third of the grass blade at a time.

7. Leave grass clippings on the lawn, to return nitrogen to the soil.

8. When irrigating the lawn, water infrequently but deeply to promote deep root growth.

9. Overseed with appropriate grass seed in fall (for cool-season grasses) or spring (for warm-season grasses).

10. Consider adding white clover to your mix, for a built-in source of nitrogen.

11. Add nitrogen as needed, based on a soil test.

12. Keep a special eye on calcium levels, which should be seven times higher than magnesium levels.

will go through periods of fast growth followed by inevitable decline.

Making a smooth transition to natural lawn care, however, usually won't happen overnight, or even in the first year. The difficulty of the transition is often proportional to your lawn's stage of addiction — in other words, if your lawn has existed for years on synthetic fertilizers and pesticides with regular applications of synthetic nitrogen, phosphorus, and potassium, then its visual appearance may suffer more when you first begin to make the change to organics. Synthetic fertilizers and natural fertilizers don't deliver their nutrients to grass in the same way, and your lawn will have to relearn the way it feeds itself.

As a homeowner, you can approach the change in two ways, either by going cold turkey and forsaking all synthetic fertilizers and pesticides on Day One or by "bridging" the process with specially formulated fertilizers that have a blend of organic and synthetic ingredients. The latter approach is a bit like human beings weaning themselves off medication. The goal is to keep the lawn green with limited amounts of synthetic fertilizers on the grass while moving toward a completely organic lawn. Organic purists feel this is cheating; others feel it's a good compromise. In any event, most of this chapter focuses on a cold-turkey switch to organics.

The Transition: Year One

This is, by far, the most important and often the most difficult year for your lawn. The soil under a synthetically treated lawn, in effect, has forgotten how to sustain itself. As homeowners and lawn growers, we have to begin by reinvigorating the life within the soil. Once it's alive, it will begin to support the life of your lawn.

I'll be honest. The results you'll receive are almost directly related to the effort you put forth, and the initial work required to transition to organics may be greater than you've done in the past. You'll have to dig, pull, or spray weeds (with a natural herbicide) individually. You'll have to water as needed, not on a preset timing. Depending on your sources and how many soil amendments you can make or acquire for free, you may have to expend slightly more effort to put down natural fertilizers, and they may cost as much as 25 to 50 percent more than their synthetic counterparts. Remember, though, with a natural lawn care system, you're creating an annuity. Effort you put in this year will pay you back for years to come. Synthetic lawn care is like term insurance; once you've spent the money, it's gone forever, and you'll have to spend it again next year.

What follow are the steps and what you can expect for a fairly intensive natural lawn program that is designed to maximize the growth and appearance of the grass. If your goal is something less than "intense" and "maximum" in your lawn approach, you can pick and choose how to spend your money, time, and energy. The great thing about a natural lawn program is that the rules and timing are not rigidly bound by a calendar. You run your lawn; it doesn't run you.

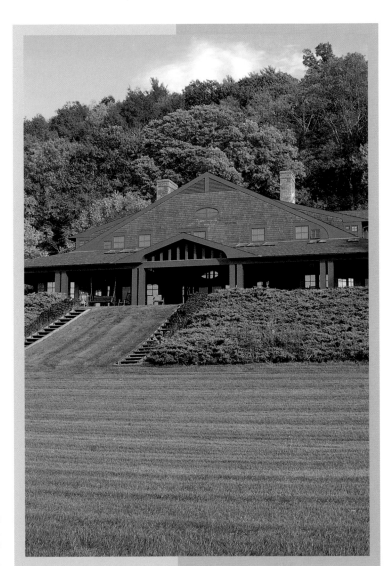

This organic lawn, which spreads across several acres of a New England homestead, rivals any sports stadium or golf course in America.

Spring Evaluation

You can begin the transformation to an organic lawn any time of year, but in North America most of us are typically oriented toward spring. The first step, always, should be to obtain a soil test (see page 45) to get a scientific evaluation of the nutrient content of your soil.

You should also look at existing soil texture and depth (pages 36 and 38) along with the weed populations. If the soil isn't deep enough, starting a new lawn from scratch may be in order (see page 74). If the soil depth is acceptable and you like the appearance of your existing grass, you may want to begin a renovation (page 94) or simply switch to a natural fertilizer, pesticide, and main-

tenance program without attempting to change the existing grass. If you have a lot of weeds, you may want to eradicate them (see pages 174–180) prior to overseeding with the grass seed that is best suited for your particular lawn situation. Be sure to add in 5 percent white clover to your seed mix (see page 183).

If your lawn is in generally rough shape and all you do is change the fertilizer from synthetic to organic, the transition to a better appearance will likely be slow. However, if your lawn is of poor quality and you take the other steps outlined in this book — top-dressing with compost, applying compost tea, adding more soil, adjusting the soil pH, eradicating weeds, overseeding with the proper grass seed — you can significantly speed up the transition.

Finding Sources

One of the former drawbacks of a natural lawn program, often cited by critics of organics, was in the inconsistency and, in some cases, the unavailability of products. While it's still true that not all organic products are the same, many manufacturers have joined the organic bandwagon in recent years. Capitalism and competition have conspired to create all sorts of great natural alternatives, from fertilizers and pest controls to seeds and soil amendments. Chapter 7 describes a broad range of naturally occurring materials, from alfalfa to granite dust, that can be incorporated into an organic lawn care program.

Todd Harrington, an organic lawn care professional, is always digging into the soil to search for signs of life.

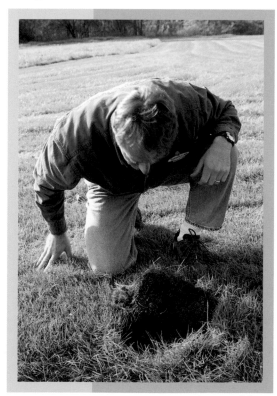

No matter where you live, though, it's wise to scout out sources first. If you have the time and patience, test the products for a few weeks or even a whole season to see which ones work best in your soil and climate. If you're unfamiliar with a particular grass species, don't conclude your research with just this book. Find someone in your community who is growing the same grass and talk with that person about the grass's performance.

You'll have made a major score if you can find a good, reliable source of bulk compost. Your town may make compost, and it may or may not be good for your lawn, depending on whether the town accepts grass clippings tainted by pesticides.

A local farmer may have compost or composted manures. Check the Internet, the Yellow Pages, your favorite local garden center, your Cooperative Extension Service, and your neighbors for references. You can also send any compost you're thinking about using off to a testing lab to determine its nutrient content.

Beginning Applications

In spring of the first year, begin by cleaning up the lawn with a hand rake or a dethatching machine (see page 97). Move all debris to the compost pile. At this point, you may also consider aerating the soil if it feels compacted (see page 98).

After cleanup, top-dress the lawn with a ½-inch layer of compost, and spray on compost tea (see page 130). Apply fertilizers and any soil amendments based on the soil test results. If your lawn is lacking in nitrogen, applying corn gluten in spring is a good idea — and you'll get an added benefit. Corn gluten is somewhat effective in preventing the seeds of annual weeds such as crabgrass from germinating (see page 125). For this same reason, however, you shouldn't use corn gluten on any areas of the lawn that you plan to overseed with new grass seed.

Don't be discouraged, though, if your lawn doesn't immediately green up. The compost and compost tea will soon begin to restore microorganisms to the soil, which will then begin to digest the natural fertilizers and soil amendments. Achieving a green lawn may be slower than what you're used to with synthetic fertilizers, but you'll need to be patient with your new program. Within a week, your lawn will be visibly greener.

My wife, Katie, makes frequent trips to our bulk pile of compost, which we replenish annually from a great local source.

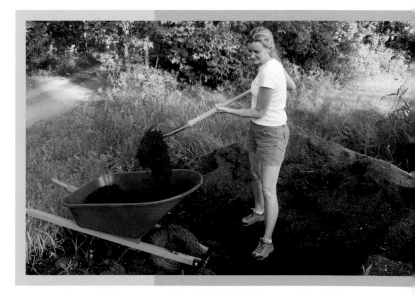

Mowing Assessment

Your mowing practices may need an easy adjustment, or you may require some entirely new equipment. The mower of choice for a natural lawn is either a reel mower for a small, manageable area, or a mulching rotary mower for a larger area (see page 224). Get used to the idea of leaving all the clippings on the lawn so that the nutrients always recycle back into the soil.

You may also need to adjust the height of your mower blade. A natural system considers the ideal mowing height for the optimum health of the grass rather than the neatly cropped appearance that is usually the priority in a synthetic lawn. Check the chart on pages 66–70 to determine the optimum mowing height for your selected grass species or mixture.

Keep in mind that you can mow your lawn lower and more frequently when there's plenty of moisture in the soil, but you'll want to leave the grass taller during warm, droughty periods. With less available water, the grass will tend to grow more slowly anyway.

Eight Billion Reasons to Have a Soil Test

FOR AT LEAST the last three generations, most homeowners and far too many lawn care professionals have tended lawns and gardens by rote. In the colder areas of North America, we have been conditioned by popular culture to fertilize from a bag, usually in spring, summer, and fall, and to apply limestone for good measure at the end of the year. In the South, gardeners tend to fertilize even more often. The Web site for a major Florida university advises people to apply nitrogen to Bermuda grass lawns during *every* month of the year to achieve the optimum appearance.

All these blanket recommendations add up to one giant guess. Eight billion pounds of fertilizer are applied annually to lawns and gardens in the United States, much of it by people who have no idea if their soil really needs it. As a nation we spend more than $8.4 billion and use nearly 100 million pounds of synthetic pesticides just in lawn care each year — up to 10 times as much pesticide per acre as farmers apply to their crops.

One thing this book won't do is to estimate how much fertilizer you should use on your grass. I don't have a clue. How could I, unless I'm standing on your lawn making a highly educated guess or, better still, reading an exact amount needed from a computer printout of a soil test? The only way to know what's going on with your soil and grass is a soil test. No test? No synthetic fertilizer. And no legitimate lawn care professional would ever sell you a synthetic fertilizer program without a test, either.

Watering Evaluation

Be honest with yourself about the availability of water on your property, as well as the impact that watering your lawn may have on the community at large. Decide early on if you're going to irrigate your lawn during times of drought or if you're going to let it go dormant.

If you make the decision to water the lawn, do it infrequently but heavily and always in the morning. Once, maybe twice, each week should be the goal.

With an organic system, your lawn's watering needs should be reduced dramatically from the amount needed with a synthetic lawn. The slow-release nature of the organic fertilizers and composts will make the grass grow more slowly, reducing the amount of water required for photosynthesis. As the soil assimilates the compost and other natural foods, it will retain moisture for longer periods of time.

Watching the Weeds

The change in maintenance and fertilizer applications may initially spur weed growth, though not as fast as you might think. If you have kept your lawn free of weeds with synthetic weed 'n' feed products, you're not likely to get a full lawn of dandelions or chickweed in the first year after you pull the plug. If weeds do start coming up, remember to listen to what they are telling you (see page 172) about the soil below. Identify the weeds. Draw a weed chart. Understand that one weed or five is not a problem; weeds are a big issue only if they really start to take over.

When you've done all that, it's okay to pull or dig any weeds manually where possible, or to spot-spray with a natural weed killer (see page 175). Maintain your watch and diligence for the first few months, and you'll gather useful information that will come in handy the rest of the first year and for years afterward.

Making a rough chart of the weed populations of your yard can be a useful tool in your lawn care strategies for the following season.

Summer Program

If all you have done in your transition to an organic lawn is switch fertilizers, the first summer is when you may begin to wince. Your lawn may not, in fact, be as green as it had been because you didn't give it that intense supply of synthetic nitrogen. Don't despair, though.

Apply your second or even third coating of compost tea to keep those populations of soil microbes building. They really love it when it's warm. Raise the height of your lawn mower blades to allow the grass to shade itself and stay

Overseeding lawns in autumn or spring, depending on where you live, is a vital part of the natural lawn care program.

cooler, and if you have the water available, maintain soil moisture to a depth of 6 inches. If your lawn has the moisture, but only if it has the moisture, you can apply an organic lawn fertilizer in summer to jump-start the greening process. If a drought is predicted, hold off on fertilizing until fall.

Autumn Renovations

Depending on where you live, rainfall totals may pick up in late August and early September — which makes this the best time of year to tackle lawn projects in much of North America. In this first year, you'll want to top-dress with compost again and spread more compost tea. If you haven't applied any nitrogen fertilizer thus far, applying the equivalent of about a pound of nitrogen per 1,000 square feet is a good idea.

If you've been on the organic plan since spring and dethatched your lawn back then, you shouldn't have a significant thatch problem by now. If you still do, take the time to dethatch. If the soil feels compacted, autumn is a good time to aerate. And if you didn't overseed in the spring, you should definitely apply the seed now. In cooler climates, fall is the best time to overseed. The new grass will have a chance to settle in prior to winter and will be established enough to tolerate the heat of summer by the following year.

Folks in warmer climates often overseed with warm-season grass seed in the spring and cool-season grass seed in the autumn (see chapter 4). The cool-season seeds (typically fescues and ryegrasses) will keep the lawn green all winter when many of the warm-season grasses go dormant and turn brown.

Many people in the East are conditioned to apply limestone to their lawns as a matter of habit every autumn. While fall is a good time to apply limestone, don't do it without first reading the results of a soil test. High-calcium limestone is almost always preferable to dolomitic lime in an organic program.

Autumn Maintenance

Temperatures are usually dropping and rainfall is increasing by September in most areas of North America. For a few weeks, at least, that will mean increased lawn growth. If you've been mowing the grass high all summer to keep it shaded and healthy, you can typically lower the blade by ½ to 1 inch, unless you're growing one of the warm-season grasses, such as seashore paspalum and Bermuda grass, that are mowed lower to begin with.

In this first year of no weed killers, watch closely for any weeds on the lawn that have gone to seed. Do everything in your power to make sure these seeds don't fall off the plant and hit the soil, where they may germinate prior to winter or next spring. Thorough hand digging is recommended. If you have a lot of weeds that have gone to seed, go ahead and mow with a bagger attached to the mower and dispose of the seeds in a really hot compost pile. I spread them in the deeply shaded woodlands on my property, where they won't germinate.

As for raking and cleanup, the idea is to leave the lawn clean. Don't let large quantities of leaves remain on the

The Hidden Cost of Synthetic Fertilizer

EARLY IN THE TWENTIETH century, two scientists, Fritz Haber and Carl Bosch, blended two emerging technologies to spawn the modern synthetic fertilizer industry. By combining nitrogen with hydrogen under extremely high pressures and temperatures, they formed nitrogen compounds that could be used as fertilizers. Creating these pressures and temperatures requires burning large amounts of fossil fuels, usually natural gas, to achieve the 750° to 1,200°F needed for the nitrogen conversion. Though the Haber-Bosch process is still considered to be the most commercially economical for fixing synthetic nitrogen, some scientists have pointed to the hidden cost of burning all that fossil fuel in the process.

Dr. David Pimentel, of Cornell University, estimates that it takes about 33,000 cubic feet of natural gas to create 1 ton of nitrogen, enough for about 150 of those 40-pound bags of 32-10-18 fertilizer. That's enough natural gas to heat the average American home for half a year. That's why every time home fuel prices increase, fertilizer prices typically follow suit.

ground; rake them or bag them with your mower as soon as they have all fallen, and add them to the compost pile. I'm not a big fan of mulching leaves and allowing them to stay on the lawn, especially if you have a heavy coating of them. Even when mulched, leaves can cause winter-kill when they're packed under a layer of snow. In warmer climates, leaving a thin layer of mown leaves on the lawn won't hurt anything, but a heavy layer can smother the grass.

Winter Preparation

As temperatures really begin to cool, grass growth will slow almost to a standstill in much of North America. The exceptions, of course, are the definite warm-season areas from Florida to Texas and southern California, where grass growth may never completely stop year round. But in regions where growth does slow, the most important factor to

remember is to mow the grass low, to about 2 inches. Long grass matted down by ice and snow is a recipe for trouble next spring. Long grass is also a haven for field mice, or voles, which will hide out in the lawn and leave telltale trails of damage in the spring.

In warm-winter areas where you have applied a cool-season grass seed for winter color, you'll want to add a nitrogen-rich fertilizer or soil amendment. In wintry regions where you did a lot of overseeding in late summer or autumn, a potassium-rich fertilizer or soil amendment is recommended. The potassium will fortify the grass heading into winter. In both cases, it's not a bad idea in the first year of going organic to have a second soil test in the late winter to see how the soil has responded so far to your new natural program.

Another application of compost tea right before winter can also help the lawn keep a maximum number of microbes in the soil heading into the cold season. Even though photosynthesis has stopped, plenty of activity takes place underground until the soil freezes solid. One final heavy watering is also a good idea if nature hasn't provided enough moisture. Once the ground does freeze, those grass roots will have to do without water until thawing in the spring. It's best if they can face winter with their reservoirs full.

Managing the Winter Load

All too often, those of us in the North tend to think of frozen lawns as pavement. We walk and park on our grass,

One year, I didn't mow the grass before the first snow; the field mice took advantage and mowed part of it for me.

or push a snowplow onto and over our grass, and wonder why the lawn doesn't emerge in the spring looking like a lush emerald carpet. Frozen grass is resilient but not foolproof.

Well prior to the ground freezing, you can't go wrong staking the edges of your lawn so the plow knows where the pavement ends and the grass begins. Also, let the person who plows your driveway know where the excess snow should go. Ideally, you'll find an area away from the most visible parts of your lawn. Huge piles can take a long time to melt in spring and cause winter-kill of the underlying grass.

Long before the snowplow arrives in winter, I take time to stake the edge of my lawn so the driver knows where to avoid.

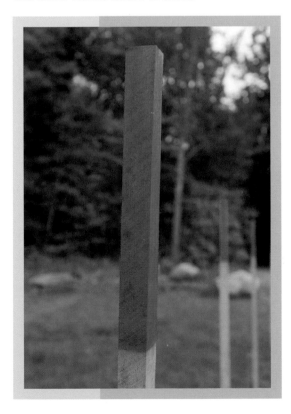

Talk to your plow operator, too, about raising the blade 1 or 2 inches when plowing over the grass. Heavy metal plow blades will easily damage grass that isn't thoroughly frozen; raising the blade will limit the risk of literally peeling back the top layer of sod that you worked all season to create.

Finally, manage your own lawn activities. Avoid parking cars, boats, or campers on the lawn, because wherever a vehicle spent the winter will surely emerge as a dead spot in spring. Repeated foot traffic over the same area of the lawn all winter can also cause compaction and winter-kill, so try to reroute pedestrian traffic.

Avoid sodium-based ice melters around lawns and other plants. Rock salt, or sodium chloride, may be the cheapest, most commonly available product in winter, but it is by far the most toxic to lawns and other plants, and also to pets according to some veterinarians I've interviewed. Calcium chloride is a better, readily available choice. All sorts of companies are coming out with environmentally friendly ice melters, which I admittedly have not tried. I tend to use sand on my walkways and driveway. It doesn't melt ice, but it does help with traction and won't hurt the lawn.

In warmer climates where snow is not an issue, some areas do experience heavy rains. The key here is to watch for soil erosion or excessive puddling and, if necessary, to take steps to improve the drainage in your yard (as outlined in chapter 3).

Mental Preparations

Next year's lawn begins now. Make copious notes on how well your lawn performed during different times this year. Remember to include special details on any trouble areas, difficult seasons, and frustrating maintenance chores. Spend the winter evaluating the lawn's size, function, appearance, and budget to be ready for Year Two of the transition.

Ask yourself how you're feeling. I'm hoping that you're proud your lawn is freeing itself of toxins, and that your organic lawn program is now far safer for you and the planet. Remember that in just one more year, your lawn will be over the hump and on the way toward greater self-sufficiency.

A spring application of corn gluten is a good source of nitrogen and can inhibit seeds of annual weeds from germinating.

The Transition: Year Two

For many homeowners, this is make-or-break time. By spring of the second year, your previously weed-free lawn may start to sprout a few weeds here or there. It may be slower to green up than your neighbor's chemically treated lawn. Or if you were that homeowner with the weed field, you may look at your lawn now and begin to wonder if the effort is all worth it — because it may not look much better yet. Hang in there.

By the second season, any residual toxins from the synthetic fertilizers, weed killers, insecticides, and fungicides will be leached away or broken down, and the barriers to a soil full of life will be gone. When you hit your lawn with a spring application of compost tea, you will probably see a quicker green-up than the year before. That tells you the bacteria in the soil are alive and happy to get a quick food source.

You may want to apply corn gluten in the second spring, as a preemergent measure to keep crabgrass and another annual weeds from popping up. Or you may decide to skip the corn gluten and go with a spring overseeding of grass seed after thoroughly dethatching and aerating the lawn. For sample calendars of the natural lawn system for cold winters and warmer winters, see page 120. It's a great guideline, but one of the major components of a natural lawn system is your input. You decide what to give your lawn and when to give it, based on the lawn's needs and your ability to provide for those needs.

In Year Two, go through all the same steps as in Year One and you should begin to feel more in tune with your lawn. A second soil test, while not absolutely necessary, will tell you if you're on the right track with your fertility program. Top-dressing with compost is still recommended at least once a year, as is overseeding. Put down an application of compost tea every other week, or at least three times a year; by the second year you will have gotten the hang of brewing it yourself, and you can just apply it to a different part of the lawn every 10 days to two weeks.

You'll have to watch for weeds and still dig or pull the ones that pop up sporadically. If you're seeing the same weeds repeatedly, see whether you can determine from chapter 9 if something in the soil is causing the problem.

Ultimately, by the fall of the second season, your natural lawn should be coming into shape. If your lawn were an organic farm, it would be just a year away from certification, proof to the world that you're doing a good thing.

Bridging the Transition:
The Synthetic-Organic Blend

SOME PEOPLE CALL THEM A COP-OUT. Others call them good business. Several companies stand on the fence between natural and traditional lawn care by creating products that combine both synthetic and organic ingredients. The percentages may vary greatly, so it's important to read labels carefully and be a good student of the language.

By law, products that call themselves organic must be derived from plants, animals, or minerals. "Organic-based" products may or may not, in fact, be organic as we have come to define it in this book. Often, they contain large percentages of synthetic materials, which accounts for a cost difference between them and true organic products. For example, a bag of organic fertilizer might cost $10; an organic-based product of similar weight might be $8. You're not really getting the same product, however. Many organic gardeners question the wisdom of putting synthetics in the same bag as organics, because the synthetics are often highly toxic to the microorganisms in the natural materials.

"I think we have a long way to go in the language of organics," says Eliot Coleman, a well-known organic farmer and author from Maine. "I'm not happy with what they've done with such a great word. Gardeners who really want to be natural and organic need to start out as smart shoppers and make sure they're buying authentic products."

The Transition: Year Three and Beyond

When spring arrives two years after you joined the natural plan, you're ready to give your lawn its first official grades. How is it doing? Is it (almost) as green as the chemical lawn you remembered, and are weeds at an acceptable level? You also need to grade yourself. How are you handling the maintenance that comes with a natural lawn? If your lawn isn't where you'd like it to be, are you applying everything you've learned from the book about watering, mowing, fertilizing, and weeding?

The good news is that by now, you're well on your way to more freedom in your lawn care program. Every lawn is different, and you should still make the same evaluations you did in Year One, but you can probably skip many of the steps. The soil test? Probably not necessary for a year or two, unless something still appears out of whack. Dethatching and aerating? They may not be necessary either, since the microorganisms you introduced to the soil with compost and compost tea are already taking care of any thatch buildup and soil compaction. You should have noticed a dramatic reduction in the amount of mowing required now that you've given up synthetic fertilizers.

Some materials should probably be applied every year. Plan on keeping up with corn gluten in the spring; it's a great source of organic nitrogen, even if weeds aren't a problem. Always put down at least a couple of applications of compost tea each year, even if the soil looks great and you don't need to top-dress with compost. Most soils will also benefit from an annual dose of calcium, unless a soil test indicates otherwise.

How much you reduce the intensive management of your lawn is really up to you. It's all about keeping your eyes open so any weeds and diseases don't get out of hand, and about a constant evaluation of your goals for the lawn and its performance. By Year Three, your lawn can look pretty close to perfect.

The Cost of Organic

ALTHOUGH THE COST of organic lawn care may seem high at first, it actually decreases over time. By contrast, the cost of synthetic lawn care increases over time, because lawns require higher quantities of fertilizer, weed-control products, and insecticides the longer they are part of a synthetic program.

The Living Lawn

HER CHILDREN ARE GROWN now, but Pat Beckett vividly remembers taking them for their first walks in her suburban New York neighborhood.

"Like many a mother pushing a stroller on the sidewalk, I was used to seeing that little yellow lawn sign, warning me to stay off the grass, to not let my children play on the grass," she said. "That's when I first started to ask questions: 'Well, what does that mean? Why are we poisoning the lawn? Why is it dangerous for a child to play on grass?'"

When Pat moved to Marblehead, an affluent coastal community on the north shore of Massachusetts, she found a lifelong town resident who was beginning to ask many of the same questions. Chip Osborne had earned a degree from the state university in greenhouse and turfgrass management and his business was among the most respected in town.

"My background was in traditional greenhouse floraculture when I started back in 1974, and to be perfectly honest, my education, and the way I conducted my business back then, involved the heavy use of chemicals inside the greenhouses," he said.

These days, Beckett and Osborne have become Marblehead's dynamic organic lawn duo. Their public park and outdoor laboratory, known as The Living Lawn, has demonstrated that organic techniques really do keep grass green and flowers beautiful. Their public awareness campaign has convinced Marblehead's board of health to ban lawn chemicals on all town property.

It's now Osborne's job to manage all the town's lawns — including the athletic playing fields — with only organic materials and techniques. He and Beckett travel endlessly, throughout Massachusetts and beyond, to share what they've learned.

"If an organic program can be accepted in this town, with people who like things just so, then any town in America can adopt an organic program," said Osborne, who now teaches organic lawn care classes back at that same state university. "We know that grass is a very vigorous plant, and when properly managed and grown in a natural manner, it has the ability to crowd and choke out weeds."

The Natural Lawn Care Calendar

Use the following chart as a seasonal guide to the natural lawn care system, but understand that the timing may vary greatly in your area, as much as a month in some cases. The activities below are designed for an intensive, highly maintained natural lawn in its initial years. Actual activities may vary depending on the individual requirements of a lawn and the desire, time, and budget of the homeowner.

	Cool Regions (Cold, Snowy Winters)
December to February	◆ Don't park or walk excessively on the lawn.
March	◆ Rake up leaves and debris. ◆ Begin regular mowing with blade low.
April	◆ Apply corn gluten when forsythias bloom. ◆ Pull weeds by hand or spot-spray as needed. ◆ Apply compost tea.
May	◆ Apply calcium-rich fertilizer and other amendments per soil test results. ◆ Dethatch and aerate as needed. ◆ Consider top-dressing with compost. ◆ Consider first overseeding or wait until late August. ◆ Apply beneficial nematodes for grub control.
June	◆ Stay vigilant with weeds. ◆ Begin irrigation as needed. ◆ Monitor billbug, chinch bug, sod webworm, and other insect pests. ◆ Raise mower blade. ◆ Apply compost tea.
July	◆ Monitor irrigation. ◆ Monitor insects.
Late August	◆ Evaluate and pull or dig summer weeds. ◆ Monitor irrigation. ◆ Apply compost tea. ◆ Dethatch and aerate as needed. ◆ Overseed with appropriate grass seed. ◆ Top-dress with compost. ◆ Apply calcium-rich fertilizer.
September	◆ Limit watering. ◆ Lower mower blade. ◆ Apply beneficial nematodes as needed.
October	◆ Begin fall cleanup.
November	◆ Mow low without scalping lawn. ◆ Remove all leaves and debris, and add to compost, or mulch leaves into lawn if not abundant. ◆ Apply compost tea.

	Warm Regions (Mild Winters)
	◆ Mow if lawn has been overseeded or isn't dormant. ◆ Apply water during warm periods.
	◆ Begin or continue mowing with blade low. ◆ Apply calcium-rich fertilizer and other amendments per soil test results. ◆ Apply compost tea. ◆ Apply corn gluten when dogwoods or forsythia bloom.
	◆ Overseed with appropriate grass seed. ◆ Dethatch and aerate as needed. ◆ Consider top-dressing with compost. ◆ Apply beneficial nematodes as needed for grub control. ◆ Pull or spot-spray weeds as needed.
	◆ Raise mower blade except on Bermuda and paspalum grasses. ◆ Begin irrigation as needed. ◆ Apply compost tea. ◆ Monitor mole crickets and other insects.
	◆ Monitor irrigation. ◆ Monitor insect pests. ◆ Apply nitrogen source if corn gluten is not used. ◆ Look for brown patch and other fungal diseases.
	◆ Apply compost tea. ◆ Monitor irrigation. ◆ Monitor insects.
	◆ Watch irrigation. ◆ Evaluate and pull or dig summer weeds. ◆ Apply calcium-rich fertilizer per soil test. ◆ Consider overseeding with appropriate seed. ◆ Top-dress with compost. ◆ Dethatch and aerate as needed. ◆ Apply beneficial nematodes as needed for grub control.
	◆ Continue monitoring mole crickets and other insects. ◆ Apply compost tea.
	◆ Lower mower blade. ◆ Monitor dollar spot, other fungal diseases. ◆ Apply nitrogen- and potassium-rich fertilizer. ◆ Overseed cool-season grasses into lawn.
	◆ Lower mower blade. ◆ Apply compost tea. ◆ Remove all leaves and debris, add to compost, or mulch leaves into lawn. ◆ Monitor for sod webworm and other insects.

7 Changing Your Lawn's Diet

t he world's reliance on synthetic fertilizers that are quick and easy to apply got its start a century ago when two German chemists, Fritz Haber and Carl Bosch, figured out how to blend nitrogen from the air with hydrogen in a laboratory. In heating natural gas to 750° to 1,200°F, they found that the nitrogen and hydrogen in the gas fused to make ammonia, which could be used in making fertilizers. After World War II, the Allies were able to adopt the Haber-Bosch process for themselves. A revolution in agriculture, gardening, and lawn care soon followed.

Several generations later, we now know that synthetic fertilizers are often out of balance with nature and often more harmful than helpful in lawn care. We also face limited supplies of and rising prices for natural gas, making it more important than ever to cut down on our use of synthetic fertilizers.

Clever marketing has made us especially voracious when it comes to feeding our lawns. We spread billions of pounds of synthetic chemicals on grass, and the total increases every year. So, too, does the cost. For many of us, being part of a kinder, gentler approach to the environment is one reason for switching to a natural system.

The good news is that you can achieve both goals. With natural lawn care, once you own your mower, trimmer, and other tools, you may conceivably never have to shop again for lawn care products. As you'll see when you check out Free Lunches, on page 138, it is possible to grow a completely product-free lawn by picking the right lawn seed mix that includes clover and then recycling the grass clippings back into the soil. That doesn't mean you're giving up lawn care, or even a decent-looking lawn. It just means you're letting the lawn feed itself. It can be that simple.

Sometimes, though, your lawn may need a boost. You may want to find a natural source of nitrogen for extra green-up, or your soil test may call for extra phosphorus, potassium, or one of the micronutrients. You might go shopping in the aisle filled with natural lawn care products and wonder what all those ingredients really do for your lawn. In this chapter, we'll take a look at the burgeoning world of organic soil amendments. If any of us must shop for these items, at least we should pick good merchandise.

The good news about all these natural products is the built-in safety net. Burning your lawn or harming the environment is difficult when you take synthetic fertilizer out of the equation. That's because the concentrations of nitrogen, potassium, and phosphorus are far lower with natural products. Some people may see this as a negative; it's not, though. Naturally occurring nutrients break down more slowly in the soil and therefore last longer.

The following descriptions often list percentages of nutrients, which is the amount of a nutrient per 100 pounds of the material. A 40-pound sack of alfalfa meal, which contains 3 percent nitrogen by weight, will provide 1.2 pounds of nitrogen for the lawn.

Though many organic soil amendments are sometimes not sold individually, they are often blended together to make excellent lawn fertilizers.

Plant By-Products

For years, animal-based products led the way in fertilizers. People never thought twice about manure from cows, chickens, and other farm critters. Then along came fears about mad cow disease, *E. coli,* and other pathogens associated with animal waste. Suddenly, gardeners were taking a second look at plant-based soil amendments, some of which have wide practical application for lawns.

Alfalfa Meal

Often available in pellets containing approximately 3 percent nitrogen, alfalfa meal is readily available at farm stores as an inexpensive animal feed. It works well as a lawn soil amendment, probably because it's a grass product.

Corn Gluten

A by-product of the milling of corn syrup products, corn gluten has been marketed as a weed suppressant since 1991. A thin layer of the material applied on lawns and gardens inhibits the germination of seeds. High in proteins, corn gluten also contains a significant amount of nitrogen, up to 10 percent. Just don't apply it at the same time you're trying to overseed your lawn; the seeds won't come up.

Cottonseed Meal

A rich source of nitrogen at 7 percent, cottonseed meal is popular as a fertilizer in some areas of the South where cotton is grown. Most organic certifiers reject cottonseed meal, however, since the majority of cotton in the United States is sprayed heavily with pesticides.

Soybean Meal

A component of many natural fertilizers because of its high nitrogen content, about 7 percent, soybean meal is on the expensive side.

Alfalfa meal

Corn gluten

Cottonseed meal

Seaweed Products

The anecdotal evidence has always been there. Gardeners in England and Ireland, where seaweed is plentiful, gather every speck they can find. If you've ever seen one of their gardens, you'd have to believe the stuff works. I'll never forget visiting the organic gardens of Olympic gold medal marathon champion Joan Benoit Samuelson, who lives by the shore in Freeport, Maine. She harvests seaweed by the bushel and lays it in the rows between her plants, and her soil is amazing.

Much of the new generation of bagged fertilizer products has embraced seaweed as one of the key ingredients. Myriad studies have shown that kelp contains all 16 elements needed for plant growth as well as a particular hormone known as cytokinin, which is responsible for cell division and cell enlargement. Cytokinin is often lacking in lawns that have suffered root decline and kelp can help restore root vigor. Many organic lawn specialists also point to increased seed germination and seedling vigor when seaweed products are applied.

Dried seaweed contains about 1 percent each of nitrogen and phosphorus and 5 percent potassium.

Kelp meal

Wood ash

Wood Ash

Readily available to people who burn wood to heat their homes, wood ash is often used in place of limestone to raise the pH of soil. Wood ash contains about 2 percent phosphorus, 6 percent potassium, and 20 percent calcium. Beware, though: Don't use wood ash from unknown sources, and avoid wood ash if your soil pH level is already adequate or high.

Animal By-Products

Call me old-fashioned, but I still take all the manure I can get from the farmers in my town. I grew up on a dairy farm and helped my grandfather spread cow manure on everything from the cornfields and hay fields to my grandmother's vegetable and even flower gardens. I'll never forget my grandmother's proper sister, Aunt Evelyn, who marveled about the size and quantity of the blossoms in Gram's garden. She took off her white gloves, reached down to scoop up some soil, and exclaimed at the rich material in her fingers. "It's so nice and dark and healthy-looking," she said.

"It's cow manure," said Gram.

Her sister turned white and instantly went inside to wash her hands.

On lawns, animal manures are used mainly as composted amendments. Some other animal by-products can be useful if you can find them at a reasonable price, though it is still a good idea to know the source of any animal by-products.

Blood Meal

Dried slaughterhouse waste containing about 12 to 15 percent nitrogen and 3 percent phosphorus, blood meal should not be used as a top-dressing because it might burn the lawn. However, you can work it into the soil when establishing a new lawn or use it to help activate a compost pile. Blood meal is expensive.

Bonemeal

Containing approximately 22 percent phosphorus and 22 percent calcium and used during seed, sod, sprig, or plug establishment but not as a top-dressing, bonemeal can help roots establish themselves. Like blood meal, it is very expensive.

Feather Meal

A common by-product of the poultry slaughter industry, feather meal shows up fairly often in natural fertilizers because of its nitrogen content of 8 to 15 percent. Feather meal is slow to break down, so the nitrogen is released extremely slowly, which can be good or bad, depending on your soil's needs.

Fish Products

Growing up on the Maine coast, I vividly recall a foul stench at certain times of year when visiting the shorefront of many communities. Low tide always has a distinctive odor, but this was something more: fish-processing factories. By-products would pile up outside, and depending on which way the wind was blowing, the smell could stick with you all day.

By the early 1990s, manufacturers of compost and fertilizer gobbled up the fish waste as fast as it was produced. Fish emulsion, as it is often called, may contain as much as 10 percent nitrogen and 6 percent phosphorus, with high levels

Blood meal

Bonemeal

of calcium and micronutrients. In New England alone, at least a dozen companies are now making fish-based fertilizers. Across North America, dozens more are including fish in the fertilizer mix, especially when the goal is a high nitrogen count.

A primary benefit of fish in fertilizer is that it is available to the grass plants more quickly than organic fertilizers that first need to be decomposed by microbes in the soil. The fish-based products, in other words, can provide a quick green-up because the nutrients are predissolved in the water and ready for the grass plants immediately.

If you've got a spot to have it dumped, buying compost in bulk can save a lot of trips to the garden center.

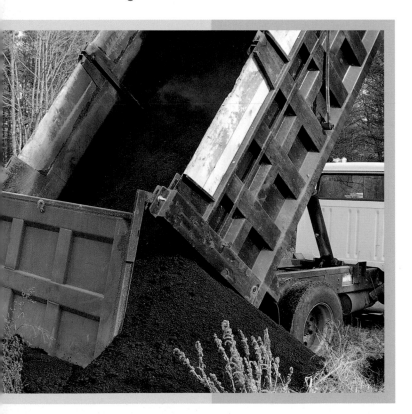

Compost

Mentioned hundreds of times in this book, compost is the basis of all organic gardening. I submit that the conscious creation of compost and the subsequent addition of compost to the soil is humankind's primary contribution to the health of the planet as a whole. Plants can't get too much.

One quick aside . . . Years ago, when world-famous homesteaders Helen and Scott Nearing were farming in Maine, they would faithfully send a sample of their soil to the Cooperative Extension Service at the state university. When the authors of *The Good Life* got their results back, they were always the same. "Too much organic matter!" they would exclaim together, and then laugh out loud like children.

An optimum goal for lawns, according to numerous agronomists, is 5 percent organic matter mixed in with the particles of clay, silt, and sand in the soil. Because most compost is 25 to 40 percent organic matter by volume, you need to mix it in liberally to achieve 5 percent organic matter in the overall soil profile. And if you go above 5 percent, it won't hurt the lawn one bit. Organic matter is constantly cycled by soil microbes, which will quickly devour any extra they get.

The challenge for the homeowner these days is to find a good bulk source of really fertile compost. The least expensive material may contain a high percentage of biosolids (see page 143). Some of the poorer-quality composts may contain high levels of sawdust, which is good for growing trees and shrubs but should not be used in abundance on grass. Compost should also be "finished." That means it should smell sweet and earthy, not pungent or like ammonia, and it shouldn't be hot with steam rising from the pile as it pours off the truck.

Some companies do make decent bagged compost, but bagged products are expensive when used on areas as large as a lawn might be. Turn to page 77 for a breakdown on how much compost is required for a ½-inch top-dressing for spring and fall. For example, you'd need 1½ cubic yards of compost to top-dress a 1,000-square-foot area ½ inch deep. That amounts to 40.5 cubic feet, or almost 14 bags each containing 3 cubic feet.

Once you find good compost and can afford it, don't skimp. Applying compost builds soil structure and adds soil life. In addition to the organic matter, most compost also has some nutrient value, usually about 1 percent each of nitrogen, phosphorus, and potassium. Compost does it all in an organic lawn program.

"Think of it this way," says Todd Harrington, a noted organic lawn care professional from Connecticut. "Ninety-nine percent of the growth in grass happens in the organic matter of your soil. If you don't have enough organic matter, you have limited your lawn's potential right from the start."

A Compost Primer

A DISCUSSION OF COMPOST could fill a volume unto itself, but in basic terms, *compost* is defined as decomposed organic matter. Loaded with micronutrients, compost is useful both in improving soil structure and for providing nutrition for plant growth. To create your own compost, here are a few tips:

1 Anything that was once living and breathing, plant or animal, can be composted.

2 You'll want to blend nitrogen-rich "greens" such as grass clippings, weeds, and food wastes with carbon-rich "browns" such as leaves, twigs, and bark; the browns should outweigh the greens by at least a 2 to 1 ratio, or else the pile may start emitting a foul odor.

3 The pile should be kept evenly moist but not constantly wet.

4 You'll need to allow for air movement, either by manually turning the pile, or by allowing air to hit the pile from all sides. I use a simple pile system of four pallets nailed together, but I also own a compost tumbler, which is essentially a trash can with holes in the sides that pivots on a metal fulcrum. Finished compost can be achieved in a month or so in a tumbler, but can take a year or longer in a more passive system.

5 Always include some native soil in the compost pile to introduce the native microorganisms into it.

6 Adding a "compost starter," such as a high-nitrogen organic fertilizer, will speed the decomposition process.

Compost Tea

My grandmother never knew why compost tea worked. But she *knew* it worked and used it religiously. In its simplest form, compost tea is no more difficult to make than a cup of tea for a person. You fill the "tea bag" — in Gram's case, her old nylon stockings or burlap seed sacks worked great — with compost or aged manure and steep it in a 5-gallon pail of water. After a week or so at room temperature, the resulting liquid can be sprayed on plants or lawns, or used to drench the soil.

Recently, as compost tea has become more scientifically understood, the brewing process has become more refined.

Many organically minded lawn care companies now routinely spray compost tea several times per year as a part of their program.

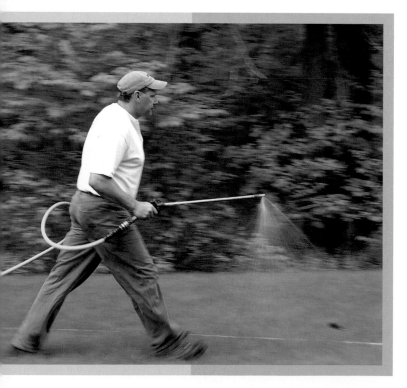

Constant aeration or occasional stirring of the solution is recommended, as is "feeding" the mixture with rich organic materials — for example, molasses, kelp, rock dust, and organic by-products known as humic, or fulvic, acids (see page 141) — especially just prior to applying the tea to the lawn. By feeding the microbes in the compost and keeping air moving, the brewing process grows populations of beneficial microorganisms such as bacteria, protozoa, and fungi.

Spraying this solution on your lawn accomplishes two primary objectives: It spreads beneficial microbial life into the soil or onto the foliage of plants and it extracts nutrients from the compost and suspends them into the tea in a form that makes them immediately available to the grass plants. Dry compost, by comparison, must be consumed by microorganisms in the soil before the nutrients become available. That's part of the reason why top-dressing with compost and spraying compost tea are both recommended as part of a good natural lawn program, especially in the first few years in the transition from a synthetic lawn care program to a natural one.

Brewing good compost tea does take practice, sort of like brewing good beer or coffee, and it's imperative to begin the process with a good source of compost.

Worm compost, also known as vermi-compost, is among the best. It is possible to create anaerobic tea (lacking oxygen; often recognizable by the smell of alcohol or ammonia or a general stench) if you don't stir it or aerate it enough. Do not use bad-smelling tea; it could harm your grass and soil. A safe and sure way to make tea is to use a small electric motor to pump oxygen into the water; aquarium pumps work well, or you can find specialized tea-brewing pumps at garden supply stores. With an oxygen pump in a 5-gallon pail, your tea should be brewed in 24 to 36 hours.

Good tea is worth the trouble to brew because it can transform your lawn and garden. Frequent spraying of about 1 quart per 1,000 square feet, especially during the first two years after converting from a traditional lawn care program, will help restore life to the soil and also help fight off fungal diseases such as dollar spot and brown patch.

Once you really begin to understand compost tea and its beneficial organisms, you can even modify the tea to benefit not only your lawns but also the other plants in your yard. Expert brewers know how to add more fungal properties to the tea to benefit trees and shrubs or more bacterial content for certain lawn soils. It's not unlike the beer-brewing process, in which a master brewer can create distinctly different flavors by blending various percentages of hops and yeast.

Compost vs. Compost Tea

DRY, AGED COMPOST is often loaded with micronutrients and can contain up to 50 percent organic matter. Those qualities make compost amazingly helpful in growing plants and also in improving soil structure. If you apply dry compost to the lawn, either as a top-dressing or by mixing it into the existing soil at the time of planting, it will often take time — a few days or weeks — before you see the benefits of greener, healthier grass. That's because the soil organisms need to digest the organic material and smaller organisms in the compost before the grass plants get the benefit of the micronutrients.

To speed up the process, many lawn professionals and backyard gardeners create compost tea. By suspending the micronutrients of the compost in a liquid form, the grass plants and soil organisms can access the benefits of the compost far more quickly. Applying compost tea will also help speed up soil's digestion of granular organic fertilizers and soil amendments, and, as an added benefit, scientific studies have shown that compost tea is also beneficial as an inoculant against many insects and diseases that can attack grass.

Making Compost Tea: A Step-by-Step Guide

MY GRANDMOTHER BREWED her own compost tea simply by sticking an old nylon stocking filled with aged manure into a bucket of water. She'd give the stocking a stir every day and within a week or so, she'd apply the solution to her gardens. These days, many garden supply stores sell tea-brewing kits with an electric motor than can shorten the brewing process to about 36 hours.

Tools of the Trade

- Mesh bag
- High-quality compost
- Plain bucket or compost-tea-making kit with aerator (shown)

1 Fill the mesh bag with a large scoop of high-quality compost.

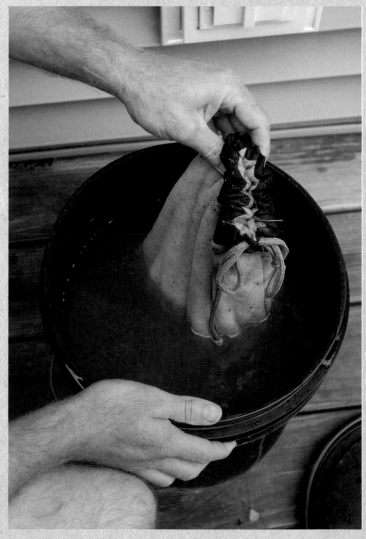

2 Sink the bag into a bucket of water.

3 Lower the pumice end of the aerator mechanism into the water, close the lid, and plug it in.

4 The pump will circulate fresh air into the tea, encouraging the growth of beneficial organisms.

5 The finished tea can be sprayed on the lawn with a hose-end sprayer or through a sprinkler. A siphon draws the tea out of the bucket and into the hose.

Mineral Powders

Generally embraced by the organic gardening community as a judicious use of natural resources, numerous mined minerals are valued for their nutrient content. Some are obscure or regional in supply; others are available at nearly every garden center in North America.

While many of these minerals can be great soil or compost amendments, they do lead to some confusion about just how much nutrient value they provide for the soil. In some cases, the nutrients are locked so tightly in the minerals that it can be months or years before the soil microbes unlock the value. Before you spend a great deal of money on any one mineral, be sure you talk to an Extension agent or someone with experience with whatever mineral you're considering.

Granite Dust

Used by some organic farmers as a slow-release form of potassium, this stone dust contains from about 3 to 5 percent potassium. I know of some golf course superintendents who include granite dust as part of their top-dressing regimen in the autumn. The good news is that it's not highly expensive.

Greensand

This mineral, known as glauconite but marketed as greensand, is extremely expensive but a good slow-release source of potassium, about 8 to 10 percent. Some organic gardeners swear by it as an autumn fertilizer and tell me it does magical things to improve the structure of clay soil. I don't have a lot of experience with it; it would cost a small fortune to apply to a lawn of more than a few thousand square feet.

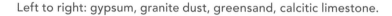

Left to right: gypsum, granite dust, greensand, calcitic limestone.

Gypsum

A common ingredient in products from toothpaste to wallboard, hydrous calcium sulfate, better known as gypsum, has been used as a fertilizer in the United States ever since Benjamin Franklin, the great experimenter, used ground raw gypsum — then called land plaster — on his Pennsylvania farm. The gypsum industry estimates that homeowners use 188,000 tons of its product each year in lawns and gardens.

Mined from ancient saltwater deposits in Michigan and elsewhere around the world, gypsum is marketed as an elixir for heavy clay soils and marketed for its high content of approximately 22 percent calcium, which grass plants use in quantities third only to nitrogen and potassium. The professional lawn care community, however, is somewhat divided about the extent of its ability to improve soil. The Iowa Cooperative Extension, for example, tells lawn growers in the East that gypsum offers little benefit, and instead to use compost and other organic matter to break up clay soils. In the West, though, gypsum comes highly recommended for improving sodic soils, which have poor structure and drainage caused by a high salt content.

Most of the organic gardeners I have interviewed have good things to say about gypsum, and it's a recommended mineral by the Northeast Organic Land Care Committee, which produced the nation's first-ever organic land care standards. Besides, could Ben Franklin really be wrong?

Langbeinite

Extracted from the Great Salt Lake in Utah through a specialized evaporation process, this form of potassium sulfate is marketed under multiple brand names, including SulPomag and K-Mag.

Potassium is often applied during seed establishment or to give the lawn vigor heading into winter. This form is said to be somewhat less water soluble than muriate of potash, the most common conventional potassium fertilizer, which means langbeinite won't leach out of the soil as quickly. Langbeinite contains 22 percent potassium along with 18 percent magnesium and 27 percent sulfur. Be careful with using this product without a soil test. Too much magnesium can cause soil compaction and too much sulfur can increase acidity.

Limestone

A regular component of lawn care, especially in the East where soils are often acidic, limestone raises the pH level and adds magnesium and calcium to the soil. Some folks put it down in the fall like clockwork, but it should not be added without a soil test.

Organic gardeners recommend calcitic lime rather than dolomitic lime, which may contain high levels of magnesium, an element that grass does not need in large quantities. Most limestone contains about 30 percent calcium, with the magnesium content in dolomitic limestone averaging about 6 to 15 percent. As a reminder from the soil chapter, the best ratio of calcium to magnesium for healthy lawn soil is about 7 to 1.

Because lime is slow to move through the soil, it's best applied in autumn for benefit the following spring. To avoid breathing limestone dust when applying powdered limestone, wear a dust mask and use a drop spreader (never apply powdered limestone with a rotary spreader). A newer option, and one that avoids clouds of dust, is pelletized limestone, which dissolves and moves through the soil more quickly than powdered limestone.

Rock Phosphates

Derived from ancient marine deposits, rock phosphates can contain as much as 30 percent phosphorus, but only about 2 percent of that may be available to the soil in a given year. A similar mineral, colloidal phosphate, consists of clay particles surrounded by natural phosphate. Advanced organic farmers and gardeners often add colloidal phosphate to composting manures to stabilize nitrogen in the compost.

Zeolites

These mined minerals containing significant amounts of potassium (3.2 percent), calcium (2.5 percent), aluminum, and silicon are an emerging soil amendment. Used for years in Europe to reduce nutrient leaching in sandy soils, they are gathering favorable reports in a few U.S. soil journals. At least one company is known to be mining zeolites in Utah and incorporating them into fertilizers.

Soil Inoculants

Rarely talked about a generation ago, especially in lawn care, soil amendments known as inoculants are playing an increasingly important role in the dawning age of natural lawn care. It's important to understand the distinction between them and fertilizers. To fertilize a lawn, in general terms, means to feed or nourish it. To inoculate is to introduce a characteristic, typically a support mechanism — sort of like a flu vaccination for the lawn. An inoculant may aid in the feeding process, offer disease or pest resistance, or help promote overall vigor. When you spread compost tea, in effect you are inoculating your grass and soil with all sorts of beneficial organisms. The other inoculants described below may be added to compost and compost tea or they may be applied directly to the lawn on their own.

Algae

Scientists discovered long ago that certain algae could fix atmospheric nitrogen just as legumes such as peas, beans, and clovers do. Companies now offer soil-building products that contain billions of single-celled algae that grow rapidly when sprayed on the soil surface. By grabbing nitrogen from the atmosphere, the algae can make 30 to 60 pounds of nitrogen per acre available to the soil. They also help reverse soil compaction at the same time. Algae-containing products, which golf course greenskeepers have been using with great success, are now available to homeowners. See Resources, page 262.

Mycorrhizae

The real up-and-coming inoculants in the new millennium are mycorrhizae. Beneficial fungi that live on or in plant roots, these superfine structures help plants absorb water and nutrients more efficiently. As a result, plant growth rates as well as disease and pest resistance can skyrocket. Organic lawn professionals often incorporate mycorrhizal fungi into their fertilizer blends, and university researchers have been amazed at their findings in study after study.

"Results of the inoculation were striking," according to a mycorrhiza report about golf course greens released by the University of Rhode Island in 2004. "Establishment of young turf was enhanced by inoculation with mycor-rhizal fungi and differences were apparent within three weeks after seeding. Turf older by several months continued to grow more vigorously with mycorrhizae. In addition to improved growth, mycorrhizal turf was greener than non-mycorrhizal turf and possessed up to 60 percent more chlorophyll . . . Mycorrhizal turf survived drought far better, and recovered more quickly after a drought."

Interestingly, the report also showed that the benefits of mycorrhizae were dramatically reduced or lost altogether in the presence of synthetic weed and insect killers.

Future research into the refinement of various strains of mycorrhizae will lead to wider application. Several companies do offer these inoculants already, and they are certainly worth trying, especially when preparing the soil for a new lawn. A key point to remember is that the mycorrhizae need to establish root contact to be useful to the plants. The only way to get the mychorrhizae near the roots of existing lawns is through heavy core aeration (see page 98).

Too small for the naked eye to see, mychorrhizal fungi are suspended in clay particles that are easy to apply. For best results, apply mycorrhizae when planting a lawn from scratch.

Rhizobia

Bacteria known as rhizobia are common, naturally occurring inoculants of legume plants such as clover. The bacteria penetrate plant roots and form root nodules that then allow a plant to fix nitrogen from the atmosphere. While this does happen naturally, gardeners can also purchase rhizobia from various sources and apply them to their soil to help increase the ability of the lawn to fix its own nitrogen.

Free Lunches: 12 Money Savers for the Lawn

THE FOLLOWING MATERIALS all provide fertilizer value to the soil, either through direct application or through addition to the compost pile:

1 **Grass clippings.** According to studies at Ohio State University, allowing grass clippings to remain on the lawn recycles nutrients back to the soil in approximately a 4-1-3 ratio, meaning 100 pounds of grass clippings can account for about 4 pounds of nitrogen, 1 pound of phosphorus, and 3 pounds of potassium. Gathering other people's clippings and adding them to the compost pile won't cost a nickel; leaving your own clippings on your lawn will account for a quarter to a half of your lawn's fertilizer needs for the year. If you do gather other people's clippings, be certain they have not been contaminated by weed killers; residue from the weed killers can impede the growth of your lawn.

2 **Homemade compost.** Though it's difficult to make enough compost to top-dress your entire lawn if it's sizable, every little bit helps. The rule is that just about everything that used to be alive is fair game for compost. All the other items on the Free Lunch menu, for example, can be composted prior to use. Leftover items from your own meal can also be added to the compost (meat and oily foods can attract animals, however, and are best avoided). Even newspapers, uncoated paper plates and cups, and napkins will quickly biodegrade.

3 **Compost tea.** You can make it yourself, quite easily in fact (see page 132). This is basically compost in liquid form and extremely useful in jump-starting the life and fertility of your soil.

4 **Leaves.** I'm not a fan of allowing autumn leaves to remain on the lawn or even mulching them back into the lawn in fall. Mulch them with your mower and rake them into a pile away from the lawn. Allow them to decompose for a year or add them to a compost pile, and then reapply this finished compost to the lawn. Leaving whole leaves on the lawn, can promote winterkill of the grass.

5 **Seaweed.** My friends Eliot Coleman and Barbara Damrosch, two well-known authors and organic gardeners from Maine, gather all the seaweed they can from the shore. If you live by either coast, see if you can find a good access point to the ocean. It's a good idea to obtain permission to gather seaweed; some local ordinances do not allow random harvesting.

6 **Wood ash.** By some estimates, a cord of wood generates about 20 pounds of wood ash, depending on the tree species and the efficiency of your woodstove. That's enough to cover 1,000 square feet of lawn for a year. Apply it only in regions where the soil is inherently acidic. Wood ash is not recommended where soil pH is above 7. Wood ash is also a good source of potassium and calcium. It's a smart idea to have a soil test to make sure your soil needs lime; wood ash replaces lime in about a 3-to-1 ratio, meaning 18 pounds of wood ash is equivalent to 6 pounds of lime. Ash from treated or painted wood should not be used on the lawn.

7 **Sawdust.** This is a great source of organic matter, and there's no reason not to rake it into the lawn at a low rate of no more than a ¼ inch deep. People point to the nitrogen deprivation that occurs when nitrogen is used up during the breakdown of wood, but as long as your lawn appears healthy and is getting nitrogen from other sources, a light coating of sawdust can be beneficial.

8 **Animal manures.** If you have a nearby farm with a manure pile, it doesn't hurt to ask if you can bring some home. Never apply the material directly to the lawn because it may burn the grass. Also keep in mind that certain manures contain weed seeds that can affect your lawn's appearance; composting the manure first, however, makes it a good free score.

9 **Green manure.** A term for plant material that is grown only to be returned to the soil as an enriching amendment, green manures such as clover, barley, and wheat can be highly useful in preparing the soil for a season before planting a lawn. If you're considering starting a lawn around a newly constructed home where the soil is poor, you may be better off planting a cover crop for a year and starting the lawn in the second year. Though technically not free, since the seeds do cost money, the cover crop can be mowed like a lawn for that first year for a decent appearance and plenty of low-cost fertility in the meantime. There are hundreds of references available about cover cropping.

10 **Legumes.** As mentioned elsewhere in this book, certain plants such as clover and bird's-foot trefoil have the ability to fix, or store, atmospheric nitrogen within their roots. A lawn consisting of 5 percent clover can create up to half of its own nitrogen for the year.

11 **Coffee grounds.** Ever wonder what happens to all those spent coffee filters full of used ground beans at the corner coffee shop? Many times, they're free for the asking. They contain as much as 5 percent nitrogen as well as many micronutrients. The only downfall is that they're acidic, with a pH as low as 3.5. Be sure to apply them with wood ash or lime if you put them directly on the lawn or, better yet, add them to the compost pile.

12 **Weeds.** Yes, weeds. The same ones you pull or dig out of the ground can be added to a really hot compost pile to be recycled as lawn food, provided they haven't already gone to seed. Weeds that have gone to seed should be carried off into the woods where they'll simply rot without germinating in the shaded forest soil. If your compost pile isn't hot, drown your weeds in a pail of water for a week or more before adding them to the pile.

Other Soil Conditioners

In chapter 8, I spend a fair amount of time talking about wetting agents, which help reduce the surface tension in water and help soils absorb water more efficiently. Wetting agents can be effective in some cases where the soil repels water, but not when the soil is highly compacted. You may not know if these products will work on your soil until you try them, so experiment first. Wetting agents can be expensive, and they also may not be allowed in purely organic systems if they are synthetically derived.

One soil conditioner that is universally embraced by organic lawn care professionals, however, is humate — a term that's often used interchangeably with *humic acids* or *fulvic acids*. Technically speaking, these are minerals found naturally in soils and also mined from freshwater and ocean sources for use as soil conditioners. Formed from the natural breakdown of animal and plant life, humates make up a large portion of the organic matter found in most soils. Humic acids are now found in more and more natural lawn care products (see Resources, page 262).

What About Peat Moss?

THIS STATEMENT IS considered heresy by many longtime gardeners, but I would use this time-honored soil amendment on my lawn only if I had absolutely no other choice. Yes, I know. Your grandparents used it. Your parents used it. You've probably used it, too. It's just that with the total embrace and understanding of compost in the past two decades, sales of peat have dropped dramatically

. . . and that's probably a good thing. Compost is a renewable resource; we'll never run out of things to add to the compost pile. Peat is mined from precious bogs of finite size and life.

Because of this, the Northeast Organic Farmers Association, which established the nation's first organic landscape standards, officially denounced the use of peat with this statement:

"Although peat moss is widely used as a soil conditioner, we do not recommend it because the harvesting of peat moss destroys increasingly rare bog habitats."

I don't recommend it as a top-dressing for lawns because it easily blows away when dry and it is acidic. Peat is still a valued component of potting soils and is sold by many companies that employ responsible mining practices.

Bridge Products

These are fertilizers and soil amendments that dance in the gray area between natural and synthetic. They exist for two reasons: Organic sources of nitrogen are more expensive than synthetic sources in some cases; and synthetic forms of nitrogen bypass normal soil processes and become available to a plant more quickly than some natural forms of nitrogen. By including both kinds of nitrogen in the same bag, marketers are trying to sell you the best of both worlds — and they are extremely clever with their use of the language on the bag. By itself, *organic* means the nutrients are derived from plants, animals, or minerals. Expressed as "organic-based," this phrase means the nutrients have some portion of natural origin, but not necessarily all.

Many reputable companies produce these products. Though the products are not allowed in pure organic farming and gardening, they are at least a step in the right direction. As refinement of purely organic sources of nitrogen increases, bridge products will likely become less prevalent in the marketplace.

When reading product labels, be sure to ask questions about "other" or "inert" ingredients that may, or may not, be toxic.

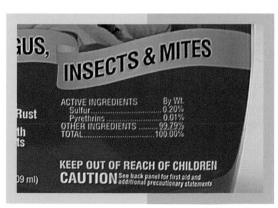

Humic Acids: Vitamin C for the Soil

HUMATES ARE THE Father Time of horticulture. Soil scientists have found that humates are the most stable form of organic matter, where 99 percent of plant growth occurs in soil. Unfortunately, they are not practical as a bulk soil amendment. It is possible to get many of the rich benefits of humates, however, through the application of humic acids to our composts and soils.

In addition to supplying nutrients and improving soil structure, humic acids (also known as fulvic acids) have been shown to enhance photosynthesis, root functioning, and seed germination. They are especially useful in soils that are low in organic matter and during times of stress. Soil is like the bloodstream of our bodies. When we have a cold, vitamin C helps deliver deficient elements back to the body by facilitating absorption. Humic acids serve the same function for the soil by promoting photosynthesis and nutrient retention. Applying humic acids can shorten the recovery time from various lawn stressors. Many of the new lawn and garden fertilizers contain humic acids in their formulation.

Elise Craig

APARTMENT DWELLER Elise Craig said she never paid much attention to lawn care prior to the birth of her son, Michael, in 1998. As a new mother, she did take note of the keep-off-the-grass signs that popped up outside after applications of lawn pesticides, but never understood why they mattered. When Michael turned 4, that quickly changed.

"My son started having sudden episodes of loss of bowel and bladder control, disorientation, and short-lived tremors, which had a direct correlation to the weed -and-feed treatments on our lawn," said Craig, a Portland, Oregon, resident and self-taught authority on pesticide applications. "The symptoms would gradually fade over a few weeks and then return suddenly after the next lawn treatment. I had been led to believe that lawn chemicals 'disappear' after a few days. However, after the fourth time this happened, I realized this was a clear pattern I had best not ignore, and I had better take this seriously."

Craig rallied the support of her neighbors, who included a veterinarian, an organic gardener, and several other young parents, and eventually persuaded her landlord to cease the lawn chemical applications. Not stopping in her own yard, she lent her voice to a citywide natural lawn care initiative that includes billboards urging residents to avoid lawn pesticides.

"It took quite a bit of work to organize, present the science, and garner support, and there was vocal opposition," she said. "But the [apartment] community eventually voted to stop using the lawn chemicals."

As Michael has grown older and her family's needs have changed, Craig said it remains a challenge to keep her son healthy. Everywhere she turns, she said, she finds common ground with other parents and concerned citizens — but continues to have some difficulty persuading larger, public bodies such as city hall and the school boards.

"It is more of a problem with schools," she said. "Unfortunately, school bureaucracies really suffer from poor information and indifference in this area. We are fortunate, however, to live in a city that has several parks designated as pesticide-free, a mayor who supports sustainability, and a public recycling organization."

Craig said she will continue to follow as many scientific reports as possible and urges other parents to get all sides of the story before making their own lawn care decisions. She applauds the efforts of many organizations, such as Environment and Human Health, Inc. of New Haven, Connecticut, that are speaking out.

"More than ninety percent of pesticides and inert ingredients are never tested for their effects on developing nervous systems," said John Wargo, director of the Yale Center for Children's Environmental Health and author of "Risks from Lawn-Care Pesticides," a report from EHHI. "Children are more affected by exposure to such chemicals because they are smaller and their organs are not mature."

Biosolids and the Lawn: Natural or Nasty?

DEPENDING ON YOUR point of view, biosolids are either the answer to one of humankind's greatest waste challenges or one of the most manipulative ruses of our time. They're the material left behind after human waste passes through a treatment facility. Further treated or composted, they're also the main ingredient in millions of pounds of lawn fertilizers and soil amendments.

In the community of certified organic gardening, biosolids and their by-products are not allowed. Regulations adopted by the federal government in 2002 specifically eliminate biosolids along with genetic engineering and irradiation as components of any food and fertilizers labeled *organic.*

When it comes to using biosolid-based lawn products, though, the debate rages loudly. The Environmental Protection Agency (EPA) steadfastly approves of biosolid fertilizers as a dramatic improvement on past practices and has lobbied to have many forms of biosolids declared organic. Until 30 years ago, human waste was routinely discharged into rivers, lakes, and oceans. According to the EPA, a one-time pollutant has now been turned into a prized commodity. "The controlled land application of biosolids completes a natural cycle in the environment," it states. "By treating sewage sludge, it becomes biosolids, which can be used as valuable fertilizer, instead of taking up space in a landfill or other disposal facility."

Opponents of biosolids point to reports of contamination with various toxic substances, including heavy metals and nonbiodegradable PCBs, a group of known cancer-causing compounds. Some folks, frankly, can't stomach the idea of having decomposing human waste applied anywhere on their property. The biggest issue, for many, involves clarity. If biosolids are allowed to be labeled organic, consumers may not know what is inside the product.

"Sewage sludge isn't just human waste; it's also everything else that people flush into the system — a fact the industry tries to obscure," says Ellen Z. Harrison, director of Cornell University's Waste Management Institute. "Many of these other materials never, ever break down. I don't feel enough testing has been done. Very little data exists about the long-term effects of biosolids and land treatment."

Having used biosolid-based composts on lawns for more than 15 years, I always believed the material provided a low-cost alternative to synthetic fertilizers. While biosolid compost is nowhere near as effective as many, often more expensive composts, I felt that applying these materials to lawns was a great way to recycle wastes — and to help deal with a material that will always be in abundance. Research for this book, including Harrison's comments, will make me rethink my position.

"I have not personally tried them on lawns, but I can see where biosolid composts could make your lawn grow well," she says. "If I were near retirement age, maybe I would put it on my lawn. If I had young children crawling around on the lawn who would be far more susceptible to potential contaminants, I would have a different view."

Natural Foods: The Nutrient Content

Here is a breakdown of the percentage content by weight of the macronutrients nitrogen (**N**), phosphorus (**P**) and potassium (**K**), along with the secondary nutrients calcium (**Ca**), magnesium (**Mg**), and sulfur (**S**) for many common natural materials. These are approximations derived from research at many state universities. Actual content can vary greatly depending on the temperature as well as the source and the age of the material. Raw materials sold at farm and feed stores may not have the analysis printed on the label. By federal law, any materials sold as fertilizer must have the analysis of **N-P-K** printed on the front of the bag or other container.

Plant-based materials

	N	P	K	Ca	Mg	S
Alfalfa meal	3	0.5	3	8	0.3	0.1
Corn gluten	9	0	0	0	0	0
Cottonseed meal	7	2.5	1.5	0.5	1	0.2
Soybean meal	7	1.2	1.5	0.4	0.3	0.2
Seaweed	0.7	0.8	5	0.2	0.1	0
Wood ash	0	2	6	20	1	0

Animal-based materials

	N	P	K	Ca	Mg	S
Blood meal	15	3	0	0.3	0	0
Bonemeal (raw)	3.5	22	0	22	0.6	0.2
Feather meal	15	0	0	0	0	0
Fish products	10	6	0	6	0.2	0.2

Mined minerals

	N	P	K	Ca	Mg	S
Granite dust	0	0	4	0	0	0
Greensand	0	1	8	0.5	3	0.1
Gypsum	0	0	0.5	22	0.4	17
Langbeinite	0	0	22	0	18	27
Limestone (dolomitic)	0	0	0	25	9	0.3
Limestone (calcitic)	0	0	0.3	32	3	0.1
Rock phosphates*	0	25	0	0	0	10
Zeolites	0	0	3.2	2.5	0	0

Recycled materials

	N	P	K	Ca	Mg	S
Coffee grounds	2	.3	.3	.1	.1	0
Grass clippings	4	1	3	8	3	.5
Leaves	.8	.4	.2	0	0	0
Sawdust	.2	0	.2	0	0	0
Compost	1	0.5	1	0.3	0.2	0.3

Manures

	N	P	K	Ca	Mg	S
Chicken manure	2	1.5	.5	2	.2	.1
Cow manure	.5	.2	.5	.2	.1	.1
Green manure**	.75	.2	.5	1.5	.5	.1
Horse manure	.6	.2	.5	.5	.1	.1
Sheep manure	1	.3	1	1	.1	.05

* Some rock phosphates, such as Carolina phosphate, contain high levels of calcium, as much as 35 percent.

** Green manure, which is a planted crop such as clover, barley, or wheat, may produce a considerable amount of nitrogen underground in addition to the nutrients in the portion of the plants growing aboveground.

8 Watering Dews and Don'ts

Water, simple as it may seem, plays several profoundly important roles in plant growth. Combined with sunlight and carbon dioxide, water is among the primary ingredients that make photosynthesis possible. Inside plants, water moves upward from the roots to the tips in a cooling and breathing process known as transpiration. Outside the plants, water functions as a carrier, collecting nutrients and delivering them to the roots.

When water is plentiful for the lawn, we rarely give it a thought. For many communities, however, water is not always abundant. The reservoirs are under municipal water restrictions; rivers, lakes, and underground aquifers are being drained; and climate change is altering annual rainfall totals in many areas. Flying around the United States to research this book, I found stunning differences when I aimed my camera at the landscapes below. Rainfall in the sand bowl known as Phoenix, Arizona, is barely 5 inches a year. Parts of lush Washington state are washed with nearly 50 inches from January to December, while arid New Mexico receives less than an inch per month for half the year and only about 13 inches total. The single unifying landscaping element in all those locales remains the lawn.

Keeping in mind that water, just like soil, is a precious resource — even in areas with plenty of rainfall — in this chapter I'll focus on water conservation techniques and strategies for growing lawns. The truth, ironically, is that any lawn professional will tell you overwatering lawns is generally far more of a problem than thirsty lawns when it comes to the overall health of your grass. Applying moisture in the right amount at the right time is good for a lawn, and good for the planet, too.

Maintenance Considerations

When it comes to lawn care, how you maintain your grass will be the biggest determining factor in how much water you need to apply. If you use synthetic fertilizers with high nitrogen content, for example, your lawn will require a lot of water to help the plants process the fertilizer. And if you apply synthetic pesticides, many of those products require extra water to wash them deep into the soil. Even when you don't use any synthetic products and instead follow an organic lawn care system, several considerations come into play.

Timing

Traveling around the country, I have seen water flying everywhere at all hours of the day and night, especially in the evening when homeowners return from work. We are creatures of convenience; most of us water our lawns and gardens whenever we have the time.

Make no mistake, though. The best time to water lawns is in the wee morning hours, from midnight to 9 a.m. Watering in the morning allows the grass and soil surface to dry off throughout the day; watering at night when dew has already settled may promote the occurrence of fungal diseases, which are often related to excess moisture. Keeping the surface constantly wet, except when establishing a new lawn from seed, sod, or sprigs, should *not* be the goal of a good watering program.

Watering during peak sunshine hours is worst of all; much of the water will be wasted through evaporation before it ever reaches the soil roots.

Amount

You'll see mentioned in many books that lawns and gardens need about an inch of water per week, but that is really far too general to be taken as a blanket recommendation. If you are doing your own lawn maintenance, you'll want to take the steps necessary to determine how much *your* lawn needs. Five primary factors are involved: sunlight, soil type, grass species, natural rainfall, and evapotranspiration. Other determinants, to be discussed in more detail in this chapter and elsewhere in the book, include mowing height, wind, and fertilization.

Remember that sandy soils require more water than clay soils, and that species such as buffalo grass, fescues, Bahia grass, and centipede grass require less water than bluegrass or Bermuda grass. The chart on pages 66–70 lists the water requirements for each species, but those will still vary depending on soil type. Adding organic matter such as compost will increase the soil's capacity to retain water for longer periods of time.

Each locale also produces a certain amount of natural rainfall and loses a certain amount of moisture through evaporation from the soil and transpiration through the plants. A certain amount of water is lost during the process of photosynthesis, as well.

Watering the Natural Lawn:
12 Questions You Should Ask

1 When should I water?
In general, early-morning watering is always best for grass.

2 How much, how often?
Each grass species differs in its water needs, as does every soil type. Every locale gets a certain, somewhat predictable amount of natural rainfall. Every locale experiences water evaporation and transpiration, combined as "evapotranspiration," which is somewhat predictable in each region. To be reliably successful, your watering program should factor in soil type, grass species, rainfall, and evapotranspiration. The amount of sun and shade that the lawn receives will also affect watering.

3 Should I buy a timer?
This can be a high- or low-tech device designed to turn your watering system on or off when you're not home or before you get up in the morning.

4 Are all sprinklers created equal?
From tiny tractors that use a garden hose as a track to run on to automatic sprinklers that remove most of the labor from the process, garden centers are filled with good and bad watering gadgets.

5 What are wetting agents?
Emerging technologies and products are designed to help soil absorb water more efficiently.

6 Is gray water good for my grass?
Some recycled water from clothes washers, bathtubs, showers, and bathroom sinks can be used to irrigate lawns, though some municipalities have zoning restrictions that limit or restrict gray water usage.

7 Do I need to dethatch and aerate?
Turf can choke itself on too much unhealthy buildup of dying grass, and the soil can become compacted. If so, you may need to take mechanical action.

8 Which grass, where?
For areas with little natural rainfall, more and more drought-tolerant grass species and varieties are available. Where water is ample or even in abundance, other grasses may be better.

9 How low can I mow?
Some grasses tolerate the mowing height of a golf course green, but most grasses grown around homes aren't as tolerant: you'll need to raise the mower blade for them.

10 Where will I get my water?
Whether you get your water from a well or a city source may affect your ability to irrigate, as well as the health of your lawn grass.

11 Is xeriscaping right for my yard?
Derived from a Greek term meaning "dry scene," this relatively new concept in landscaping utilizes drought-tolerant plants rather than lawn grasses, which crave water.

12 Can I deal with dormancy?
Sometimes, when water just isn't available, it's best to let the lawn turn brown and go to sleep for a while. Can you look the other way?

The National Climatic Data Center (NCDC) tracks rainfall by month in each state and further breaks it down by region; coastal areas of California, for example, get far more rain than inland desert regions of the state. The U.S. Geological Survey (USGS) publishes evapotranspiration rates, also by month. "Estimates of average statewide evapotranspiration for the United States range from about 40 percent of the average annual precipitation in the Northwest and Northeast to about 100 percent in the Southwest," according to the USGS. "During a drought, the significance of evapotranspiration is magnified, because evapotranspiration continues to deplete the limited remaining water supplies in lakes and streams and the soil."

In other words, naturally available water is always ebbing and flowing, and if we are intent on growing lawns, we have to be on the ball. I know some folks who attempt to accomplish this by measuring rainfall and sprinkler flow. Every garden center sells some version of the

Average Annual Precipitation

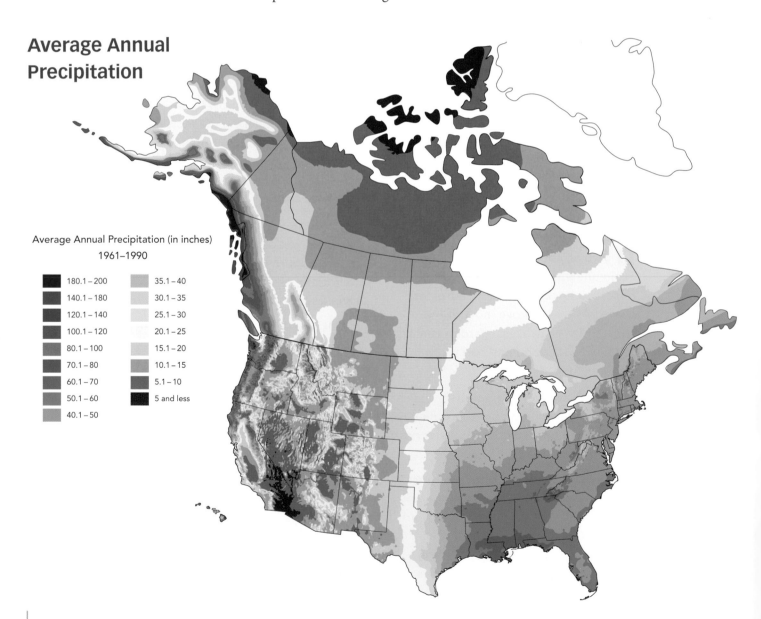

Average Annual Precipitation (in inches)
1961–1990

180.1 – 200	35.1 – 40
140.1 – 180	30.1 – 35
120.1 – 140	25.1 – 30
100.1 – 120	20.1 – 25
80.1 – 100	15.1 – 20
70.1 – 80	10.1 – 15
60.1 – 70	5.1 – 10
50.1 – 60	5 and less
40.1 – 50	

rain gauge. You can easily monitor your sprinkler output by placing jars or tuna cans out on the lawn. If the jars fill with ¼ inch in a half hour, it's easy math to deduce that they'll provide the full one inch in two hours. I have also provided a convenient equation known as the Watering Calculator on page 154.

That's useful information. It's best, though, to also become a good observer of your soil and lawn and look for visual clues (see page 152). If you want to spend money, buy a soil probe, which you use to lift a sample of soil out of the ground. You then see whether the soil is moist. A fully watered lawn should be moist to the bottom of the root zone, at least 4 inches deep; if it's not, apply more water.

Remember, too, that not all areas of your lawn may require the same amount of water. An area of full sun will use far more water than an area of partial shade. That's why you have to throw the inch per week as a blanket rule out the window; probing the soil with a special tool or an old-fashioned spade is the only true measure.

When we water frequently, we encourage roots to stay near the lawn's surface, where they're more susceptible to drought and disease. By watering infrequently but deeply, we encourage roots to grow downward in search of the moisture.

Frequency

Sprinklers programmed to go off every morning or gardeners who reach for the nozzle every evening drive professional horticulturists crazy. The goal of a good watering program should be to apply water as infrequently as possible, still making sure that the root zone gets moisture on a consistent basis. Put a lot of water down all at once, but ensure the soil is taking in the water and that water is not running off on driveways or into ditches. If you begin to see puddles form while you're watering, turn off the faucet and wait for the water to soak in.

Frequent, superficial watering causes plants to produce shallow roots that cannot survive the heat and dry conditions of summer. Repeated deep watering clogs the pores of the soil and drowns roots. By watering deeply but infrequently, you'll encourage roots to probe deep into the soil to get the water, yet allow them to dry out slightly between waterings. In the long run, you'll have deeply rooted, more drought-resistant plants as a result.

During the growing season, a good rule is to water the lawn weekly in regions where 25 inches or more of natural rainfall occurs annually. Twice weekly watering will likely be required in regions where rainfall is below that amount and in regions of the country that have defined rainy and dry seasons. Folks in southern California may get all kinds of rain from October to April but none at all for the six months of summer. After the growing season, watering can be less frequent. Monitoring should

Thirsty Lawns: The Visual Clues

MANY PLANTS TEND to wilt when dry; lawns don't so much droop as pout. Here are three sure visual signs that your lawn needs a drink:

1 Leaf blades are folded in half lengthwise in an attempt to conserve moisture.

2 Footprints remain visible in the grass long after you walk across the lawn.

3 Grass appears bluish gray rather than green before turning to brown (a yellowing lawn is usually a sign of different problems; see chapter 10).

be maintained, however, so the soil never completely dries out. In cold climates, it's a good idea to water the lawn heavily just before the ground begins to freeze. Once the soil is frozen on the surface, the roots will not have access to water until the spring thaw.

Wind

Windy sites generally require a higher level of water management because they dry out far more rapidly. If more water is not available, consider installing a windbreak such as a row of trees or a fence.

Wind also affects the amount of water that makes it to the soil upon application. Avoid using oscillating sprinklers during periods of heavy breeze; much of the water will be lost to evaporation or to the neighbor's yard.

Mowing Heights

Mowing heights are discussed in detail in the chart on pages 66 through 70, but it's always worth revisiting the settings on your lawn mower when water is an issue. Though this concept may run counter to reason, taller lawns require far less water than shorter lawns. The higher the blade of grass, the more it shades the neighboring blade and the soil below. Short-cropped lawns allow the soil to dry out more quickly; lawns kept consistently short are always spending their energy

trying to regrow the plant instead of establishing deep roots.

I know. I know. I know. Golf courses mow low and look great. They are also not low-maintenance, natural systems. The superintendents are out there daily spending time, money, and all sorts of resources because their job calls for near perfection. Your lawn does not.

Fertilizing

This subject also got its own treatment, in chapter 7. As it relates to watering, though, you have to remember that applying fertilizer, even organic fertilizer, encourages lawns to feed and grow. Actively growing lawns require more water. The higher the percentage of water-soluble nitrogen in your fertilizer, the faster your lawn will want to grow — which will require even more water.

Never apply nitrogen-rich fertilizers in times of drought, or even during months of the year when rainfall is expected to be low and evapotranspiration rates are high, which is generally in summer.

Excess nitrogen fertilizers can cause thick layers of thatch, which then block moisture and nutrients from getting to the grass roots.

Dethatching and Aerating

These techniques are important for lawn care, not just for watering but also for your lawn in general. They can go a long way toward making your watering program efficient and successful. Dethatching removes the mat of decaying material that is one of water's main impediments; a heavily thatched lawn will shed water before it has a chance to reach the soil surface. Aerating compacted soil allows air and water to get to the roots of the grass more readily by opening air holes into the lawn's soil.

Dormancy

The most natural approach to lawn care is to allow the grass to turn brown and rest during times of drought. For periods of up to four to eight weeks, most lawn grasses have a survival mechanism that tells them to shut down and preserve energy; when normal rainfall resumes, lawns will reliably turn green.

In periods of prolonged drought, however, grasses will eventually die. This usually doesn't happen in areas that receive more than 25 inches of water annually. Approximately a third of the United States falls into the extended-drought-prone category, and homeowners in these regions need to be prepared to make a decision: will you accept dormancy, with a slight risk that you'll lose your lawn completely, or will you proactively apply water no matter what? This is a conclusion you should reach well in advance of the dry season; once a lawn has gone completely brown, it is extremely difficult to bring it out of dormancy with watering alone.

If your lawn has gone totally dormant, it's a good idea to give it about ¼ inch of water every two to three weeks to keep the crown of the plants alive. If you give it too much water all at once, the grass may try to break dormancy prematurely and ultimately waste energy.

The Watering Calculator

To calculate how long the sprinkler should run to achieve your desired water coverage, simply plug your numbers into the following equation:

$$\frac{C \times W \times .052}{HR} = \text{Sprinkler Minutes}$$

C	coverage area (area in square feet covered by your sprinkler setting)
W	water depth (the desired water depth in inches)
.052	.052 (it takes 52 gallons per 1,000 square feet to soak an area 1 inch deep)
HR	hose rate (gallons per minute coming out of your hose)
=	sprinkler time (how long you should run your sprinkler in minutes)

Sample Calculation:

2500 (coverage area) x .5 (water depth) x .052 / 1 (hose rate) = 65 minutes

Some warm-season southern lawns also go dormant in winter, not from lack of water but because of cold weather. They'll turn green again when the weather warms. Some southerners who just can't stand a brown lawn overseed with annual or perennial ryegrass or tall fescue, which grows well in most southern winters.

Quality and Quantity

I live in the country, where my family draws water from a drilled well for drinking, washing, gardening, and lawn irrigation. Most years we have plenty of water for all our needs; in drought years we have to be careful to keep the well from running low. You may live in a city that draws water from a lake, a river, or an underground reservoir like the giant Ogallala Aquifer, which stretches under parts of eight states from South Dakota to northern Texas. Scientists as far back as the 1930s were concerned that the Ogallala would someday run dry, and many still predict doomsday scenarios.

Water availability is just one issue in lawn care, though. The kind of water is also a factor; whether it's hard or soft, or contains fluoride or chlorine, may affect the growth of grass. It's a complicated topic; this section covers just the basics.

Hard vs. Soft Water

Those of us with hard water in the home recognize it when we bathe or wash dishes. Soap won't suds up readily, making it difficult to get things clean. We'll occasionally add water softeners so our T-shirts come out white and our hair feels silkier. Lawns actually prefer hard water because it contains high levels of calcium and magnesium, two secondary elements required for plant growth. When water is softened, sodium replaces the calcium and magnesium. Too much sodium will turn the grass yellow and, in severe situations, can ultimately harm soil structure and kill plants.

Watering a Slope

I'LL NEVER FORGET the first lawn I ever mowed for hire. Across the street from my mother's house, we would go sliding on the hill in winter and I somehow managed to wrestle a mower up and down its steep terrain in summer. I've avoided growing lawns on slopes ever since.

Depending on the severity of the hillside, watering can be a special challenge. If you simply set a sprinkler on a slope for the same amount of time as sprinklers on the rest of a flat property, much of the water will probably run to the bottom. Dry, brown patches of grass will invariably result.

To try to get even, deep saturation into the soil on a slope, split your watering into multiple cycles. If your normal watering cycle is 30 minutes, you might split the cycle into three 10-minute phases, with a few hours in between. Or you can simply water the slope until it begins to run off. Start watering again a few hours later and stop when the runoff is visible.

Because of the slope's natural propensity to shed water, soil quality becomes especially important. Sandy soil and heavy compacted clay are both recipes for disaster. Work as much compost into the soil as possible. Wetting agents (see page 159) may also be useful. Then again, you could replant the slope altogether; consider an alternate ground cover (see page 241) or a xeriscape (see page 248).

To overcome a problem with soft water, you can occasionally water your lawn thoroughly with rainwater collected in barrels to help dilute the sodium. Adding plenty of compost will build the soil's own drainage capacity, diminishing the likelihood of a sodium buildup.

Wells vs. Municipal Water

Wells contain whatever kind of water Mother Nature wanted to give us. Testing your water will let you know about mineral and sodium levels and help alert you to any potential problems with sodium or fluoride. Water from municipal sources may contain chlorine (added as a disinfectant) and fluoride (added to prevent tooth decay). Call your local water district to determine what has been added. Even then, you might consider getting a water test.

Although chlorine is one of the 16 elements required for plant growth and is found naturally in small amounts in healthy soils, too much is toxic to grasses and other plant life. The problem with excess chlorine is detection; it's really difficult to tell if chlorine is damaging your lawn. If you suspect excessive chlorine to be a problem, allow the water from your tap to sit in a large open container overnight before applying it to your lawn; the chlorine will evaporate from the water.

I'm frequently asked about watering lawns with pool water, especially in the autumn when families drain pools. As long as the water has been sitting without a fresh application of chlorine for a couple of days, it should be fine to use.

Fluoride is generally far more of a problem on lawns than chlorine. Excessive fluoride will concentrate in the tips of the grass plants, causing them to burn and turn yellow. It's a phenomenon known as necrosis. The best solution is to add lime or wood ash to the soil to get the pH as close to 7 as possible. At this neutral pH level, the fluoride is converted to a form that is unavailable to plants. I also know some folks who have elaborate mineral filters installed to their water systems to remove fluoride and other mineral deposits from water; they're expensive but may be worth the cost to you.

Novel Ideas

Faced with the unassailable reality that lawn care as usual simply isn't possible in many locales, innovative residents are rethinking the lawn care watering system. Here are three emerging technologies that can work in many places.

Rainwater Harvesting

With extended periods of drought now common in even the rainiest climates, the age-old practice of capturing and reusing water is gaining new momentum. Virtually every garden center sells some version of the rain barrel, which is used to collect storm-water runoff from downspouts. Homeowners can easily siphon water from the barrels to apply to lawns and gardens, but several barrels are needed to gather enough water to irrigate a substantial lawn. You'll require approximately 52 gallons to apply 1 inch of water to 1,000 square feet of grass, or about 2,260 gallons per acre.

In arid regions, many lawn aficionados have underground water storage tanks installed. Fitted with pumps, these tanks allow homeowners to pump water up to the lawn so it stays green in all seasons. After the initial cost of purchase and installation, these systems may be seen as affordable, especially in municipalities with high water costs or restrictions on watering.

Gray Water

Many homeowners are turning to a practice known as gray water irrigation. Collected from clothes washers, bathtubs, showers, and laundry and bathroom sinks, the water is generally safe to apply on lawns, trees, shrubs, and flower gardens, but it is not recommended for use on edible plants. Gray water should not be confused with black water, which is wastewater from toilets, kitchen sinks, and dishwashers. Untreated, unfiltered black water should never be reused, because of possible contamination by viruses and other toxic pathogens.

Gathering gray water can present certain practical challenges. First, check with your local code enforcement officer to see if the practice is allowed in your community. If so, consider whether you want to use gray water on a large scale or only occasionally. The easiest place to collect gray water is from the discharge hose on your washing machine; it will

Scott Calhoun, a garden designer in Tucson, Arizona, uses inverted culverts as cisterns to collect rainwater in his yard.

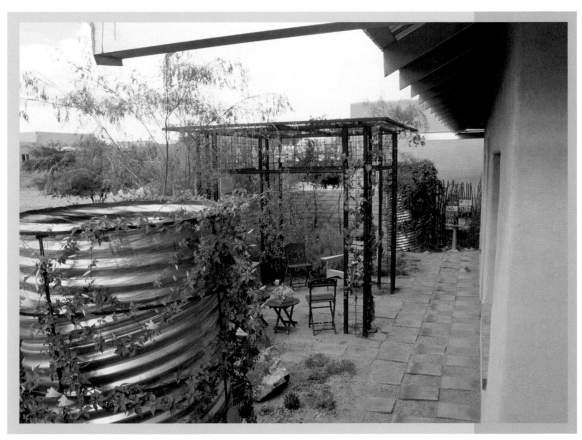

Gray Water: The Arizona Standard

You may use gray water for household gardening, composting, and lawn and landscape irrigation, but it should not run off your property.

Do not surface irrigate any plants that produce food, except for fruit and nut trees. These plants can filter the water through the tree roots, trunk, and branches.

Use only flood or drip irrigation to water lawns and landscaping. Spraying gray water is prohibited.

When determining the location for your gray water irrigation, remember that it cannot be in a wash or drainage way (that flows to other properties).

Gray water may only be used in locations where groundwater is at least 5 feet below the surface.

Label pipes carrying gray water under pressure if confusion between gray water and drinking water pipes is possible.

Cover, seal, and secure storage tanks to restrict access by small rodents and to control disease-carrying insects.

Hazardous chemicals, such as antifreeze, mothballs, and solvents, cannot be in gray water. Do not include wash water from greasy or oily rags in your gray water.

Gray water from washing diapers or other infectious garments must be discharged to a residential sewer or other wastewater facility, or should be disinfected prior to its use.

Surface accumulation of gray water must be kept to a minimum.

Should a backup occur, gray water must be disposed into your normal wastewater drain system. To avoid such a backup, consider using a filtration system to reduce plugging and extend the system's lifetime.

If you have a septic or other on-site wastewater disposal system, your gray water use does not change that system's design requirements.

Courtesy of the Arizona Department of Environmental Quality

Connecting the discharge hose of your washing machine to a 50-gallon drum is an easy way to make use of gray water.

emit up to 60 gallons per wash depending on model and load size. The bathtub is another reasonably easy place to save water, by either bailing with a pail or siphoning the water with a hose.

It is also possible to engineer the plumbing in your home to direct all eligible gray water to an underground tank; the wastewater would still flow to a standard septic system or the sewer main. This, again, would require the approval of your code enforcement officer or plumbing inspector. If you're considering using gray water for irrigation on a small or large scale, take a moment to read the gray water regulations developed by the Arizona Department of Environmental Quality and reprinted here with permission. That state used to have strict gray water rules, but found that tens of thousands of homeowners were using gray water anyway, without adverse health effects to people or plants. The Arizona standards (see opposite page), developed in 2001, are similar to those in many other states and in municipalities around the country. The average home generates between 35 and 45 gallons of gray water per person per day; it could well be a valuable resource in your lawn watering program.

Observe the health of your lawn frequently when utilizing gray water. Though not likely, it's possible that excess bleach and detergent residues in the water will harm the grass. Yellowing and curling of the leaf tips is often the most visible effect. Test the gray water on small areas of the lawn before trying it out on the whole lawn.

Wetting Agents

Depending on their structure and texture, soils have varying capacities to absorb water and nutrients and therefore support plant life. Some are like wax paper, which repels water; other soils are like newsprint or tissue paper and are easily saturated. Constant baking in the sun often forms a surface crust on soil, even healthy soil, limiting the lawn's ability to accept water even when it rains. If water tends to run off your soil's surface or leach quickly through the upper layer, your lawn might be a good candidate for a wetting agent, also known as a surfactant. This type of compound allows soil to absorb water more readily by releasing the surface tension in the water that promotes beading and puddling. Particularly useful during dry seasons, a wetting agent can reduce water needs on lawns by up to 60 percent.

Wetting agents are not a replacement for fertilizer or the necessity to replenish the soil's organic matter, and they generally aren't practical as an ongoing watering substitute. They may not help much at all if your heavy clay soil is overly compacted, either. If your goal is to keep a healthy established lawn green during a prolonged drought, however, this product is best applied as soon as the grass is visibly stressed from lack of water — in other words, when it begins to turn brown. Wetting agents are also tremendously helpful when establishing a lawn from seed because the soil should never be allowed to dry out prior to seed germination.

Both granular and liquid wetting agents are available, but check the labels to determine the formulations; some synthetically based products may not be safe for the environment. No matter which wetting agent you choose, you'll want to test a small area of your lawn before treating the whole thing; different grass species have varying tolerances. Various sources also recommend applying certain soaps to the lawn as wetting agents, but this practice is specifically denounced by Colorado State University, among other researchers.

"The use of dishwashing detergents and other soaps in place of turf-type wetting agents is not recommended and may damage heat- and drought-stressed lawns," concluded Dr. Anthony J. Toski, a turf specialist with Colorado State University in Fort Collins, who published his findings in February 2004.

Depending on the site, any number of sprinklers can come in handy from time to time.

Tools of the Trade

Anyone committed to growing a healthy lawn will likely, at some point, have to apply water above and beyond what Mother Nature provides. Entire sections of garden centers are now devoted to the task. Every metropolitan area — even in areas with 40 or more inches of annual rainfall, mostly during the growing season — will have as many as 200 irrigation companies competing to install a watering system around our homes. These days, the water world is a jungle.

Hand Watering

A variety of hose nozzles and watering cans are available to the home gardener, but they're of little practical use in lawn watering. I've got better things to do, and you probably do too. Remember that it takes about 52 gallons to water 1,000 square feet of grass, or 260 gallons to water 5,000 square feet, about an inch deep. At my house, it takes about 45 seconds to fill a gallon bucket with water from the hose, which means it would take about three and a quarter hours to soak my 5,000-square-foot lawn.

Portable Sprinklers

On the one hand, we've come a long way since Joseph Smith patented the first oscillating lawn sprinkler in the 1890s. Just out of curiosity, I typed "lawn sprinkler" into my Internet search engine and found nearly 6,000 different images. When you look more closely, though, you'll see we haven't really come that far at all. I couldn't track down a photo of Joe Smith's model, but I have a sprinkler in my basement from the 1940s, and it's suspiciously similar to some of today's "new" models. It spins around and sends water upward and outward.

Portable sprinklers come in four basic designs: oscillating, rotary or impulse, stationary, and spinning. All models are limited by the water pressure coming out of your hose, but the coverage varies greatly, from about 100 square feet to nearly 8,000 square feet. The smaller the coverage area, the faster the sprinkler applies the water to that area. If you know that different parts of your lawn have different water needs, you may opt

A watering timer is an essential tool for busy homeowners who won't be available to shut off the water spigot.

for a sprinkler with a small coverage area. If your entire lawn needs approximately the same amount of water, you'll probably want to go with a sprinkler capable of wide coverage.

Always test your coverage area. Set out jars or tuna cans at various points to see how far and how fast the water is hitting each section of the lawn. You should also avoid the rather lazy oscillating sprinklers that send water high into the air when they hit the median point in their cycles; these models waste water through evaporation and are most prone to loss of water from wind gusts (see page 163).

Timers

If you're a homebody with a lot of time on your hands, maybe you don't need one of these. And if you don't water your lawn, don't bother with these, either. Otherwise, a hose timer should be one of your next lawn care purchases. By using the Watering Calculator on page 154, you can tabulate exactly how long your sprinkler should run. If, for example, you want to spread ½ inch of water before heading to work, you need two numbers: the amount of water in gallons per minute coming out of your sprinkler and the coverage area of your sprinkler. If your hose puts out 1 gallon per minute and your sprinkler covers 2,500 square feet, the Watering Calculator tells you that it takes 130 gallons to cover that area 1 inch deep or 65 gallons for ½ inch. You can then set your timer for 65 minutes before you go to work and not have to worry about whether or not the sprinkler shuts off or wastes water.

A Sprinkling of Sprinklers

Stationary. As the term suggests, these sprinklers don't have moving parts other than adjustable heads. Some are ring shaped with holes in the top; others spray unique measurable patterns, usually squares, rectangles, or circles. Although they are generally low in cost, their holes may be prone to clogging. Impractical for large lawns because they would have to be moved frequently, they'll work for small lawns and spot watering.

Novelties. The brass "art" sprinklers have become all the rage lately and may be okay for a small lawn, but they are not practical for large area. I've had a lot of fun with my rain tractor, a spinning sprinkler that moves along the ground using a garden hose as its track. Children love it, and it can be set up to do a good job delivering water to a lawn. I also found, though, that I grew tired of setting up the hose track time after time . . . and if you're not home when the tractor gets stuck or reaches the end of its track, a lot of extra water gets wasted in one area.

Spinning. Also good for small lawns and spot watering, these sprinklers deliver water through nozzles in circular patterns anywhere from about 5 to 60 feet in diameter. If you opt for this type of sprinkler, be sure to purchase one with a stable base; the cheaper plastic versions tend to tip easily when delivering full water pressure. More expensive models have adjustable nozzles to allow for flexibility of coverage.

Rotary and impulse. Both of these deliver water in potentially large circles or portions of circles. I like rotary sprinklers because they're quieter, whereas the impulse sprinklers give off a characteristic machine-gun rat-a-tat that sounds like a rattlesnake. The difference is in the internal mechanics. Rotary sprinklers contain a water-powered gear system to move the spray stream back and forth. Impulse sprinklers operate with a spring-activated counterweight bouncing off the stream of water: hence the rattlesnake sound. Either type is ideal for large lawns of 5,000 square feet or more. You can usually pick a central location and let the sprinkler run for up to four hours, depending on coverage area and the amount of water needed.

Oscillating. Still a best seller because of its graceful, sweeping delivery, this type of sprinkler generally wastes too much water through evaporation and wind gusts. Because many models seem to pause at both ends of the sweeping cycle, they also tend to spread water disproportionately.

Hybrid. This sprinkler is buried at ground level, and like many professionally installed sprinkler heads, it connects to your garden hose aboveground. When you turn on the water, the quiet rotary sprinkler emerges and sprays water in a circular pattern. The sprinkler can attach to both the male and female ends of the hose at the same time, which allows you to run multiple sprinklers in a series. That alone is an ingenious idea.

Timers can just do the basics — meaning they shut off after a pre-set amount of time — or they can do a whole lot more. The more technical models allow you to preprogram the on and off times well in advance, which makes them ideal for vacationers or busy homeowners.

You should always be home the first time you use your timer, just to make sure you've set it properly and that applying all that water at once doesn't create unexpected runoff.

Hoses

In the same way extension cords are, well, an extension of your home's electrical system, the hose is an extension

All hoses are not created equal; the small, thin vinyl hoses will typically wear out quickly, while larger composite hoses may have a lifetime warranty.

of your home's plumbing. I bring this up only to illustrate the idea that you need to have the right hose for the job. You wouldn't run an electric lawn mower, a chain saw, or a hedge trimmer off the same thin, 12-foot electrical cord that you would use for a TV or computer. You shouldn't run a substantial lawn watering system through an inadequate, cheap vinyl hose. The inexpensive versions will kink, crack, leak at the couplings, quickly wear out, and generally cause frustration.

Pick a length that suits the size of your lawn. For my 5,000-square-foot lawn out front, I like to have about 200 feet of hose; I have two 100-foot sections connected end to end, but I wish I had purchased a 250-foot hose in the first place because the hose couplings always seem to wind up in the middle of the driveway, where they can easily be run over. Pick a quality hose that will withstand lying around in the hot sun all summer in case you're like me and aren't always home to roll it up. A hose constructed with a combination of reinforced rubber and vinyl should give you years of use.

Irrigation Systems

Even though I'm at the risk of alienating every irrigation contractor I know, I'd like you to read this quote from the official University of Florida lawn guide: "While automation is becoming increasingly necessary in many areas of our lives, automatic sprinkler systems and improper watering practices are undoubtedly the single biggest factor leading to the decline of home lawns."

As much as we desperately want to install a system and be done with it, responsible lawn care doesn't work that way. How often have you seen a lawn sprinkler going off in the rain? Or spewing water onto a driveway or roadside? How often do you see your neighbor's sprinkler heads pop up *every* single morning like clockwork?

As I've already detailed, lawns need a certain amount of water, but not more. Water is a precious, limited resource that shouldn't be wasted. So, please, if you take anything away from this chapter, remember this: You should not abuse a sprinkler system by thinking you can have it installed and then leave it alone.

That said, I think sprinkler systems are great tools for the lawn and garden, and I plan to have one put in at our new home. Installed properly with high-quality components and aimed well toward areas that really need water, sprinkler systems can be the best and most efficient watering system on the planet, other than a slow, steady rain. Just plan to turn on your system manually, and only when the lawn needs watering, or invest in the new generation of timers, which can sense exactly how much rainfall, evaporation, and transpiration have occurred. These timers won't even allow the system to turn on if the timer says the soil already has enough moisture.

Though many stores sell do-it-yourself lawn irrigation systems, I cannot endorse their use any more than I would tell you to attempt your own indoor plumbing. I have friends who have tried and succeeded, but they're few and far between.

The Submeter:
A Money-Saving Water Tip

YEARS AGO, when I started mowing lawns for a living, I never understood why one particular customer had two water-usage meters attached to his single-family home. Since he paid me only $10 to mow his lawn, I might have guessed: the two meters allowed him to save money.

Many municipalities charge customers extra for water that winds up in the sewer system. If you have only one meter on your home, chances are you are being billed under the assumption that *all* your water is going into the sewer. Installing a second meter, often known as a submeter, allows you to differentiate between water used indoors and water used outdoors to irrigate lawns, fill pools, or wash cars and windows. In both cases, you'll be billed for the water, but with a submeter, you'll save substantially on your sewer bill.

You will usually need to contact your local water district to purchase a submeter; installation by a professional plumber is also recommended. The initial cost may be great, but if you frequently irrigate your lawn, the submeter will be worth it in the long run.

Getting Started

The ideal time to install an irrigation system is before the lawn and garden are even planted. Most contractors will recommend setting aside a portion of the new home construction budget for at least the bones of an irrigation system, which can be modified at a later date. A landscape plan is a virtual must if you're going to put irrigation in the ground; try to construct a 5- to 10-year plan for the landscape, even if all aspects will not be built right away.

It's far more agonizing and expensive to tear up the lawn and garden after the fact, but it is certainly possible with the right equipment. Whether you install the system yourself or hire a professional, you'll want to take care to avoid large roots and utility lines. For a big lawn, you'll probably want a system that features pop-up sprinkler heads that can spray water great distances but not too high in the air. You should know that pop-up heads, however, are prone to malfunction and to lawn mower damage — especially some of the inexpensive, do-it-yourself models — and you'll want to spend the money on the best equipment you can afford. You'll also want to have your system serviced professionally in the spring and fall if possible. Winter drainage of the system is absolutely necessary in cold climates.

Choosing a Contractor

It's likely that a number of companies are lined up to sell you a full range of systems, from a few dollars to a few thousand dollars. As with anything else, you get what you pay for. Even if you do hire a professional, you'll still want to keep an eye on your system and stay in touch after the installation. Leaks can occur, and pipes can get plugged with calcium deposits and other debris. You might assume an area is getting plenty of water, only to see plants fail due to a malfunctioning system. More plants suffer from having no system, however.

Make sure the contractor is installing a rain sensor, maybe one of the new high-tech timers (see page 161), as well as a backflow prevention device approved by the local plumbing inspector. Backflow devices keep water that has entered the sprinkler system from reentering your drinking-water supply. Insist on getting a certificate of insurance from the contractor that includes liability and workers' compensation coverage. Your homeowner's policy probably will not cover workers injured on your property, and it may not cover damage if your contractor's backhoe nicks a power line or knocks out cable TV in the neighborhood. Be sure, too, to get a contract. Everything should be in writing, including materials, warranty (three years is standard), and the start and completion dates.

San Antonio, Texas

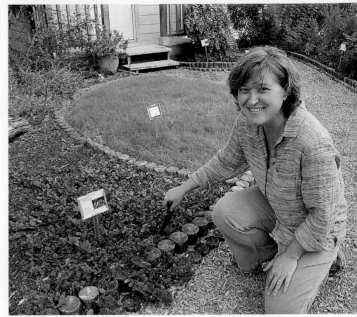

LOTS OF TOWNS and cities talk about water conservation and many have laws that severely limit when and how much water the residents may apply to their lawns. In San Antonio, Texas, the local water district found a way to take the sting out of its restrictions.

"Plain and simple, we pay people," said Dana Nichols, the conservation manager for the San Antonio Water System. "I'd estimate that we've awarded at least $200,000 in rebates since SIP [Seasonal Irrigation Program] started."

To earn a rebate, home- and business owners must comply with several landscape guidelines. No more than 50 percent of the landscape, for example, may be planted with lawn grasses. St. Augustine grass is banned; more drought-tolerant grasses such as Bermuda, buffalo, and zoysia are allowed.

"People here now take water conservation very seriously," said Nichols. "Water is an endangered resource, and through educational programs, we've really been able to make a difference."

In the mid-1990s, the average San Antonio resident consumed 160 gallons of water per day; in 2006, that total had been reduced to 130 gallons — but Nichols and her department are not finished. In 2007, the city will implement an ordinance that forces builders to use only drought-tolerant grasses around new homes. Nichols personally oversees the most popular exhibit at the San Antonio Botanic Garden, known as WaterSaver Lane, which showcases drought-tolerant alternatives to the traditional Texas landscape.

"I've been thrilled with the response," said Nichols. "It's my favorite thing I've ever worked on. The exhibits put the alternatives to lawns in context and get people thinking about a reduction, in general, in the size of their lawns. You think about how big your patio will be, or your flower bed, or your swimming pool. Think about your lawn, too, and don't necessarily use turf as your default feature in your landscape. That kind of thinking is working here in San Antonio."

9 Listening to Your Weeds

for many of you, this is probably the definitive chapter of the book. When it comes to natural lawn care, the real question isn't so much about how to grow grass, is it?

The real challenge is how to eliminate everything else that wants to grow in your lawn. We have long called these unwelcome plants "weeds," which in the famous quote by Ralph Waldo Emerson are defined as "any plants whose virtues have not yet been discovered."

Emerson was clearly from the nineteenth century. In this modern world, in which some of us barely take the time to meet our next-door neighbors, we're not all that interested in getting to know the virtues of any new plants, especially anything that is roguishly trying to invade our outdoor carpet of green. We're a society of grass snobs who want every blade in the lawn to look and feel exactly the same. I was one, and still am, to a degree. In this environment, a weed is defined as any plant trying to sneak in a little diversity.

Traditional lawn care since the late 1940s has feasted on a one-size-fits-all approach to weed control that paints every plant with the same broad stroke. Grass is good; everything else is bad. It's a simple tactic, requiring as little brain matter as possible on the part of the homeowner, the turf professional, and the marketing industry. It's also about the most unnatural thing in the outdoor world.

This chapter, like the rest of this book, will ask more of you. For the minimalists, I'd have you ignore the fact that not everything on your lawn is grass and just mow whatever is managing to grow. That's natural lawn care in its simplest form. To achieve the greater goal of a natural "weed-free lawn," however, you may be required to think, to meet some new plants, to occasionally use physical exertion, to learn some new techniques and products, and possibly to look at the world outside your door in a whole new way. And what a blast it is when you do. It's all about tracking the clues provided by nature, as if your lawn were a giant board game. Colonel Moss. In the shade. With compaction. Mystery solved!

Approximately 1,775 plants in the United States have been classified as weeds, and entire wonderful books have been written on the subject. *Weeds and What They Tell*, written in the 1950s by a German biochemist named Ehrenfried E. Pfeiffer, is especially enlightening. "Weeds are weeds only from our human egotistical point of view, because they grow where we do not want them," he wrote in his introduction. "In nature, however, they play an important and interesting role."

The RILE Approach

The Weed Identification Guide, starting on page 184, focuses on only about 40 of the most common lawn weeds, including what they look like, methods of control, and, most importantly, what the weeds tell us about our soil. This guide is the cornerstone of what I call the RILE approach to weeds: *Relax* before you act, *identify* your weed, *listen* to your weed, and, if necessary, *eradicate* your weed. If you can develop a basic understanding of RILE, you'll be armed against all weeds and off to a great start in your quest for a natural lawn.

Left: From a distance, the Great Lawn at Tower Hill Botanic Garden in Boylston, Massachusetts, looks green and great.

Right: Up close, the lawn reveals a large population of creeping Charlie — but no one seems to mind.

Relax

A devilishly inventive advertisement for a popular synthetic weed killer depicts a man climbing the sheer face of a high mountaintop. After braving the elements and exerting himself to the highest degree, the climber finally reaches his destination and pulls his spray bottle of herbicide from his holster as if it were a six-shooter. Heroically, he sprays the single dandelion emerging from a crack in the granite.

The ad's message, clever as it may be, is also tragically sad. As this chapter details, many plants actually provide significant benefit to the soil and therefore your lawn. Wide swaths of just turfgrass, if left alone, are dependent systems with no ability to feed or sustain themselves. Add in a little white clover or bird's-foot trefoil, though, and you'll give your lawn the tools it needs to take care of itself — except for the mowing, of course.

The best first step in natural weed control is to take a deep breath and make an honest evaluation of your weed population. A rule of thumb is that if you have anything less than 10 percent weeds in your grass, you don't have a weed problem worth treating. Anything more than 90 percent perfection isn't even reasonable to expect in a backyard setting. If you have 10 to 60 percent weeds, you may want to take some of the actions outlined later in the chapter. If more than two-thirds of your lawn is covered with weeds, in our lawn-as-a-board-game scenario, do not pass "Go," do not collect $200, and go straight to jail. You can come out only when you've reread chapter 5 about how to start over the right way.

Identify

Let's begin with a primer. On the one hand, lawn weeds are generally convenient to classify. They are either grasses, such as crabgrass, quack grass, and Bermuda grass, or they are broadleaf weeds, such as dandelion, ground ivy, and chickweed. Botanists will further explain that weedy grasses are monocots, meaning they emerge from their original seed with a single seed leaf. Broadleaf weeds are dicots, meaning they have two seed leaves at the time of germination. That's good to know when plotting your natural approach to weed eradication, because you always want to get rid of weeds when they're small. You also want to know if the weed is an annual, biennial, or perennial in your climate, because this will affect your method of control.

Annual weeds germinate from seed, grow, send up flowers, and produce new seed all in the same growing season if we allow them to live that long. They'll ultimately be killed by frosts. With annual weeds, therefore, careful management of the weed seeds is critical to reducing populations of the plant. Never allow a weed to produce seeds if at all possible; mow or pull the weeds instead.

Biennial weeds have a two-year life span. They store food reserves in the roots for the first year and then flower and set seed in the second year. Their control is most closely associated with that of annuals. In other words, if you don't let biennials go to seed, you've got a leg up in the battle.

Perennial weeds also germinate from seed, but they can also populate themselves through runners known as underground rhizomes and aboveground stolons. They won't die off in the winter, which generally makes them far more of a nuisance to control, even through traditional synthetic chemical treatments. If you simply try to dig them out and don't get every speck of rhizome or stolon, they'll typically grow back even stronger. The best tactics, therefore, involve changing the soil conditions that are allowing a weed to thrive.

If you read about soil in chapter 3 and are beginning to think of your lawn as a living body much like your own, you know that not all plants and soils can be treated equally. Part of the reason so many people fail in traditional lawn care programs is that they attempt to treat the entire yard with the same chemicals, which don't always work on all plants. Broadleaf herbicides won't touch weed grasses, for example, and generally do a poor job of eradicating many perennial weeds. Preemergent herbicides, similarly, won't do a bit of good on a perennial weed that's already established.

Having said all of this, I should tell you that you can grow a decent natural lawn without ever knowing the name or type of a single non-grass plant. Treat the soil well (chapter 3), pick good grass seed (chapter 4), and generally follow the rest of this book's advice, and it won't matter terribly if you don't know creeping Charlie from bugleweed. But if you're going to go to war with lawn weeds, it's imperative to know what you're fighting. To meet some of the likely suspects, turn to the Weed Identification Guide, on page 184. Your local Extension agents, most of whom are now online, will usually have fact sheets on other weeds prevalent in your area but not listed here.

Listen

The essence of organic weed control comes down to this premise: Most of those other plants that pop up in your lawn are trying to tell you a story about your soil. Sure, you can kill the messengers by instantly eliminating the weeds from the lawn with the right tool. But pulling or spraying the weeds doesn't change the underlying tale that

Got Moss?

IF SO, YOU LIKELY have one of six conditions in and around your soil: compaction, low fertility, acidity, excess moisture, inadequate soil depth, and shade. Organic moss killers do exist; they're usually soap products with a high phosphorus content. Until you correct some or all of the inherent soil and site conditions, however, it's not worth killing the moss.

"To control moss, you have to consider the reasons why it began to grow in your lawn," says Peter Landschoot, associate professor of turfgrass science at Pennsylvania State University. "Moss usually thrives under conditions that aren't conducive to good turf growth."

One alternative, of course, is to embrace the moss as a valid turf alternative. It's green, soft, and utterly low maintenance.

the plants are trying to convey. Just as your grass needs certain conditions to thrive — from a balanced pH to adequate organic matter, moisture, soil life, and fertility — weeds have their own needs, and their presence in your lawn should be seen as valuable indicators.

Have you ever wondered, for example, why crabgrass always seems to crop up right next to the driveway? Maybe you dig up the crabgrass, but then a new batch grows right back. It's because the crabgrass is trying to tell you the soil is compacted from all the feet, automobile tires, and plow blades that wander off the edge of the pavement. Until the compaction is remedied, you will always have crabgrass — or plantain, chickweed, or knotweed — in abundance. I have a nice neighbor who has been by a few times to expedite my landscape projects with his backhoe. Bless him. During one recent visit when I wasn't home, though, he drove the tractor right across my new lawn out front. I'm not generally a violent guy, but I wanted to strangle him. If I don't aerate the soil under those tire tracks, his visit will be marked by telltale trails of plantain for years to come.

The stories of weeds are many. Before you ever get a soil test, the presence of certain plants can tell you about all of the following: soil pH, soil life, moisture or drought, soil temperature, drainage, organic matter, fertility, tillage, soil structure, and the aforementioned compaction. To learn the story every plant has to tell in detail, I realize, is a tall order for anyone except the most dedicated of horticulturists. I have

Alien Invaders:
Exotic Invasive Weeds

IF YOU'RE THINKING of letting part of the lawn go "back to nature," you might want to be on alert. The plants that move in to replace the grass may not be all that natural.

In the past 50 years, weeds known as exotic invasive species have proliferated throughout our lawns, gardens, fields, and forests. If you let your existing lawn become a field on its own, chances are at least a few exotic invasive weeds will be part — or most — of your landscape.

By definition, exotic species are any plants or animals that originated elsewhere. Americans have consciously imported tens of thousands of plants for food, fiber, or ornamental purposes, including most of the grasses commonly used for lawns. All too often, though, the imported plants outcompete native plants and threaten natural ecosystems. An estimated 5,000 introduced plant species have escaped human cultivation and now exist in the United States on their own, according to the National Wildlife Federation, which has begun promoting the use of native plants.

Just one of these pest weeds, the European purple loosestrife, *Lythrum salicaria*, is estimated to be spreading at the rate of 50,000 acres per year — putting 44 common native plants and wildlife in danger and costing more than $50 million per year in control costs and forage losses, according to the National Sustainable Agriculture Information Service. In California, yellow star thistle, *Centaurea solstitalis*, now dominates more than two million acres of northern California grassland, resulting in the total loss of this once productive pastureland.

What can homeowners do? The first thing is to learn to identify the most invasive exotic weeds in your area. Make an effort to remove the plants from your landscape, by either digging, spraying with natural weed killers, or solarizing the plants (see page 176). It is far easier to remove the weedy plants when they're small than when they're full grown. Several sources can help you identify the most noxious plants; www.invasive.org is a great place to begin the education process.

observed many weed tendencies myself through my years as a landscaper and homeowner, but I have also learned much from the work of others. A special thanks again to Ehrenfried E. Pfeiffer, who was a protégé of Rudolf Steiner, the father of biodynamic farming and gardening, and to people like the late agronomist Carey Reams, who taught us that each weed species is genetically programmed to replace specific deficiencies in the soil. These groundbreaking scientists showed us that nature is always trying to find a balance. They proved that if your lawn is missing nitrogen, nature will often send in clover or one of its cousins in the legume family of plants, which can trap and process nitrogen from the atmosphere (see page 183). If your lawn, conversely, has too much nitrogen, nature will likely give you an

abundance of dandelions — and insects — to feed on the excess. Listening to your weeds can be an enormously powerful tool.

Eradicate

My friend Pat Lewis still remembers his first day of classes at the Stockbridge School at the University of Massachusetts in Amherst, back in the early 1980s. Dr. Joseph Troll, the renowned instructor, told the would-be golf course greenskeepers that "the best tool against weeds is a healthy grass plant." This is a point on which the traditional lawn care industry and the natural lawn care practitioners agree. A nice, lush stand of turf will resist weeds by blocking the light needed to germinate weed seeds. Getting to that verdant green carpet is where the two lawn care communities differ. Killing weeds by synthetic means often requires multiple applications of chemicals each

Because grasses hate soil compaction, growing lawns next to highly traveled walkways is often a challenge.

year, and no one chemical application will work for all weeds. The EPA estimates that only 2 percent of the active ingredients in weed killers, which are called herbicides, ever reach the target plant. The other 98 percent goes into the soil, the groundwater, and the atmosphere; onto other nontarget plants; or elsewhere in the environment.

After many years as a successful superintendent at golf courses in New England and countless sessions dressed as a white-suited spaceman atop the chemical sprayer, Pat Lewis reached a watershed conclusion.

"I thought Dr. Troll was right," he said. "But maybe there had to be a better way to get the grass healthy."

Pat proceeded to take the lead in converting his course, the Portland Country Club, in Falmouth, Maine, to a natural approach to growing grass. In time, his course became the first in Maine to be certified by the Audubon Society's Cooperative Sanctuary System, which requires limiting weed killers and other pesticides. Hundreds of other courses around the country are also now certified. I tell you this by way of example. If a golf course can create championship conditions without using weed-killing chemicals, you can certainly grow a nice natural lawn around your home.

Getting Rid of Weeds

If you have relaxed, identified, and listened to your weeds and are now ready for eradication, you have six primary tools at your disposal:

1. Total weed wipeout with nonselective sprays or solarizing techniques
2. Spot weeding with nonselective sprays, flaming, or mechanical tools
3. Preemergent weed control in spring and fall
4. Soil modification that gets to the root of the problem
5. Overseeding with new grass seed to crowd out weeds
6. Mowing at appropriate heights and only occasionally using a bagging attachment on your mower

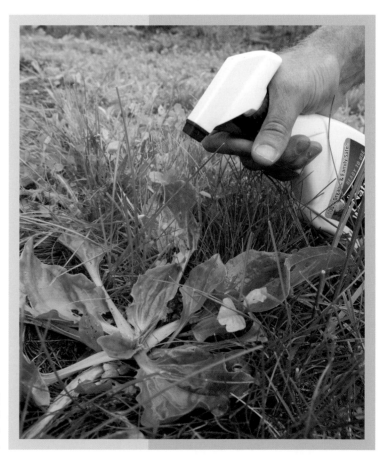

Newer vinegar-based or orange-oil based formulations of nonselective weed killers can be useful in spot spraying for plantain and other challenging weeds.

Solarization:
The Rubber Roundup

I CAME UPON this technique quite by chance back in my landscaping days in the early 1990s and have practiced it since with great success. The accident was leaving a pond liner spread out on the lawn area for just two warm days of summer. Oops. The grass, the weeds, everything underneath the pond liner was already dead or dying.

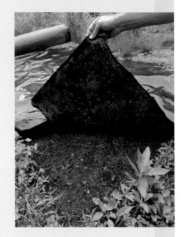

I have since used scraps of pond liner to kill vegetation on purpose. Whether it's to dispatch a patch of poison ivy near the edge of the woods or to clean out a potential lawn area that needs a complete overhaul, spreading the pond liner works far better than black or clear plastic. Sold as either pond liner or roofing underlayment at your local building supply store, this heavyweight (ask for 45-mil EPDM) black product will smother and fry all vegetation. Because it's heavier than plastic and doesn't allow any air to pass underneath, it will also trap all the gases being released from the soil and plants. Depending on temperatures, total dieback can take anywhere from one week in the heat of summer to two months in the cold of winter.

After removing the rubber blanket, it's important to work fresh compost or to spray compost tea into the solarized soil to restore life to the growing zone. Replant the area immediately with fresh grass seed or else weeds will quickly try to reestablish themselves.

Though the pond liner or roofing underlayment can be expensive initially, as compared with plastic, it will last far longer — 20 years or more — making it a great investment.

Total Weed Wipeout

Sometimes, when the weeds are just so bad, it's best to completely remove them before you plant new grass seed or put down new sod. In this scenario, you nonselectively kill every plant before starting your lawn program. For many years, glyphosate (most commonly marketed as Roundup) has been the synthetic chemical of choice, and depending on whose report you read, the compound is either benign or moderately toxic.

Fortunately, in recent years researchers and entrepreneurs have begun to manufacture natural alternatives that function in a similar manner. Mixtures of horticultural vinegar and citrus or vinegar and clove oil have all shown great promise. These products work most efficiently when air temperatures are warm, above 65°F. They are now available in large quantities and can be effective over a sizable area.

If the temperature is adequate, you spray the products directly onto the plants, soaking all parts of the foliage. Within 24 hours, the affected plants will show visible signs of browning and decline and will usually die within 48 to 72 hours. Multiple applications may be necessary in some cases, especially if it rains after an application or if the weeds are really large.

A word of warning: Even though these products are natural and won't harm the environment or the user, they can harm any nontarget plants. In other words, if you spray the weeds near the lawn, the lawn will also suffer dieback if some of the product hits it.

In cases where sprays are deemed either too costly or impractical, or if air temperatures are not high enough for these natural controls, the best alternative is solarization of the area. Basically, solarizing bakes the weeds to death by trapping the sun's heat. I've seen people try to spread out sheets of either clear or black plastic for this, but the best material is flexible rubber (see page 176).

Whether you use sprays or solarization to kill weeds, it is important to revisit the concept of listening to your weeds before you reestablish the lawn with seeding or sodding. Try to determine the identity of the predominant weeds so you can further understand the underlying soil conditions. If you haven't had a soil test already, get one. In general, a good follow-up to nonselective weed eradication is to work quality compost into the affected area. This will restore soil life and add nutrition, structure, and organic matter (more on these topics in chapters 3 and 7).

Although a rototiller has its uses in soil improvement and establishing a lawn, it is not a tool for eradicating perennial weeds. Always kill perennial weeds prior to tilling your yard.

Rototilling: The Pros and Cons

IN DAYS OF OLD when mammoth rototillers were still in fashion, it was the accepted practice to begin the renovation of a lawn by bulling the machine through any existing grass and weeds. After three or four passes, the plants' foliage had disappeared and all that remained on the surface were pulverized powdery soil and the illusion that our problems were gone. Maybe we would overseed the area, cover it with straw, and expect the weeds to magically stay away. Most often, they didn't.

Today we have a greater understanding that rototilling can, in some cases, do more harm than good. Tilling, for the sake of tilling, never has any long-term benefit and actually often ruins soil structure. If you're going to till, it should be because you're adding soil amendments and want to quickly work them into the root zone of your intended crop: in the case of lawns, usually 6 inches deep. Keep in mind that tilling weeds, especially perennial ones, without killing them first is just asking for trouble. Many perennial weeds spread by underground runners known as rhizomes. Either the roots or the rhizomes of the plants can break off the parent plant and quickly rejuvenate into a complete plant, so instead of a small patch of creeping Charlie you then have an entire colony.

If you do rototill to work in amendments or turn over dead foliage, be sure to roll the lawn afterward with a steel or plastic drum roller. This will give you a uniform grade, reduce air pockets, and ensure contact between seed and soil if you have overseeded.

Spot Weeding

Many times, even in healthy established lawns, weeds will randomly appear for any number of reasons. Maybe a long-dormant seed worked its way to the surface, maybe the wind carried it to your lawn, or maybe the soil conditions are now ideal for the establishment of that weed. Remember to relax, not panic.

If a weed or two pops up, try to take note of what it is and simply dig it out. The best tool for eradication of a single weed is the dandelion weeder, which looks something like the tail of a skinny fish. This implement can dig down to the bottom of most plants with taproots like dandelion and Queen Anne's lace, and it can also be useful in teasing out the fibrous roots of weedy grasses and some broad-leaved weeds like lamb's-quarters.

My long-handled fishtail weeder makes quick work of removing a large dandelion.

When weeding by hand, the key is to disturb as little of the soil surface as possible, so that you don't encourage other weed seeds to grow — and so you don't ruin the appearance of your lawn. Plenty of other hand-weeding devices are available, especially for vegetable gardeners, but for lawn weeds, the dandelion weeder is the one you want. You can also "flame" your weeds (see page 180).

If an entire colony of weeds appears on your lawn and it seems impractical to remove them by hand, you can spot-weed with the same products you'd use for a total weed wipeout. Just take care not to spray unintended areas, which you can do by screening them with a piece of cardboard, and try to understand why the colony of weeds appeared in the first place. If leafy spurge or speedwell is moving in, maybe that area isn't getting enough water; if wild strawberry appears in summer or hawkweed in fall, the soil pH or fertility, or both, may be too low. That's where listening to your weeds and studying the Weed Identification Guide will come in handy time and time again.

Preemergent Control

By employing this often misunderstood tool, you're simply attempting to cut off weeds at the pass, before the seeds germinate and begin to emerge from the soil. Primarily marketed by the traditional lawn care community as a weapon against crabgrass, this cocktail of synthetic chemicals creates barriers at the soil surface through which seeds cannot come to life. Preemergent weed killers are powerful, but nonetheless often fail because their use requires proper timing of application and patience. By their nature, these products do not break down quickly in the soil and are therefore among the most controversial lawn care herbicides.

In the natural lawn care community, the only preemergent control of note is based on corn gluten, a protein-rich by-product of the cornmeal-milling process. Marketed under a variety of brand names (see the resources section on page 262), corn gluten was patented for use on weeds by Iowa State University in 1991. The results, frankly, have been mixed. Natural turf care professionals use corn gluten effectively because they understand the issue of timing: the product must be on the ground two to three weeks prior to the expected germination of the target weed. For crabgrass in the North, that date can vary from early April to early May, whenever the forsythia and daffodils begin to bloom. For crabgrass in the South, the product should be applied around mid-March, when the flowers open on dogwood trees. If your target weeds generally emerge in different seasons from crabgrass, corn gluten may be also be utilized at other times of the year.

Potential corn gluten users must be aware of four key points:

1. The product inhibits seed germination of all types and therefore cannot be used within six weeks of overseeding a lawn. That means that in any given spring or fall, you will usually decide not to apply corn gluten but rather to spread new grass seed.
2. Corn gluten does absolutely no good combating previously established perennial weeds or annual weeds that are already growing.
3. Researchers at Iowa State admit that, on average, corn gluten is only about 65 percent as effective as synthetic preemergent weed controls.
4. Corn gluten is an excellent source of nitrogen and needs to be factored in to your lawn's overall fertilizing program for the year. A 40-pound bag of corn gluten generally contains 8 to 10 percent nitrogen, or between 3 and 4 pounds per bag. For some natural lawn care professionals, a spring application of corn gluten is the only nitrogen they apply on a customer's lawn all season.

A spring application of corn gluten will help control weeds, as well as supply a healthy dose of nitrogen.

Flaming Your Weeds

DO YOU LOATHE DIGGING, pulling, and spraying weeds? Here's one more solution: zapping them to death with a portable propane torch that heats to 2,000°F and often kills young annual weeds in less than a second by boiling the water in the stems and foliage. Older annuals and perennial weeds with elaborate root systems will likely take multiple flamings, but will eventually succumb.

Flamers are available at most hardware stores for $50 to $100 and should include a hose and a burning tip that produces a fine flame. Tanks vary in size from small handheld canisters to larger containers typically used to heat gas barbecue grills.

Here are a few usage and safety pointers to consider:

1 Look for a flamer with an ignition switch and avoid using matches; I've scorched the hairs on my hand more than once by lighting a flamer with matches.

2 Never flame weeds during dry periods, on windy days, or when the lawn contains excessive dry thatch.

3 Avoid using a flamer near dry bark mulch, which can ignite quickly.

4 If your flamer has an extension hose, keep the flame away from the hose and the tank.

5 The younger the plants, the more quickly and easily they'll die back after flaming.

6 Just a split second is needed to scorch a weed; holding it longer may damage soil organisms and nontarget plants near the weed.

7 The flamer tip will remain hot long after the flaming stops, so be careful not to touch the tip or leave out the tool where others, such as curious children or pets, might come in contact with it.

Soil Modification

At the beginning of this chapter, I cited the example of crabgrass growing in the compacted soil near the edge of the driveway. Nothing keeps crabgrass from recurring completely until the underlying soil is improved. This may require a soil amendment such as compost, gypsum, or limestone, along with a soil manipulation such as aeration, or the addition of more topsoil to improve drainage and overall depth. Review chapter 3 about the importance of proper soil for your particular climate and grass variety.

Make no mistake. What is going on underneath the soil surface will have the biggest impact on what is going on above the ground. Oftentimes the solution to removing weeds can be found by adding relatively small amounts of nutrients that scarcely anyone ever talks about. We hear about the macronutrients nitrogen, potassium, and phosphorus, which are listed as N-P-K on the front of fertilizer bags, yet soil scientists tell us other nutrients are equally or more important. Some lawn care professionals are able to conquer dandelions, for instance, by adding calcium to the soil.

Jay McCaman would agree. In his report *Weeds and Why They Grow,* the Michigan agronomist found that 90 percent of the most common lawn weeds appear due, in part, to a deficiency of calcium in the soil. That's why many of the new organic lawn care programs emphasize multiple applications of calcium each year.

An abundance of dandelions may indicate a lack of calcium in the lawn soil.

Overseeding

Other than building healthy soil, applying new grass seed over an existing lawn is the best long-term strategy against weeds. Even in healthy soil, overseeding is often necessary to combat certain perennial weeds, such as creeping Charlie, ragweed, and chicory, that will grow well in the same conditions that turfgrasses enjoy. New seed, applied every fall, will generally outcompete weeds if you have otherwise created good soil conditions. Revisit chapter 4 to decide which seed varieties are best around your home, as well as when and how much to apply.

Mowing

Remember what Dr. Troll, the instructor at the Stockbridge School at UMass, told Pat Lewis and his other students about battling weeds, that healthy turf is the

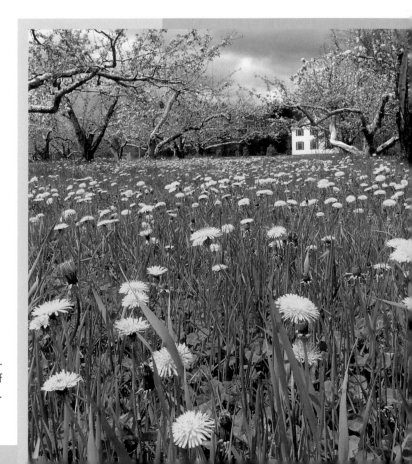

first line of defense? Well, the quickest way to ruin healthy turf, other than compacting it with heavy equipment or spilling toxic compounds on it, is through poor mowing techniques. Cutting back anything is an unnatural act, and it takes time even for grass to recover. But if you mow properly, grass recovers quickly, in fact much faster than many weeds. Mowing gets its own treatment in chapter 11. You'll also need to review chapter 4, because each grass species grows best at different heights.

Bag it or not. In general, I rarely recommend using a bagging attachment when mowing the lawn. As with many rules, however, exceptions apply. You get three free passes a year when it comes to using a bagging mower.

The first time is during your initial mowing in spring, before the true flush of new growth pushes out. It's a good idea to mow a still-dormant lawn with the bag attached to collect any snow mold, leaves, and other debris that linger from winter. Removing this debris and adding it to the compost pile clears the way for your lawn to grow freely.

The second time to attach the bag comes when the dandelions go to seed, usually about mid-May in wintry climates. We all recognize them, the little white puffballs that explode into millions of seeds as soon as we touch them. Having the bag attached helps collect these seeds and keeps them from spreading throughout a lawn. Of course, if you don't have dandelions in your lawn, you can turn in this free pass at the door. If you do use the bagger to collect dandelion seeds, don't add the contents to your compost pile unless you're sure the pile is heating to 130–150°F; if possible, simply spread the material out in the shade of the woods and let it decompose naturally.

The final time to use the bagger comes at the end of the year, when you're collecting any leaves on the lawn. Raking is hard work, and a bagging mower can be an efficient tool to vacuum up fallen foliage from maples, oaks, and their deciduous brethren. This is great material for the compost pile, especially since the leaves are all prechopped by the mower blades. One caution, though: If weeds on your lawn have gone to seed at the end of the year and these seeds have made it into your mower bag along with the leaves, don't add the refuse to the compost pile. Take it to the woods instead.

Keeping a mower on its higher settings allows grass to grow tall and shade out weed seeds.

Clover: The Best Weed Money Can Buy

ONCE UPON A TIME, before the advent of synthetic weed killers for the lawn in the late 1940s, most American lawns contained white clover. Because no formulation of weed control could be developed that left grass and clover but killed everything else, clover was then lumped in with the weeds in subsequent marketing campaigns. The scientist who developed 2,4-D, the most common synthetic herbicide, was publicly apologetic because his new product had the unfortunate side effect of eliminating clover.

"The thought of white Dutch clover as a lawn weed will come as a distinct shock to old-time gardeners," wrote Dr. R. Milton Carleton in his 1957 book, *A New Way to Kill Weeds*. "I can remember the day when lawn mixtures were judged for quality by the percentage of clover seed they contained. The higher this figure, the better the mixture . . . I can remember the loving care which old-time gardeners gave their clover lawns. The smug look on the face of the proud homeowner whose stand was the best in the neighborhood was really something to behold."

"Milt," as his friends called him, reportedly also carried around a flask of pure 2,4-D, from which he would take a pull from time to time to prove to naysayers that the compound was "safe enough to drink." He lived to be 87 and would, no doubt, debate any claims that the product has negative side effects other than killing clover.

What is not in doubt are the many benefits of white clover, among which are:

Nitrogen fixing. Clover and other legumes are infected by soil bacteria known as rhizobia, which allow them to form nitrogen-fixing nodules on their roots. Nitrogen fixing enables the plants to convert nitrogen gas in the air to a form that plants can use as nutrition.

A lawn that contains 5 percent clover can create the equivalent of approximately 2 pounds of nitrogen per 1,000 square feet annually. Most lawns need about 4 pounds of nitrogen per year per 1,000 square feet. This means that if you grow clover and use a mulching mower to recycle the clippings, your lawn probably has enough nitrogen without additional fertilizers. You can tell if nitrogen fixing is happening on your lawn by digging up a clover plant and cutting into a root nodule; if the inside of the nodule is red, then nitrogen fixing is occurring.

Nutrient efficiency. Nitrogen provided by clover is far less likely to leach from the soil than nitrogen from synthetic fertilizers. Naturally produced nitrogen will also not reduce the pH of your soil, which can happen when large amounts of synthetic nitrogen are applied.

Evergreen color. Clover remains green all year round, even in times of drought.

Masking. Clover generally outcompetes other lawn weeds and hides the presence of other non-grass species.

Disease resistance. The presence of clover in the lawn, along with the absence of synthetic fertilizers and weed 'n' feed, generally helps the grass fend off pests and diseases. Excessive synthetic nitrogen attracts pests and disease, and both the synthetic nitrogen and weed 'n feed may negatively impact the vigor of the grass roots. Clover even resists "dog spot," which occurs when female dogs urinate on the lawn.

Though clover is rarely included in premixed bags of grass seed, it is readily available by the pound from seed supply stores and garden supply catalogs. To achieve the goal of about 5 percent clover in your grass, apply about 1 ounce of clover seed per 1,000 square feet.

Weed Identification Guide

USE THE FOLLOWING INFORMATION to positively identify weeds growing in your landscape and to potentially develop an action plan against them. Remember, a few weeds are not cause for alarm; simply dig them out if they bother you. If large colonies of weeds are growing, or if many weeds that thrive in the same kinds of soil conditions are present, then it may be time to take action. The information listed here is gathered from personal observation and from feedback from nationally recognized lawn care professionals including Todd Harrington of Connecticut and Phil Catron of Maryland, as well as published studies by the U.S. Department of Agriculture, Cornell University, and McGill University and published texts by authors Charles Waters, Ehrenfried E. Pfeiffer, and Jay L. McCaman (see page 261). Keep in mind that the soil indicators listed below are not absolutes. Weeds that often indicate low levels of calcium, for example, may grow in areas of high calcium if fertility is low.

Many weeds have multiple common names, but all have only one botanical name, which is listed in italics. If you remove any weeds mechanically or by hand, soil amendments and immediate overseeding with proper grass seed are highly recommended. Although many weeds are listed as edible, they should not be consumed or used medicinally without the proper guidance or experience. It is a good idea to allow any perennial weeds to dry in the sun or to drown them in a pail of water prior to adding them to a compost pile.

Barnyard grass

Barnyard grass

Echinochloa crus-galli
annual

Appearance: Thick-stemmed grass branches at the base; leaf blades ½ inch wide; greenish purple flower heads resemble a bristle brush; plant can reach 4 feet tall; fleshy roots
Reproduces: By seed
Range: Southern Canada and entire U.S. except southern Florida
Soil indications: Low calcium, phosphorus, humus, bacteria; high potassium, magnesium, sulfur
Removal: Add calcium, compost, compost tea; dig to remove tubers, roots; mow or trim to keep from going to seed
Benefits: Can be ground into flour

Bird's-foot trefoil

Lotus corniculatus
perennial

Appearance: Sprawling; cloverlike leaves in groups of three; bright yellow sweet pea–type flowers in summer; taproots also branch
Reproduces: By seed
Range: Upper Midwest and Great Lakes region, northeastern U.S., eastern Canada
Soil indications: Low nitrogen; poor drainage
Removal: Let it grow or add nitrogen, compost, compost tea; pull excess plants in fall
Benefits: Fixes nitrogen from the atmosphere

Bird's-foot trefoil

Black medic

Medicago lupulina
annual

Appearance: Mat forming; often confused with clover because of oblong leaves in groups of three; distinguished by long stalk on central leaflet; small yellow flowers in early summer; shallow taproot
Reproduces: By seed
Range: U. S. and Canada
Soil indications: Low nitrogen, bacteria; high magnesium, sulfur, iron
Removal: Let it grow or add nitrogen or compost; pull by hand
Benefits: Fixes nitrogen from the atmosphere

Black medic

Carolina geranium

Geranium carolinianum
annual

Appearance: Common, pretty wildflower with distinctive lobed leaves resembling a hand; small five-petaled flowers at stem ends in late spring; can grow to 10 inches tall; fibrous, shallow taproot
Reproduces: By seed
Range: Entire U.S. and southern Canada
Soil indications: Low calcium, nitrogen, humus; high phosphorus, potassium; compaction; low soil life
Removal: Add calcium, compost, compost tea; pull by hand; mechanical aeration
Benefits: Ornamental garden plant

Carolina geranium

Carpetweed

Carpetweed

Mollugo verticillata
annual

Appearance: Mat forming; clusters of narrow leaves on wiry stem; tiny white flowers at leaf joints in mid- to late summer; short taproot

Reproduces: By seed

Range: Entire U.S. and southern Canada

Soil indications: Low humus; high nitrogen, potassium, phosphorus, sulfur; anaerobic

Removal: Add compost, compost tea; pull by hand or cut off to prevent seed formation

Benefits: Edible leaves

Chickweed

Chickweed

Stellaria media
annual

Appearance: Mat forming; pairs of yellowish green leaves on trailing, slender stems; small, five-petaled white flowers in spring; sun to shade, but may die back in the heat of summer

Reproduces: By seeds

Range: Entire U.S. and southern Canada

Soil indications: Low calcium, phosphorus; high nitrogen, potassium, magnesium, organic matter

Removal: Pulls easily by hand; overseed with grass seed in late summer before weed reestablishes

Benefits: Edible, widely used as an herb

Chicory

Cichorium intybus
perennial

Chicory

Appearance: Roadside or fence-row plant with leaves resembling dandelion at the base; blue flowers on tall, wiry stems from early summer to late fall; blossoms close late in the day; deep taproots

Reproduces: By seed

Range: Entire U.S. and Canada

Soil indications: Low calcium, nitrogen, humus; high potassium, sulfur; anaerobic

Removal: Add calcium, nitrogen, compost, compost tea; dig deeply to get full root system

Benefits: Edible; coffee substitute

Crabgrass

Digitaria spp.

annual

Appearance: Stout grassy sheaths and blades branching out from a central fibrous root system; yellowish green turning bluish red in late summer and early autumn

Reproduces: By seed

Range: Entire U.S. and Canada

Soil indications: Low calcium, bacteria; high potassium; compaction

Removal: Add calcium, compost, compost tea; pull or gather before seeds drop in autumn; mechanical aeration

Benefits: Erosion control

Crabgrass

Creeping Charlie

Glechoma hederacea

perennial

Appearance: Low-growing, aggressive creeping plant with thumbnail-size scalloped leaves like tiny geranium leaves; square stems root in the soil at nodes; abundant tiny lavender flowers in 2- to 3-inch spikes in spring; minty-scented leaves; fleshy roots

Reproduces: By seed, stolons

Range: Entire U.S. except northern Florida, Nevada, New Mexico; Canada

Soil indications: Low nitrogen, bacteria; high calcium, iron, sulfur; poor drainage

Removal: Add nitrogen, compost, compost tea; dethatch

Benefits: Edible

Creeping Charlie

Curly dock

Rumex crispus

perennial

Appearance: Often confused with dandelion; long serrated leaves; greenish rosettes of undistinguished flowers in spring; taproot

Reproduces: By seed

Range: Most of the U.S. and Canada

Soil indications: Low calcium, bacteria, pH; high phosphorus, potassium, magnesium; poor drainage

Removal: Add calcium, lime, compost, compost tea; dig by hand

Benefits: Edible; breaks up hardpan

Curly dock

Weed Identification Guide

Dallis grass

Dallis grass
Paspalum dilatatum
perennial

Appearance: Grassy looking, up to five feet tall if left unchecked; rough-edged yellowish green leaf blades up to ½ inch wide; clump forming; spreads with fibrous roots and rhizomes
Reproduces: By seed, rhizomes
Range: Southern U.S.
Soil indications: Low calcium, humus; high phosphorus, potassium, magnesium; hardpan
Removal: Add calcium, compost; dig carefully to get full root system
Benefits: None

Dandelion

Taraxacum officinale
perennial

Appearance: Long, serrated "lion's tooth" leaves, which give the plant its name; bright yellow flowers in early spring; globe-shaped seed heads; deep taproot
Reproduces: By seed
Range: Entire U.S. and Canada
Soil indications: Low calcium, pH; high potassium
Removal: Add calcium, lime; dig deep to get whole root
Benefits: Edible; brings calcium and other nutrients to the surface; leaves behind canals for easy earthworm travel; early nectar sources for bees

Dandelion

English daisy
Bellis perennis
perennial

Appearance: Spatula-shaped leaves in a rosette at the plant's base; daisylike white flowers with yellow centers emerge from tall stems; taproot
Reproduces: By seed
Range: Entire U.S. and Canada
Soil indications: Low calcium, nitrogen, humus, pH; high moisture
Removal: Add calcium, lime, nitrogen, compost; dig deep; mow frequently
Benefits: Cut flowers; herbal properties

English daisy

Field horsetail

Equisetum arvense
perennial

Appearance: Two types of stems, the most visible being fernlike foliage fanning out from a central yellowish stem; overall look of a pine tree seedling; fibrous creeping roots and rhizomes
Reproduces: By spores, rhizomes
Range: U.S. except Southeast; Canada
Soil indications: Low calcium, phosphorus, humus, pH; high moisture; poor drainage
Removal: Add calcium, lime, compost; improve drainage; pull and dig repeatedly
Benefits: Herbal properties

Field horsetail

Goose grass

Eleusine indica
annual

Appearance: Clump-forming grass resembling crabgrass; develops into mats in lawns; seed heads in fingerlike spikes at stem tops; stems often lay flat on the ground as if stepped on; fleshy roots
Reproduces: By seed
Range: U.S. except most northwestern areas; eastern Canada
Soil indications: Low calcium, phosphorus; high potassium, magnesium, salt
Removal: Add calcium, compost; mow or dig before seed forms
Benefits: Edible seeds

Goose grass

Hawkweed

Hieracium spp.
perennial

Appearance: Wildflowers with numerous subspecies occurring across the U.S. and Canada; hairy, long leaves at the base of plant; bright orange or yellow flowers on leafless stems; often mistaken for dandelion but blooms much later in summer; shallow, fibrous roots with rhizomes, stolons
Reproduces: By seeds, rhizomes, stolons
Range: Entire U.S. and Canada
Soil indications: Low calcium, nitrogen, phosphorus, humus, bacteria, pH
Removal: Add calcium, nitrogen, compost, compost tea, limestone
Benefits: Herbal properties

Hawkweed

Weed Identification Guide

Heal-all

Heal-all

Prunella vulgaris
perennial

Appearance: Upright, spreading; smooth stemmed; long leafed; spikes of tube-shaped purple flowers throughout summer; fibrous roots with stolons
Reproduces: By seed, stolons
Range: Entire U.S. and Canada
Soil indications: Low calcium, humus; high phosphorus, potassium, magnesium, sulfur; poor drainage; anaerobic
Removal: Add calcium, compost; aerate soil; dig or mow frequently
Benefits: Herbal tea

Henbit

Henbit

Lamium amplexicaule
annual

Appearance: Square stems with long, fuzzy, serrated leaves; purple tubular flowers just above the leaves in late spring; fleshy roots
Reproduces: By seed
Range: Entire U.S. and southern Canada
Soil indications: Low calcium, humus, bacteria; high moisture
Removal: Add calcium, compost; pull by hand
Benefits: Edible; herbal properties

Japanese clover

Lespedeza striata
annual

Appearance: Similar to common white clover, with characteristic oblong leaflets in groups of three; firm, woody stems unlike those of white clover; inconspicuous purplish flowers in late summer; mat forming; taproot
Reproduces: By seed
Range: Southern U.S.
Soil indications: Low calcium, nitrogen, bacteria
Removal: Let it grow or add nitrogen and calcium, compost
Benefits: Fixes nitrogen from the atmosphere; erosion control

Japanese
clover

Knawel

Scleranthus annuus
annual

Appearance: Hairy or smooth wiry stems; thick, pointed, shiny narrow leaves lining the stems in pairs; nondescript green flowers spring through summer; fibrous taproot

Reproduces: By seed

Range: East coast of U.S.; Pacific Northwest; southern Canada

Soil indications: Low calcium, phosphorus, humus, bacteria; high potassium, magnesium; sandy

Removal: Add calcium, compost, compost tea; pull by hand

Benefits: Holds sandy soils in place

Knawel

Lamb's-quarters

Chenopodium album
annual

Appearance: Upright to 6 feet tall if left unchecked; egg-shaped or triangular leaves with toothed edges covered by tiny white scales; small, nondescript flowers form at the tips of main stem and branches in summer; fleshy roots

Reproduces: By seed

Range: Entire U.S. and Canada

Soil indications: Low calcium, phosphorus; high nitrogen, potassium, sulfur; healthy overall

Removal: Add calcium; dig or pull by hand

Benefits: Highly edible

Lamb's-quarters

Mallow

Malva neglecta
annual or biennial

Appearance: Low growing; mat forming; round leaves with serrated edges; pinkish white flowers in leaf joints throughout summer; taproot

Reproduces: By seed

Range: U.S. except Florida; Canada

Soil indications: Low nitrogen, phosphorus, humus; high potassium.

Removal: Add nitrogen, compost; pull or mow before seed sets

Benefits: Edible; herbal properties

Mallow

Weed Identification Guide

Moneywort

Moneywort

Lysimachia nummularia
perennial

Appearance: Trailing vine; shiny round leaves in pairs along the stems; five-petaled yellow flowers in late spring to summer; fibrous roots develop where nodes on stems touch soil
Reproduces: By seed, rooting stems
Range: Northeast and north-central U.S.; southern Canada
Soil indications: Low calcium, phosphorus, humus, and soil life
Removal: Add calcium, compost, compost tea; pull and mow frequently
Benefits: Common herb; ornamental ground cover, also known as creeping Jenny

Mouse-ear chickweed

Mouse-ear chickweed

Cerastium vulgatum
perennial

Appearance: Low growing with tiny leaves resembling mouse ears; leaves attach directly to stems; five-petaled white flowers from spring to summer; shallow fibrous roots
Reproduces: By seed, rooting stems
Range: U.S. except Deep South and North Dakota
Soil indications: Low calcium, phosphorus, humus; high potassium, salt; anaerobic
Removal: Add calcium, compost, compost tea; easy to dig and pull
Benefits: Edible; widely used as an herb

Nimblewill

Nimblewill

Muhlenbergia schreberi
perennial

Appearance: Wiry grasslike plant with spreading stems; flat leaves pointing outward, perpendicular to the stems; 2- to 3-inch feathery seed heads in autumn; fibrous roots with stolons
Reproduces: By seed, stolons
Range: U.S. except Florida
Soil indications: Low calcium, humus; high magnesium; poor drainage; anaerobic
Removal: Add calcium, compost, compost tea; dig by hand; pull or mow before seed forms
Benefits: None

Oxeye daisy

Chrysanthemum leucanthemum
perennial

Appearance: Lobed dandelion-like leaves along smooth, unbranched stems; distinctive white flowers with yellow center in early summer; fleshy taproot with rhizomes

Reproduces: By seed, rhizomes

Range: U.S. except northern Great Plains; some areas of southern Canada

Soil indications: Low calcium, nitrogen, phosphorus, humus, pH, bacteria; high potassium

Removal: Add calcium, lime, nitrogen, compost, compost tea

Benefits: Edible; common herb; cut flower

Oxeye daisy

Plantain

Plantago major
perennial

Appearance: Broad, oval, ribbed leaves in a rosette; barely visible nondescript flowers rising from the center of rosette in summer; seeds rising in tall stalks from the center in autumn; fibrous roots and sometimes deep taproot

Reproduces: By seed

Range: Entire U.S. and Canada

Soil indications: High calcium, potassium, phosphorus; poor drainage; hardpan; acidic; anaerobic

Removal: Add lime, compost, compost tea; dig deep, mechanical aeration

Benefits: Edible

Plantain

Prostrate knotweed

Polygonum aviculare
annual

Appearance: Mat forming; wiry stems with small blue-green leaves of varying shapes; taproot

Reproduces: By seed

Range: Entire U.S. and Canada

Soil indications: Low calcium, phosphorus, humus, pH; high potassium, magnesium; poor drainage; anaerobic

Removal: Add calcium, lime, compost, compost tea; aerate soil; pull or mow before seed sets

Benefits: Edible

Prostrate knotweed

Purslane

Purslane

Portulaca oleracea

perennial

Appearance: Mat forming; succulent, brownish purple tubular stems and shiny oblong leaves; tiny five-petaled yellow flowers in summer; fibrous roots and taproot

Reproduces: By seed

Range: Entire U.S.

Soil indications: Low calcium, nitrogen, phosphorus, humus, moisture; high potassium, salt; anaerobic

Removal: Add calcium, nitrogen, compost; increase irrigation

Benefits: Highly edible and nutritious

Quackgrass

Agropyron repens

perennial

Appearance: Clump-forming grass with blue-green blades; 2 to 3 feet tall if left unchecked; often confused with crabgrass, but has thicker stems; fibrous roots

Reproduces: By rhizomes

Range: U.S. except Florida and Arizona; southern Canada

Soil indications: Low calcium, humus; high phosphorus, potassium, sulfur; hardpan; anaerobic

Removal: Add calcium, compost, compost tea; mechanical aeration; cut back or mow emerging shoots frequently in early spring

Benefits: Can be used as lawn grass substitute

Quackgrass

Queen Anne's lace

Daucus carota

biennial

Appearance: Looks and smells like a common carrot the first year; flat-topped white flowers originating from same point on stem the second year in late summer; taproot

Reproduces: By seed

Range: Entire U.S. and Canada

Soil indications: Low calcium, nitrogen, phosphorus, potassium, bacteria; prolonged drought

Removal: Add calcium, macronutrients, compost, compost tea; pull by hand

Benefits: Edible roots; cut flowers; nectar source

Queen Anne's lace

Speedwell

Veronica officinalis

perennial

Appearance: Common wildflower; upright with branching stems; toothed leaves covered in fine hairs; small white to blue flower spikes in early summer; taproot can also be fibrous

Reproduces: By seed

Range: Eastern U.S. from Virginia northward; southern Canada

Soil indications: Low calcium, phosphorus, bacteria

Removal: Add calcium, compost, compost tea; pull by hand

Benefits: Common herb

Speedwell

Violet

Viola spp.

perennial

Appearance: Common ground cover with heart- or kidney-shaped leaves; deep purple, white, or pink flowers throughout spring and summer; fibrous roots and taproot

Reproduces: By rhizomes, stolons

Range: Entire U.S. and southern Canada

Soil indications: Low calcium, pH

Removal: Add calcium, lime; dig as much of root system as possible

Benefits: Many are edible; used as ornamental ground covers

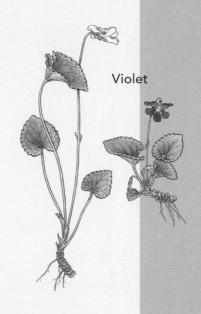

Violet

Virginia buttonweed

Diodia virginiana

perennial

Appearance: Creeping stems with pointed, narrow leaves; foliage often is purplish, but plant may have yellow cast due to persistent virus; ½-inch star-shaped white flowers in leaf joints; common name comes from the plant's buttonlike seeds; fleshy roots

Reproduces: By seed, roots

Range: Southeastern U.S.

Soil indications: Low calcium, humus; high moisture

Removal: Add calcium, compost; pull by hand in spring

Benefits: Erosion control

Virginia buttonweed

White clover

White clover

Trifolium repens
perennial

Appearance: Low growing; mat forming; round, dark green leaves in groups of three; multiple white and pink-tinged flowers in late spring and early summer; soft stems; fleshy roots

Reproduces: By seeds, stolons

Range: Entire U.S. except Deep South; Canada

Soil indications: Low nitrogen, pH

Removal: Let it grow or add nitrogen, lime, compost

Benefits: Fixes nitrogen from the atmosphere; good nectar source

Wild garlic
and
wild onion

Wild garlic and wild onion

Allium spp.
perennial

Appearance: Fleshy, tubular leaves with characteristic onion odor on both plants; hollow garlic leaves hug base of plant near the stem; purple flowers on garlic plant in spring to summer; onion leaves flatter, not hollow; distinctive bulb-like bulbils at the top of stems on onion; plant emerges from bulbs

Reproduces: By seed, bulbils

Range: Entire U.S. and Canada

Soil indications: Low calcium, humus; high potassium; poor drainage

Removal: Add calcium, compost; dig up with trowel

Benefits: Highly edible

Witch grass

Witch grass

Panicum capillare
annual

Appearance: Upright habit; spreads and branches at the base; common name derived from tall flower heads resembling a broom or the tassels on a cornstalk; fibrous roots

Reproduces: By seed

Range: U.S. except Northern Plains; some areas of southern Canada

Soil indications: Low calcium, humus; high magnesium

Removal: Add calcium, compost; hand-pull or mow before seed sets

Benefits: Edible seeds

Yarrow

Achillea millefolium
perennial

Appearance: Common wildflower; fine, feathery foliage like a fern; clusters of small white flowers atop a single stem in early to late summer; fibrous roots with rhizomes
Reproduces: By seed, rhizomes
Range: U.S. except most of Florida; Canada
Soil indications: Low calcium, nitrogen, phosphorus, potassium, bacteria; high sulfur
Removal: Add calcium, macronutrients, compost, compost tea; avoid pulling by hand
Benefits: Edible; herbal properties

Yarrow

Yellow nutsedge

Cyperus esculentus
perennial

Appearance: Glossy, pointed, yellowish green leaf blades that emerge in groups of three from the base of a central stem; white tubers and rhizomes occur on same plant
Reproduces: By seed, tubers
Range: Entire U.S. and Canada
Soil indications: Low calcium, phosphorus, humus, bacteria; high potassium, sulfur, magnesium; poor drainage; anaerobic
Removal: Add calcium, compost, compost tea; dig to remove tubers, roots
Benefits: Tubers are edible

Yellow
nutsedge

Yellow woodsorrel

Oxalis stricta
perennial

Appearance: Low and bushy; three-lobed, heart-shaped leaves like clover; small five-petaled yellow flowers all summer; taproot; slight lemon scent
Reproduces: By seed
Range: Entire U.S. and Canada
Soil indications: Low calcium, nitrogen, phosphorus, humus; high potassium
Removal: Add calcium, nitrogen, compost, compost tea; dig by hand
Benefits: Edible

Yellow
woodsorrel

10 Dealing with Thugs

t o be honest, I was tempted to eliminate this chapter altogether in an effort to make a strong point in favor of natural lawn care. In a well-executed natural lawn maintenance system, pests and diseases are rarely a problem worth treating. The deep, healthy roots of grass plants growing in fertile soil are the best defense against any kind of attack, whether from typically devastating lawn insects or the equally ruinous fungal diseases that can make our lawns look like a minefield.

From time to time, problems will arise in even the best of soils and grasses. The approach for dealing with chinch bugs (pictured top left and below) and moles (top right), or dog spot (above) and brown patch, is quite similar to the RILE technique with weeds that was detailed in the last chapter: *Relax, identify, listen,* and, if necessary, *eradicate.*

In the same way we've been trained through clever marketing campaigns to buy bagged products to make our lawns green, we've also been conditioned to rush out to purchase spray bottles to take care of whatever insect or disease is trying to turn our lawns brown. In many cases, the sprays — even organic formulations — aren't necessary. If you pause to correctly identify the nemeses and really try to understand why they're attacking your lawn, you can often devise a resolution that is not based on products. This is known as a cultural solution; if you improve the underlying condition of the soil or the aboveground condition of the grass through mowing, the visible problem with the pest or disease often will disappear.

When you do reach for a spray, and most of us have done it, be sure to select something you know will work well; cause minimal damage to nontarget insects, plants, or animals; and uphold the standards of natural lawn care. The truth is that natural products may not work as quickly in the short term as some of the synthetic chemical brands you may have used in the past; the highly toxic chemicals often spelled instant death for the ants, chinch bugs, or other pests, but they also did in many nontarget creatures such as earthworms and microorganisms that were trying to make your soil healthy. Given enough time to perform their function, natural products will kill or repel pests without leaving toxic residues.

In some cases we are being forced to change. Many of the harshest synthetic pesticides, including chlorpyrifos and diazinon, have been taken off the market by the Environmental Protection Agency (EPA), which deemed them a public health risk. For nearly 40 years, consumers used diazinon to get rid of ants, and chlorpyrifos (marketed as Dursban) to control billbugs, termites, and other insects. At the time of the ban, the EPA estimated that more than 850 products contained chlorpyrifos; consumers have been looking for alternatives ever since.

"The product manufacturers will trot out other new chemical solutions, but the bottom line is that all these products are not necessary," says Michael Surgan, the lead environmental scientist for the New York Attorney General's office. "We really try to advocate a commonsense, natural approach."

The Natural Controls

Natural approaches to pest and disease control on lawns can be broken into roughly four categories: cultural controls that focus on grass selection and soil improvements; physical controls that employ manual labor and barrier-type structures; biological controls that encourage a beneficial organism to overtake the pest organism; and botanical controls, such as sprays and dusts, which should be the last line of defense even in a natural lawn care system. All of these should be part of your RILE approach, which may sound a lot like what some books refer to as Integrated Pest Management, or IPM. The reason I don't defer to all aspects of IPM is that its approach allows for the use of toxic synthetic chemicals as a last resort; in natural lawn care, these chemicals have no place.

A few white grubs may be present in all lawns; apply control products only if you have more than a dozen grubs per square foot of lawn.

Cultural Changes

How you water, mow, and apply fertilizers and soil amendments are all part of a cultural approach to pest control. If, for example, you apply too much water or if it rains too often, brown patch may develop. If you apply too much nitrogen to force out top growth, brown patch could also be a symptom. As you read the descriptions of the various pests and diseases, you'll see that altering the culture of your lawn — for example, raising the mower blade; raking to remove leaves, debris and thatch; limiting or adding water; and adding organic matter — should be the first line of defense.

Planting disease-resistant cultivars or hybrids of grasses is also a cultural control. As detailed in chapter 4, many of the newest grass varieties will naturally fight off any problems, and some contain fungi known as endophytes that strengthen a grass plant's resolve. At least 80 percent of the time, these types of changes will lead to a permanent resolution of the pest or disease problem.

Physical Solutions

This means you have to take action. Believe it or not, if you own a Shop-Vac and see chinch bugs, leafhoppers, or sod webworm moths hopping about on your lawn, you can just vacuum up the pests, which will then be trapped in the canister. It works like a charm. You can also simply dig up an area affected by dollar spot, brown patch, and dog spot. Replace the affected soil and overseed with grass seed or patch the area with a small piece of sod, and the problem may not return.

Some lawn care professionals keep a canister of premixed seed and soil in their trucks; if they see a disease problem developing on a customer's lawn, they dig out the problem, pour in the seed-soil mixture, and water it in. It's not unlike what golfers do on the course each time they take up a divot off the tee or in the fairway.

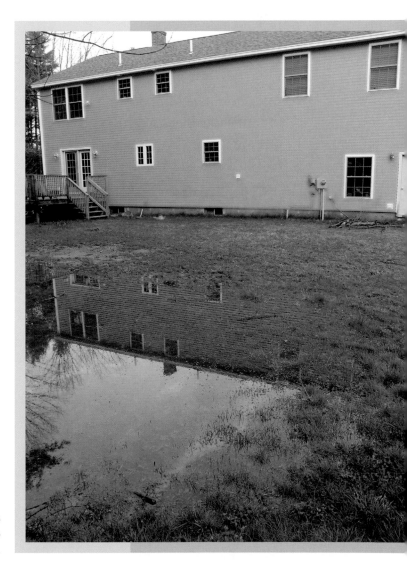

A lawn that holds water may develop fungal diseases if steps aren't taken to improve drainage.

One final physical change worth noting is altering the amount of sunlight an area of the lawn receives. If part of the lawn constantly bakes in the sun, you could create shade by planting a carefully sited tree. Far more often, though, the problem is too much shade, in which case you'll want to prune back or even remove some trees and shrubs, or take out all or part of a fence so that the lawn receives more light.

Biological Controls

Controlling pests with their natural enemies is the basis of biological pest control. When you add compost to your soil to encourage a diversity of soil life, you're practicing this form of control in its most primitive form. If you think of soil in terms of a bloodstream of red blood cells and white blood cells, the organic material you add to your lawn helps makes sure the number of organisms stays in balance. Natural lawns encourage beneficial critters we can see, such as birds, ladybugs, worms, big-eyed bugs, and minute pirate bugs, as well as all the ones we can't, like mycorrhizae and bacteria.

Sometimes you can take action by adding biological controls to the soil. For white grubs (see page 207), one of the best controls comes from applying beneficial nematodes. The microscopic creatures move through the soil in search of the grubs, eating them from inside out when they come upon their targets. The good news is that nematodes don't do any damage to nontarget pests. *Bacillus thuringiensis,* or Bt, is another common biological control. First discovered in 1911 in Thuringia, Germany, Bt combats moths and butterflies in their caterpillar stage. Caterpillars that eat this natural bacterium die when spores are activated in the insects' stomachs. Bt comes in several formulations; 100 million pounds are used each year in the United States, but you need to be sure you're using the correct strain of Bt for your target pest.

Botanical Solutions

Occasionally, even when you think you have the soil perfect and the grass seems to be otherwise healthy, pests will still appear. After exhausting all cultural, physical, and biological controls, you may decide to turn to a botanical (meaning plant based) control. With synthetic chemicals falling out of favor or being pulled off the shelves because of safety issues, a huge market has developed for sprays, soaps, traps, oils, and other products designed to kill or repel pests.

I should stress right up front that just because this new generation of products is plant based does not always mean the products are entirely safe for humans, pets, or the environment. Pyrethrin, for example, is a plant-based nerve poison used to control various chewing and sucking insects; it is moderately harmful to humans if not used carefully and judiciously. Other common botanical lawn pest controls are boric acid, neem, citrus oils, compost teas, copper, diatomaceous earth, sulfur, and many herbs, including garlic and rosemary oil.

Black Ants

Not to be confused with fire ants (see page 204), common black ants actually comprise about 400 different species in the United States alone. Though some ants are nasty pests inside the home, few cause significant lawn damage.

Natural controls: Most ants are highly beneficial because they aerate the soil and recycle organic materials, and for their efforts should generally not be seen as worthy of lawn control. The primary controls are physical, meaning you can simply rake the unsightly anthills that develop from time to time. You can also pour boiling water over the top of the hills to discourage the ants. If you feel you need to eradicate them completely, you can treat the area with a botanical solution: boric acid, which acts as a stomach poison in the ants. Either mix boric acid (common borax) with sugar or use one of the commercially available products based on boric acid. Since boric acid is reportedly toxic to humans and pets when ingested in high doses, it's best to keep the borax-sugar mixture out of reach. For a home-made trap, a tuna can covered with aluminum foil works well; poke a few holes in the sides of the can for the ants to enter and exit.

12 Common Lawn Thugs:
Problems and Solutions at a Glance

HERE ARE 12 of the most common pest or disease problems associated with lawns, with a brief description of the symptoms and remedies.

Thug	Symptom	Main Remedy
Black ants	Unsightly mounds	Boric acid
Fire ants	Skin irritant and animal health risk	Organic bait (spinosad)
Moles	Soil tunneling	Remove grubs
White grubs	Severed roots	Beneficial nematodes, milky spore
Dollar spot	Bleached spots	Repair drainage and add nitrogen
Brown patch	Round brown patches	Reduce nitrogen
Chinch bugs	Round yellow patches	Water heavily; rosemary oil
Billbugs	Yellow or brown patches	Dethatch
Sod webworms	Small, irregular dead spots	Beneficial nematodes
Mole crickets	Tunneling	Beneficial nematodes
Other fungal diseases	Various yellow or brown patches	Reduce water
Dog spot	Dead spots ringed in dark green	Yucca supplements for dogs

Fire Ants

To the naked eye, these ants simply look like a copper or red version of the black ant. Unsuspecting golfers, gardeners, and homeowners quickly learn the hard way that southern fire ants (*Solenopsis invicta*) or northern fire ants (*Myrmica rubra*) are quite different. They're fast, they're vicious, and they sting like crazy. I'll never forget my first encounter with the nasty critters when I was looking for a golf ball in the woods in Florida. My father had no sooner mouthed the words "Watch out for . . ." when I had seemingly hundreds of ants all over my legs and ankles. Veterinarians in the southern half of the United States say fire ant stings are the number one dog problem they encounter.

Natural controls: Charles Barr, a fire ant specialist with Texas Cooperative Extension, highly recommends a botanical solution known as spinosad. Made from a bacterial fermentation process that produces a nerve toxin, spinosad is used as a broadcast bait or to treat individual fire ant hills. Barr recommends putting out the product in spring or fall, or early summer mornings, whenever the ants appear to be present.

"The only surefire way to tell if it's time is to put a little bit of it out and see if the ants come to it," Barr says. "Generally, if it's less than 65 degrees, ants will not be foraging." Don't put out bait in the heat of the sun in summer because the product's oil (which attracts the ants), and its ant-killing material, will melt off.

Chinch Bugs

Adult chinch bugs, about $1/5$ inch long and black with white wings folded over their backs, mate when the temperature reaches 70°F. Females lay eggs during a two- to three-week period, with one female laying as many as 500 eggs. Young chinch bugs, called nymphs, develop into adults in four to six weeks. The nymphs, which are red with a light-colored band across their abdomen, often cause much of the lawn damage by sucking juices from the grasses and releasing a toxin that causes round yellowish patches in full-sun areas. This typically occurs in midsummer in colder regions and late spring in warm regions, especially in bluegrass and St. Augustine lawns. You can test for infestations by using a coffee can with both ends removed. Press one end of the can a couple of inches into the soil and fill it with soapy water. If chinch bugs (or mole crickets or sod webworms) are present, they will float to the surface.

Natural controls: Four cultural controls are the primary tools against chinch bugs: Water heavily, since chinch bugs will typically attack drought-stressed lawns; raise the mower blade and leave clippings on the lawn; apply any nitrogen in the fall because the insects are attracted to excess nitrogen, especially when applied in the spring; and plant grass species and cultivars that are not predisposed to chinch bug infestations. You will also find some botanical controls in the marketplace, typically insecticidal soaps and rosemary oil that can be sprayed on the lawn. If the chinch bugs are in a small, easily defined area, a solution of dish detergent (1 teaspoon per quart of water) soaked into that part of the lawn should also control the insects.

Sod Webworms

You'll most often notice the adult moths of the sod webworm when you go out to mow during springtime evenings. They'll be zigzagging across the lawn as they drop their eggs, which will hatch a couple of weeks later. With bad enough sod webworm infestations, you may begin to see small, irregular patches of dead grass about 1 or 2 inches wide. The larval stage of the webworm is when the damage occurs; mature larvae are about ¾ inch long and gray with black spots. They hide in the thatch layer of the grass during the day and come out at night to feed by cutting off blades of grass near the thatch line and pulling them into small tunnels, where they digest the grass.

Natural controls: In a well-balanced system, biological controls take care of the infestation without outside action. Birds, ants, ground beetles, rove beetles, and other predators are effective in controlling sod webworms. Beneficial nematodes, another biological control, will also eat the larvae of sod webworms (and many of the nematode formulations can do double duty by combating white grubs of the Japanese beetle). The primary cultural control is thatch removal; two botanical controls, Bt and pyrethrin, can be used as a last resort.

Black ant

Fire ant

Chinch bug

Sod webworm

Billbugs

Adult forms of this ⅛-inch-long insect are small black or gray weevils, or beetles with long snouts. It's the larval phase of the insect, white legless grubs with an orange head, that cause lawn damage in midsummer. Though the damage is similar to that of sod webworms, billbugs leave behind telltale debris that looks like sawdust scattered near the crown of the grass plant. And though the appearance of the billbug grubs is similar to that of other white grubs, these are in the soil during midsummer while the others are flying around in their adult phase.

Natural controls: Dethatching the lawn should be the first line of defense, along with raising the mower blade and maintaining high levels of organic matter in the soil. If large infestations do occur, applying a botanical control such as neem oil or insecticidal soap according to directions should help keep this pest at bay. Beneficial nematodes are also used to combat billbugs.

Mole Crickets

At 1½ inches long, the mole cricket appears similar to the common cricket, but it has a larger head and short wide front legs that are ideal for tunneling. It feeds on grass roots, but the primary damage it inflicts, especially in the South, is the tunneling similar to the damage caused by moles: hence, the name mole cricket. You'll be able to stick your finger into the holes, and often see the unshy crickets on the lawn. Your lawn may also be spongy underfoot.

Billbug

Mole cricket

White grub

Natural controls: No known cultural or physical control exists. Biological controls include applying beneficial nematodes at egg-laying time, as soon as the soil warms in the spring. The botanical control neem has also shown promise; it should be watered in deeply upon application. Various companies also market combinations of hot pepper and soap to combat mole crickets.

White Grubs

The larval phase of several insects including Japanese, June, and May beetles, white grubs all look similar: slightly curved and grayish white with a yellowish brown head. The grubs can be ½ to 1 inch long and have three sets of small legs near the head. They cause problems by chewing on roots, thereby severing the grass from its support system, and also by attracting tunneling and digging predators such as moles, skunks, raccoons, and armadillos, which see the grubs as a food source. The presence of grubs can make your lawn look like a disaster area, especially in late winter and spring, with soil and sod strewn everywhere. Dead patches of lawn caused by grubs are easy to identify: You can peel them back from the soil without resistance from any roots.

Natural controls: Two biological controls, milky spore (for Japanese beetle grubs) and beneficial nematodes, are most often utilized in cases of heavy grub infestations.

Dollar Spot

This fungal disease usually attacks lawns during the warm days and cool nights of spring and fall when excessive moisture is present. Heavy thatch and nitrogen deficiencies are other common causes of the disease, which looks like small patches of bleached-out grass. Other telltale signs are blotches on the leaf blades and white, cottony threads of fungus during the morning hours.

Natural controls: Though some people may rush out for a fungicide after a positive identification of dollar spot, such a product should not be used in natural lawn care. The key here is mainly cultural control. Improve drainage by aerating the soil. Increase fertility by adding an organic source of nitrogen, and overseed with disease-resistant grass cultivars. Allow the lawn to dry out completely between waterings, and avoid any evening watering. Applications of compost tea (see page 130) may also help.

Brown Patch

Another fungal disease brought on by excessive moisture, this appears as circular patches of brown grass in varying sizes. The leaf tips turn brown, and lesions appear on the blades. Hot, humid weather seems to ignite the problem, especially in St. Augustine lawns in the South.

Natural controls: Always allow the grass to dry out between waterings, and avoid watering in the evening. Aerate

Dollar spot

Brown patch

Rust or red thread

Dog spot

the soil to lessen thatch, improve drainage, and avoid excessive applications of nitrogen. If brown patch appears in shady areas, you have to prune tree limbs to shed more light on the grass and to improve airflow.

Other Fungal Diseases

Traveling around the United States, I heard numerous horror stories about myriad fungal diseases. In the Pacific Northwest, folks complained about leaf spot brought on by cool, wet weather. Up North, we complain about snow mold in the early spring. Kentucky bluegrass in particular seems to be prone to rust and red thread, as well as fusarium blight, pythium blight, and even something called stripe smut, which spreads masses of spores along the grass blades and turns them black.

Natural controls: The causes are almost always the same: excessive moisture, thatch, and nitrogen, caused by overzealous applications of water and nitrogen-rich fertilizers. Morning watering is critical in locales that are prone to fungal diseases. If you're in a natural lawn care program that avoids water-soluble synthetic nitrogen, fungal diseases will almost never be a problem.

Dog Spot

Some folks just can't admit that man's best friend could be a lawn's worst enemy, but your dog — especially your female dog — may well be one of your grass's worst nightmares. The symptoms are round brown dead spots on the lawn circled by lush, green growth. Since female dogs typically squat to urinate, usually all in one spot, they are more often to blame. A male dog will usually move about the yard to multiple locations, thereby spreading around the urine, which has a high concentration of ammonium nitrate, a form of nitrogen found in lawn fertilizer.

Natural controls: Veterinarians have had great luck developing a safe dietary supplement derived from a desert cactus plant, *Yucca schidigera*. The plant works naturally to bind with the ammonia in a dog's bladder to make the urine less toxic to the lawn. As a bonus, the yucca also reduces the odor of the dog's stools. These supplements are not foolproof, however. If your dog is chained or otherwise confined and must relieve itself in the same spot again and again, the lawn will suffer. The larger the dog, the worse the problem may be. The good news is that lawns tended organically are far more tolerant of dog spot; synthetically treated lawns usually have high concentrations of nitrogen, and a dog's urine quickly puts such a lawn over the edge. A study in Colorado concluded that fescue and perennial ryegrass lawns are more tolerant of dog spot than bluegrass and Bermuda grass lawns.

Mole Wars: Should You Fight Back?

I hear the exasperation from homeowners several times a week in late winter and early spring. Their lawns are littered with piles of soil that seem to appear out of nowhere. They often blame voles, but unrelated culprits, moles (shown on page 198), are the real enemy in turf wars.

Moles, voles, schmoles, you may be saying. Knowing the difference, though, is critical in your approach to regaining control of your landscape. In brief, moles are carnivores, meaning they eat meat. Voles are herbivores, meaning they eat vegetables. Voles devour roots, bark, and lower foliage to a couple of inches off the ground, but they are rarely a big problem in lawns and their tunnels are rarely a big issue in the soil. Overseeding affected areas may be required in some cases. Moles, on the other hand, just bomb about underground in search of whatever grubs, worms, and other insect life they can find. They make far more of a mess than voles do.

When people ask what to do about moles, I often respond by telling them to cheer "Go, moles, go." Moles eat the white grubs that become Japanese beetles and June beetles. In the big picture, these grubs and beetles do far more damage than moles to the overall landscape. Grubs damage grass roots; the beetles devour foliage of landscape plants.

Mole

Vole

Mole/vole tunnels

Voles

These are the true varmints of the garden. They want your plants, plain and simple. If you've ever lost a fruit tree to girdling at the base, or a prized perennial that was chewed from the roots and left for dead, voles are the likely suspects. Often called pine and meadow mice, the pine vole, *Microtus pinetorum*, and the meadow vole, *M. pennsylvanicus*, have become huge problems, especially in the East. Development has taken away their natural forest habitat and also their natural predators, including foxes, bobcats, weasels, snakes, owls, and hawks.

Pine voles are reddish brown and small, about 2 to 4 inches long, with a short tail, blunt face, and tiny eyes and ears. Meadow voles are grayer. Both have tiny yet prominent sets of eyes. Because voles don't hibernate, they feed year-round on roots and underground stems of plants. They can tunnel on their own, but often borrow tunnels already burrowed by moles, thereby creating even more confusion among homeowners. If you find exit holes on the tunnels in your lawn and garden, chances are you have voles, not moles, since moles are nearly blind and usually come up for daylight only by mistake.

Voles can bother lawns, especially if you leave the grass too long in the autumn heading into winter. Voles will see your grass as a good food source and chew the blades down to the soil surface in telltale random trails. The only viable controls are mowing the grass properly, baited traps, and owning a cat.

Moles

When you see a mole close up, the differences between moles and voles will become obvious. Take one look at the webbed front paws and claws of the mole and you'll instantly see why many books refer to the critters as "master excavators." They are also prodigious at the dinner table, able to eat up to their full body weight within a 24-hour period. Unlike voles, which travel in family packs, moles often live and work alone. They are also more active after sundown.

Their damage is usually minimal; displaced soil can be smoothed out with a metal rake. If you feel you must be rid of the moles, soaking the ground with castor oil will help, but the easiest way is to get rid of the source of food. Get rid of the grubs, and the moles will tunnel elsewhere. The most effective natural way to control grubs is to apply beneficial nematodes to the soil in May through early June or late August through September, depending on your location. This timetable can vary greatly in warm-season climates, and if you suspect grubs as a problem on your lawn, contact your local Cooperative Extension Service to determine the insect's life cycle in your area. The Extension agent should also be able to point you to a local source for the nematodes; many entomologists including Albrecht M. Koppenhofer, from Rutgers University, in New Jersey, are constantly updating information on strains of the nematodes that work the best in certain climates against specific grubs.

"White grubs, in many locations, are the leading pest of grasses by far," says Koppenhofer. "They can cause significant damage in certain situations, but people also should not overreact the first time they see a grub in the soil."

The keys to success with beneficial nematodes are twofold: Be sure you have a treatable problem and get the timing right. As a general rule, if you have five or fewer grubs per square foot on your lawn, you do not have a significant problem. You can test this by simply digging a square foot of soil to a depth of 6 inches. Break apart the soil and sod, and count any grubs you find.

OMRI:
The Organic Seal of Approval

IF YOU'RE OUT SHOPPING and trying to determine if fertilizers, weed killers, or pesticides are truly organic, look for a distinctive label with the letters OMRI on the package. The Organic Materials Review Institute is a nonprofit organization that specializes in the evaluation of substances for use in organic production, processing, and handling. Since 1998, the Oregon-based organization has published a list of approved products (see Resources, page 263).

OMRI conducts material reviews according to the standards established with implementation of the USDA's National Organic Program in October 2002. The evaluations are conducted as a transparent, third-party review. Products that do not carry the OMRI seal may in fact be organic and safe to use, but may not have been tested by anyone other than the manufacturer. Some states also have independent organic certification programs, but OMRI is now widely recognized as the default clearinghouse for organic products.

If you do act, timing is everything. Grubs spend 10 months of the year in the soil and 2 months as adult beetles aboveground. Trying to kill the grubs just before they emerge from the soil in late spring or just after they lay eggs and reenter the soil in early autumn is paramount. Treating at other times won't help a bit, whether you use a synthetic chemical or beneficial nematodes.

Applying beneficial nematodes is an easy, nontoxic exercise. You'll need a hose-end sprayer and at least enough hose to reach all infected areas of your property. Further directions on mixing and application will be available from the nematode supplier.

As an alternative, you can inoculate your lawn and garden with a white powder known as milky spore disease, but this usually takes two to three years to build up enough population to be useful. According to Koppenhofer, milky spore has shown "highly variable" results.

"Since the commercially available strain of milky spore disease is ineffective against white grubs other than the Japanese beetle," he says, "applicators interested in using milky spore disease should first make sure that their grubs are actually Japanese beetle grubs."

Yes, it's true that the same poisons that rid homes of mice will also work to kill moles and voles. When the snow melts this spring and you see tunnels and dead plants galore, you may be tempted to take out the toxins. In a word, don't. These poisons, left in the open, will be fair game for every child, cat, dog, and bird in the neighborhood.

Plants vs. Insects:
13 Natural Controls

THE FOLLOWING plant-based products are used to kill or repel insects and mammals, either alone or in combination with others. They are also often added to strengthen the properties of insecticidal soap, which consists of salts of fatty acids. Most often applied by soaking the soil, they penetrate the bodies of many soft-bodied insects, including sod webworms, billbugs, white grubs, and chinch bugs. Most do not work as quickly as synthetic pesticides but are nowhere near as toxic to the environment.

Boric Acid
Mixing equal parts borax and sugar, with about a tablespoon of sugar in a quart of water, makes a nice solution for an ant trap. Keep this mixture out of the reach of children and pets.

Canola Oil
Used as a base for numerous natural insecticides or further refined to repel and kill on its own, this promises to be a major component of pest products in the future.

Castor Oil
This extract of the castor bean plant's seeds, the basis of many herbal remedies for people, is also used to repel moles, voles, and other critters.

Cedar Oil
Extracted from the Eastern red cedar, this oil is used to repel ants in some formulations and mosquitoes in others.

Clove Oil
Combined with castor oil and thyme oil, clove oil makes a powerful ant killer to be applied directly to the soil. The combination of the three oils can kill grass and the foliage of other plants.

Diatomaceous Earth
Mined from the ocean floor, this sharp skeletal material is useful in combating a variety of lawn pests, especially ants. Because it is razor sharp, the diatomaceous earth cuts the insects' exoskeletons and causes dehydration.

Hot Pepper
Primarily used to combat larger mammals, including rabbits, squirrels, and gophers, cayenne also shows up in mole repellents. Usually combined with a food-grade wax, it is safe to apply anywhere.

Lemon Juice
Used in numerous formulations to repel fire ants, caterpillars, earwigs, Japanese beetles, and other insects, lemon juice is a component of many newer natural products.

Neem
Extracted from the seeds of the neem tree, *Azadirachta indica*, neem is gaining popularity as both an insecticide and a fungicide and also as a repellent.

Orange Peel
The active ingredient d-limonene — orange peel extract — destroys the wax coating of an insect's respiratory system. Primarily used on ants, d-limonene also repels many other insects.

Peppermint Oil
Combined with clove oil, this is a primary ingredient in insecticides that act as nerve agents.

Rosemary
A refined oil from this aromatic plant is used, often in combination with peppermint oil, to control chinch bugs in heavy infestations.

Sabadilla
Derived from sabadilla plant seeds and known for low toxicity, extract from this plant is commonly used to kill sod webworms and chinch bugs.

11 Mowing and Maintenance

i often joke that the only thing I really knew when I started my own landscaping company two decades ago was how to walk in a straight line behind a lawn mower. The straighter the lines, the better. The lower the mower blade, the cleaner the lawn appeared. I laughed out loud when I saw Forrest Gump riding back and forth, up and down on the white and red Snapper mower in the magical 1994 movie starring Tom Hanks. Others in the theater laughed, too. Mowing, for many Americans, has become a primal urge, a seemingly simple ritualistic act.

To mow and mow properly, however, is one of the primary components of a successful lawn care program. We take it for granted that the lawn will always bounce back after a mowing, and grass is certainly remarkable in its capacity to rejuvenate itself. But cutting a plant, even grass, is an unnatural act that necessitates a recovery period. During this weakened state, grass plants can become prone to insect infestation, fungal diseases, or crowding from weeds. The key to a good natural lawn program, therefore, is to limit the recovery period so the grass can fend for itself. If you mow low to get that smooth look, root growth will slow to almost zero while the top of the plant pushes out new shoots from the crown. If you let the grass grow too tall and then attempt to cut it back to its regular height all at once, the roots will become similarly stunted.

Mow Like a Pro

"Everyone mows, but hardly anyone seems to do it well," says David Mellor, one of the most visible lawn mowing professionals in the world in his position as head groundskeeper at Fenway Park, home of the Boston Red Sox. "You shouldn't do it on a set schedule, at a set mowing height. You should learn to let the grass tell you when it needs to be mowed. If you do that, it is the best tool for having the green, healthy lawn you really want, without a lot of pressure from weeds."

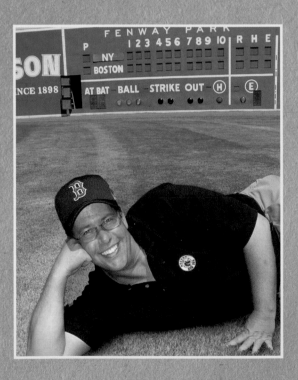

You also need to decide on your primary piece of equipment, the mower. Nothing against the Snapper Company, which makes fine lawn mowers, but Forrest Gump's gas ride-on model really isn't all that versatile or maneuverable. Get the lowdown on mower types on pages 224–225 before you make a purchase.

In the end, after you've considered all the factors and tools involved (see page 222), you may ultimately decide to leave the job to someone else. The world has become full of lawn care professionals who are eager and capable of doing a great job of mowing your grass. It may not be all that easy to find a teenager like me when I started to mow lawns, ready to make a buck by pushing a lawn mower and hauling a gas can from house to house. In reality, that's not a bad thing. Today's lawn care professionals, the good ones anyway, adhere to a set of standards developed by universities and associations all across North America. To help with your selection of a lawn care professional, see pages 230–231 for a list of questions to ask a contractor.

Ultimately, though, I do hope you do your own mowing. Forrest Gump had it right. Mowing is one of the best ways on the planet to be alone with your thoughts while you enjoy the intoxicating scent of a freshly cut lawn.

Mowing Well: The 12 Basics

Part common sense and part professional technique, good mowing practices can make all the difference in the appearance and overall health of your lawn.

1 *Check Your Mower*

Be sure the blade is sharp; in general, the blade will need a tune-up after every 8 to 12 hours of use. If you're using a gas mower, check the fuel and oil levels before you begin; avoid refilling the mower while it is parked on the lawn because any spilled gas will kill grass and harm the soil. It's a good idea, too, to clean out the undercarriage of the mower if it wasn't cleaned after its last use; layers of grass often cake above and around the mower blade.

2 *Check Your Lawn*

Move any sticks, stones, children's toys, and hoses and other lawn tools before you even start. Take note of the moisture level as well as the lawn's height and any uneven areas. Grass doesn't always grow evenly in all parts of the lawn.

3 *Mow at the Right Time*

Early evening, after the heat of the day and before dew fully settles, is the best time to mow if you're able to do it then. Avoid the heat of the day, which is tough on grass; in the mornings, dew may be heavy and can clog mowers. Avoid really moist days in general; you may spend too much time cleaning out your mower. If you haven't had any rain for a week or more and none is predicted anytime soon, don't mow. Keep the lawn blade really high if you do mow. Tall grass is the lawn's best protection in a drought. Also, check any noise restrictions in your neighborhood, and be considerate of the neighbors' quiet time.

4 *Adjust the Height*

Every grass species has an ideal height for optimum lawn performance. Bermuda grass, bent grass, and seashore paspalum can be mowed to 1 inch or less; most others are 2 inches or more. Check chapter 4 to determine the best mowing height for your lawn. Remember, too,

Mowing with a dull blade will leave ragged grass blades that are prone to damage from insects and diseases.

that you'll want to vary the height during different times of year. When the grass is actively growing in the spring, the blade can be lower; in the heat of summer, when the temperature rises and growth slows, the blade should rise. Prior to the onset of winter, in areas where snow is expected, you'll want to mow low to about 2 inches high.

5 Pick a Line

Vary your mowing direction each time you mow, either parallel to, perpendicular to, or diagonally from your house. This will maintain an even cut through the season and avoid uneven tire-track compaction. It's a good idea to mow the perimeter of the lawn prior to picking the line so that you have room to turn around without stepping into a bed or other planted part of the garden. Avoid mowing in a circular pattern; it's an inefficient use of your time and a waste of gas or electricity. It also doesn't look as good when you're done.

Vary the direction of your mowing each time to avoid tire compaction and an uneven cut.

6 Overlapping

Using your tire track as the line, overlap by about 2 inches as you mow in the opposite direction. Lift the front wheels of the mower when you make the turn at the end of each pass. Avoid lifting the rear wheels of the mower while the mower blades are operating; that tends to throw grass clippings, sticks, and stones back at you. If you're using an electric mower with a cord, always keep the cord behind you as you mow, and work away from the outlet.

7 Push, Don't Pull

Although this isn't a critical rule with rotary lawn mowers (see page 224), the blade spin of all rotary mowers is set up to mulch, bag, or discharge the grass most efficiently when the mower is moving forward. Reel mowers (see page 224) won't cut at all when pulled backward. The biggest reason to push and not pull your mower, however, is safety. If you pull the mower toward you and fall, the blade may imperil your feet.

8 Mulch Your Clippings

Use a bagger attachment for the first mowing of the year, again when the dandelions or other pesky weeds set seed, and finally when the leaves drop in the fall; otherwise, allow the clippings to remain on the lawn to recycle the nutrients. Grass clippings are among the best lawn fertilizers. If the lawn is tall and lush and the clippings appear to be too thick, you may need to rake some areas of the lawn and add the clippings to a compost pile, or you can use the rake to scatter the clippings across wider areas of the lawn. Thick piles of clippings left on the lawn can suffocate the living grass below.

9 Don't Overcompensate

If your lawn gets away from you because of vacations, frequent rainstorms, or general apathy, don't try to cut down the lawn to its optimum height all at once. The rule is never to cut more than a third of the grass plant on any one day. If you keep your lawn at 3 inches but it grows to 6 inches, then cut it back to 4 inches on one day and then down to 3 inches a few days later. This is important. Many grass species will suffer greatly if you cut off too much at once.

10 Avoid Scalping

Even worse than cutting off too much of the grass at one time is cutting the grass almost down to the soil surface. Scalping most often occurs near the edges of the lawn when the mower tires slip into ruts; when you're using a riding mower with a large, wide mowing deck; or through the improper use of a power string trimmer. To avoid scalping, become aware of low or uneven points in the lawn. Learn to use your trimmer properly by keeping its head a safe distance above the soil surface.

Left: Never remove more than one-third of the grass blade at a time.
Below: Mowing uneven lawn surfaces can result in scalping.

11 *Keep Your Eyes Open*

Part of a good natural lawn program, and an excellent reason for mowing your own lawn, is always to be on the look-out for grass invaders such as weeds and insect pests. If you notice something new, or something askew, it may be time to RILE (see page 170). It's also a good idea to keep a lawn mowing chart, with the dates you mowed, trimmed, sharpened the blade, changed the mower oil, and applied any fertilizers and pesticides. Take special note of the date that you noticed any insects or diseases, so you can be better prepared to deal with them next year.

12 *Maintenance*

When you're done mowing and if you still have the energy, go ahead and clean the mower from top to bottom with a garden hose after disconnecting the spark plug wire. If you use an extension cord for an electric model, check the cord periodically for any dings that might need taping. Gas mowers, of course, will need to have their oil and filters changed according to instructions in the owner's manual. If you change your own oil, dispose of the used oil properly at a waste recycling center.

Manual Edging

How we edge our lawns defines a lot about who we are. Formal, straight lines say one thing. Free-flowing curves say another, and no edge at all . . . well, you're probably already caring for your lawn naturally and perhaps didn't buy this book. As for me, I like to take out the garden hose and play with curves until I find the edge shape that fits the space. It's fun, and best done when you're starting a lawn from scratch or in the middle of a major renovation.

Maintaining that edge after the fact can be a challenge. Ever since the arrival of power edgers and string trimmers, which make relatively quick work of defining the line between lawns, gardens, driveways, and walkways, permanent edging materials have become less chic. I know that in my days as a landscaper, more and more clients yanked out their plastic and aluminum borders in favor of having me trim the edge on a constant basis.

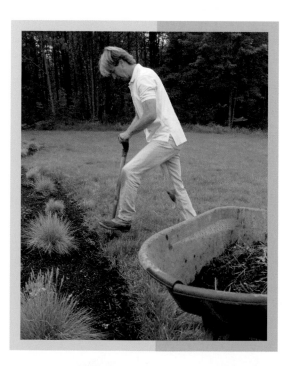

I occasionally use a gas-powered edger to reestablish the line between lawn and garden. Homeowners with a smaller yard can simply edge their lawn with a straight-bladed spade.

I have to say that as a matter of personal taste, I do like the au naturel look of a beveled edge freshly cut about 2 or 3 inches below the soil surface. These days I cut that edge with a flat-bladed spade because I feel guilty about burning fossil fuel in my 20-year-old Sears gas-powered edger. I've yet to find a good power edger with an electric motor, but someone probably makes one somewhere.

If you're averse to repeated hard work, the most practical solution is to install some sort of permanent edging so that you're not a prisoner of edging labor. Materials suitable for edging include plastic, brick, concrete, stone, copper, aluminum, and wood.

Keep Clippings, Remove Thatch

No matter what anyone tells you, thatch and clippings are not the same — and clippings do not cause thatch. Lawn thatch is the dead grass and root tissue between the green vegetation and the soil surface. In layers of ½ inch or thicker, thatch blocks water, air, and nutrients from reaching the roots. Grass roots contain lignin, a substance that decomposes slowly and causes thatch. Grass clippings, the cut out portion of the mown grass, are about 90 percent water, so they begin to decompose almost immediately after hitting the ground.

Many grass varieties in a traditional synthetic lawn care system tend to build thatch layers quickly. Excessive nitrogen pushes out excessive top growth, but it limits life in the soil and therefore slows decomposition of roots even more. The process of dethatching, with either a bamboo rake or a power machine, removes the thatch, which you can then gather and compost.

Some thatch is common and acceptable in all lawns. Natural lawn systems that add life into the soil will rarely have issues with excessive thatch. The beneficial microorganisms found in compost, compost teas, and other forms of humus will feed on the thatch.

Leaving the clippings on the lawn actually contributes to a natural lawn system by providing food, especially nitrogen, to the soil. Clippings can, in

A heavy layer of thatch, often evident in spring and fall, should always be removed. Thatch will rarely be a problem in an organic lawn, however.

fact, return anywhere from a quarter to a half of your lawn's annual nitrogen needs. This is known as nutrient cycling, a form of recycling that helps keep yard waste out of landfills. The Environmental Protection Agency (EPA) estimates that yard waste — primarily leaves and grass clippings — is second only to paper in the municipal solid waste stream. Many communities are beginning to ban yard refuse from landfills.

We've all had times when clippings are too thick and too unsightly to leave on the lawn. If the clippings are too heavy, they will smother and potentially kill the grass. In these cases, you should rake to gather or scatter the clippings. If you care for your lawn naturally and don't apply synthetic weed killers, the clippings are a great source of mulch for the flower or vegetable garden or can be added to the compost pile.

Grass clippings can either be left on the lawn or added to the compost heap.

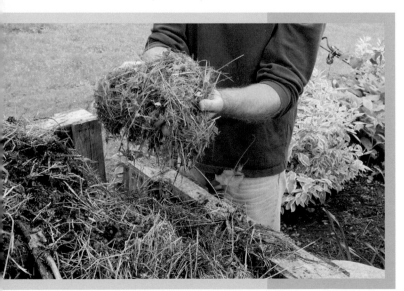

Tools for the Natural Lawn

For most North Americans, lawn care is the number one home maintenance activity. Its our connection to the neighborhood and the outdoors, and our own stamp on the environment. As you've learned in this book, the decision to care for your own lawn cannot be taken lightly. For beginners, however, the weight of that choice may first be felt at the hardware store, before a blade of grass is ever cut.

Fertilizers, herbicides, and pesticides aside, it's easy to tell if someone cares for a lawn naturally just by peeking inside that person's shed or garage. Here are a few considerations as you approach the ocean of choices in the marketplace.

Mowers

More than 30 years ago, my first Briggs & Stratton mower, purchased used for $10, took me to the promised land of many reliable $5 paychecks, hour after hour, day after day. I certainly wasn't thinking about ozone layers, pollution levels, or greenhouse gases, or even the splash of fuel that hit the ground every time I hurriedly refueled my quart-size gas tank. The state of California, which offers rebate programs for homeowners who willingly trade in their gas mowers for electric models, estimates that a 21-inch lawn mower running for 1 hour causes up to 10 times the pollution of a car running for the same period of time. To top it off, lawn and garden equipment users in that state spill 17 million gallons of fuel each year while refilling their outdoor power equipment. That's more petroleum than the *Exxon Valdez* spilled in the Gulf of Alaska.

These days, we should know better. With the improved quality of electric equipment, gas-powered motors should soon be a thing of the past. You can purchase electric mowers with cords, or with rechargeable batteries with enough life to mow for two hours or more. You can purchase electric ride-on mowers, or find conversion kits that allow you to retrofit your gas model to electric. Electric mowers are cleaner and quieter, and start with the push of a button — definitely the way to go. If you're still dedicated to a gas mower, be sure to use one with an efficient four-stroke engine; the two-stroke engines that require a mixture of oil and gas are the biggest air polluters.

After you've decided on electric versus gas, that leaves only three primary discussions about mowers. First, decide whether to purchase a powered or fully manual model; if your lawn is 2,000 square feet or less, a manual mower should suit your needs. Second, consider whether to go with a unit that bags clippings, mulches them back onto the lawn, or discharges them out the back or side; many manufacturers actually make that decision easy by producing adaptable electric units that combine all three options. Finally, decide whether to go reel or rotary with the blades, taking into account that once the grass gets above 2½ inches tall, most reel mowers don't do a good job.

Greenscaping: The 4 Rs

THE EPA, CONCERNED about the impact of traditional lawn care and landscaping on the environment, has coined a new term known as greenscaping, which has four primary components.

1. **Reduce.** Use manual garden tools instead of gas- or electric-powered devices; rent or borrow rather than own large equipment that you use infrequently; reduce or remove all toxic pesticides from your landscaping.

2. **Reuse.** Use rain barrels to collect rainwater from your roof; use gray water (see page 158) wherever and whenever possible, if it is legally allowed.

3. **Recycle.** Don't throw anything in the trash that can be recycled or that may have other uses, especially leaves and grass clippings and even the used oil and tires from your landscaping vehicles and equipment.

4. **Rebuy.** Rethink your purchasing habits by focusing on products with recycled content. Many garden hoses, edging materials, stepping-stones, lawn chairs, and mulches are made from recycled goods, which reduces reliance on fossil fuels and raw materials. Buying recycled goods only encourages more recycling, and everybody wins.

Mowers: A Basic Guide

HERE ARE A FEW QUESTIONS to ask yourself before you make a purchase: Do you need maneuverability to get around obstacles on your lawn — for example, trees, planters, patios, walls, and swing sets? Do you need a self-propelled mower to get up and down a sloped lawn? Do you like mowing? Are you capable of walking or do you need to ride? Can you complete maintenance tasks, such as oil and filter changes and blade sharpening? How big is your budget? How long will you own your home?

With those answers in mind, here are basic mower types available in the marketplace. *Note:* It's a good idea to rent a few different mowers first if you are unfamiliar with their use.

Reel Mower

This type of mower uses blades on a revolving cylinder to cut grass. As the mower moves forward, either by muscle or by engine power, the reel spins in a clockwise direction and the blades pass over a stationary bar, known as a bed knife, that is parallel to the ground. The grass is held up by the bed knife, and cut by the shearing action of the reel blades, which usually come in combinations of three, five, or seven blades per reel. Reel mowers give the cleanest, healthiest cut for the grass and are the best option if the grass needs to be mowed low (as is the case with seashore paspalum, Bermuda, and bent grass).

Pitfalls: Blade adjustment can be temperamental on a reel mower. If the bed knife is too close to the rotating blades, the blades will often bind; if the bed knife is too far away, the grass will not shear and instead will just fold over. Reel mowers are a challenge to sharpen by hand; the task is most often left to a professional.

Reel mowers are the only option for non-engine models. You'll need to keep the grass at 3 inches or less to comfortably operate a push-type reel mower.

Rotary Mower

By far the most common type of mower, the rotary mower uses flat, horizontal blades that move at a speed controlled from above by an engine. A typical configuration is to have an engine sitting on top of a mower deck with the engine shaft protruding through the deck to the blade below. More elaborate models use reconfigured decks and blades to mulch clippings back onto the lawn; I highly recommend these. Sharpening is generally easy with a tool known as a "bastard" mill file and a rotary bench grinder.

Pitfalls: The primary knock against rotary mowers is the cutting action, which tends to tear the grass rather than cut it; sharpening the blade often will help.

Walk-Behind

This means you, the user, walk behind either the reel or rotary mower. No-engine, push-type reel mowers are the lightest and often the least expensive. They're good for the environment, require almost no maintenance other than blade sharpening and a little lubrication, and are a great source of exercise.

Electric- or gas-powered rotary mowers also come in walk-behind models. Electric models require almost no engine maintenance; gas models require at least annual oil changes and tune-ups, depending on the number of hours of use throughout the season.

A walk-behind mower is generally lightweight and will not cause excessive soil compaction, the way a ride-on mower might.

Mulching, bagging, and self-propulsion are the three most common mower options. Mulching is a requisite in a natural lawn system, bagging is a nice option up to a few times a year (see page 182), and self-propulsion — which means the mower pulls or pushes itself along the lawn — is a personal decision. If your lawn is sloped or you have a heavy gas-powered model, you're probably going to want help in propelling the mower. Electric mowers are generally so lightweight that self-propulsion isn't necessary. Self-propelled reel mowers are generally found only on golf greens and can be quite expensive, but some homeowners use them nonetheless.

Pitfalls: Some folks just don't have the strength to maneuver a walk-behind mower.

Ride-on Mower

More and more popular, ride-on mowers come in numerous configurations, from tractors that tow reel mowers for golf courses, public parks and large estates, to small dedicated lawn machines with a "zero-turning radius" for the ultimate in maneuverability. They come with all the features of walk-behind models, but with the added benefit of being able to tow attachments or a lawn cart.

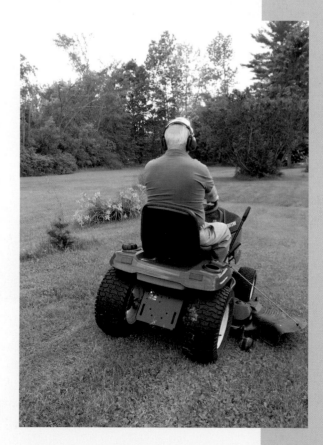

Some companies are now making electric ride-ons, and some gas-powered models can be retrofitted with electric mowers to make them more environmentally friendly.

From beverage holders to padded seats and deluxe suspensions, your mower can be as comfortable and convenient as you'd like it to be. Talk to your mower dealer about ease of access to the mower deck; large, heavy models can make it difficult to change blades for sharpening. Other models have easy, quick-pin releases on their mower decks.

Pitfalls: Ride-on mowers are expensive, and they are heavier than other types of mowers and thus may create soil compaction. They also beg the question: Do you really need to mow *all* that lawn?

Sharpening Your Own Rotary Mower Blade:
A Step-by-Step Guide

ROTARY MOWER BLADES should be sharpened often, so that grass blades are always cleanly cut. Although many homeowners take their mower blades to be professionally sharpened, it's not hard to learn how to do it yourself.

1 **Remove the spark plug and blade.**
Clamp a 2-by-4 or similar piece of wood to the inside of the mower deck to keep the blade from turning as you remove it. Using a socket wrench, turn the blade bolt counterclockwise to remove the blade. If the bolt resists turning, lubricate the bolt head with penetrating oil and allow it to sit for 15 minutes to work its way into the threads. Mark the bottom of the blade for ease of reinstallation. Examine the blade; if it is cracked or misshapen, discard it and purchase a new one.

Tools of the Trade

- Clamp
- 2-by-4
- Socket wrench
- Penetrating oil
- Bench vise
- 10-inch bastard mill file
- Balancing tool

2 **Clamp the blade into a bench vise, and sharpen.**
Sharpen the blade edge with a 10-inch bastard mill file. Use long, smooth strokes away from your body, from the center of the blade toward the outer tip. Use the same number of strokes on each side, and keep the angle consistent.

3 **Balance the blade.** With a special balancing tool from the hardware store, or on a nail pounded horizontally into a post or wall, balance the blade. If the blade appears to be out of balance, remove excess metal from the end of the blade opposite the cutting edge.

Note: Sharpening reel mower blades may take considerably more effort and experience, though some manufacturers recommend a relatively simple process of "blacklapping," which involves applying a polishing compound to the blades and the knife edge and using a special tool to spin the mower blades backward. Check the operator's manual for your reel mower prior to attempting to sharpen the blades on your own.

Grinding a Blade

IF A BLADE IS NICKED, you may need to grind down the tapered cutting edges of the blade with a rotary bench grinder. Carefully follow the factory angle of the edge. Work slowly, applying minimum pressure, and don't overheat the blade (turning it red). Keep a bucket of water nearby to cool the blade after each pass. Wear protective goggles.

If you're not successful in sharpening or balancing the blade, don't use it in the mower. An uneven blade can damage the engine. You'll be better off taking the blade to a professional sharpening center. It's a good idea to keep on hand a second blade for your mower, so that you always have a sharp one ready to go.

Power String Trimmers

The same argument against gas mowers goes double for trimmers. Because the gas in trimmers is often mixed with two-cycle oil, the air pollution is even worse than in mowers. Some manufacturers have improved emission standards with cleaner-burning four-stroke engines, but for most average-size lawns, electric is still the way to go.

Electric trimmers, like mowers, come in corded models and cordless versions with rechargeable batteries. If you're careful and pay attention to the cord, then a corded model is still the more practical for a lawn of any size. I tried a cordless trimmer that offered only a half-hour of battery time on a full charge. Depending on the size of your yard, that may not be enough.

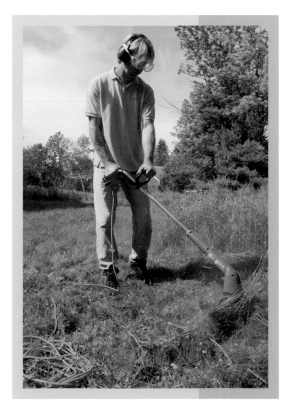

By angling the cutting head on a string trimmer, you can create a nice beveled edge. Safety goggles and earmuffs should always be worn while trimming.

Other Tools

Eye and Ear Protection

It amazes me how many people I see power-trimming lawns, also known as "weed whacking," without eye or ear protection. These tools, even electric models, are loud and dangerous. Purchase a comfortable pair of quality earmuffs and shatterproof goggles. Cheap sunglasses don't cut it.

Even though mowers may not present the same eye danger as power trimmers, they can be especially damaging to hearing. According to the National Institute on Deafness and Other Communication Disorders, sounds louder than 85 decibels — on a scale from 0 to 140 — can cause temporary or permanent hearing loss. A gas mower averages about 90 decibels, a gas trimmer puts out about 110 decibels, and an electric model comes in right on the border at 80 to 85.

Gas Cans

California, which began regulating gas cans in 2001, estimates that portable gas cans account for about 87 tons per day of smog-forming pollution in that state alone. That's equal to emissions from about a million automobiles. The newer no-spill cans reduce fumes and spills and therefore pollution; they are now required in several states beyond California.

Watering Utensils

Check out chapter 8 for a full discussion of hoses, nozzles, sprinklers, rain gauges, and timers. With water becoming more and more of a precious resource, it's important that every drop go where you intend for it to go, and not off into the driveway, drainpipe, or downhill to the neighbor's yard.

Wheelbarrows

Every home needs at least one, and you should consider its primary use before making a purchase. The earth's most efficient simple machine, combining levers and wheels, the wheelbarrow can move soil and compost, collect grass clippings and weeds, and tote tools back and forth to the shed.

Rakes

Every lawnkeeper's shed needs at least three kinds of rakes, and possibly four: a leaf rake, a metal rake, and a bamboo rake, and maybe a landscape rake.

Shovels and Spades

You'll need, at a minimum, two digging tools in your shed. The classic long-handled, round-pointed shovel is the workhorse for creating holes; filling wheelbarrows; and moving soil, compost, gravel, and just about anything else. Flat-bladed spades are used for edging or cutting through turf. These also come in long or short handles and should be selected on the basis of length, weight, and durability.

Specialty Items:
Rent, Don't Own

Lawn roller. As detailed in chapter 5, a steel or plastic drum roller is an excellent tool for lightly compacting and leveling soil prior to planting seed, sod, plugs, or sprigs. You really don't need to own one, though, unless you're planning several lawn renovations or patio installations.

Dethatcher. In a healthy, natural lawn environment, thatch is never a problem and regular dethatching should not be necessary. If you have a buildup worth treating or want to thoroughly scratch the soil prior to overseeding, then renting one of these machines for a day will save all sorts of labor with a bamboo rake. You can also purchase dethatching attachments that fit on the front of many lawn mower models.

Aerator. When transitioning to a natural lawn program, aerating the soil with a "core" aerator in spring and fall can help lessen the effects of compaction. The cores create holes in the soil to allow air, water, fertilizer, and soil amendments to get down to the root zone more quickly. Avoid aerators that do not cut a core; aerators that simply poke holes have little value. Core aerators are more rugged to use than lawn mowers and dethatchers, so you'll need to be in good physical condition to use one well.

Rototiller. Installing or renovating your lawn should be the first and last time you use a rototiller on the lawn, if at all (see page 177). Owning one makes little sense unless you're a hard-core vegetable gardener on the side.

Power edger. If you're absolutely dedicated to the appearance of a freshly cut beveled edge on your lawn, you may want to own one of these. Otherwise, rent one once in the spring and in the fall and you'll be set.

Questions for Your Natural Lawn Contractor

IN JUNIOR HIGH, when I started mowing lawns for a fee, I wasn't supposed to know anything; I just showed up and mowed a lawn for $5, and the customers were happy. When I started my own professional lawn care company as an adult, I still didn't know anything. I simply bought a truck and a lawn mower and began calling myself a landscaper. Though the industry does have several professional associations, few states require any kind of certification before landscape contractors can open for business. In other words, when you're searching, you're on your own. Here's a checklist of questions to ask potential lawn care providers:

What is your experience?

Beginners aren't all bad; some may have a newly minted degree from a technical college or university. Beware the people who sold insurance last year and who want to try their hand at lawn mowing this year.

May I have references?

It is amazing how many homeowners are apathetic about checking credentials because they're just so happy someone called back. Take the time to do at least a small background check.

Do you have licenses and insurance?

The insurance is for your protection, not his. If a contractor gets hurt on your property, the contractor's insurance should pay all medical expenses. Also, anyone applying any kind of weed killer, insecticide, or fungicide on your property should be licensed by the state pest control board; the license often requires a special rider on the contractor's insurance policy as well.

What are your professional affiliations?

Membership in professional organizations such as the Professional Lawn Care Association of America (PLCAA) and your state's landscape association is a solid indication that a contractor is taking steps to conduct business as professionally as possible.

Do you offer a natural, pesticide-free lawn care program?

If the contractor says "no" or "sort of" or generally stammers around the answer, you're better off picking someone else. Some companies will talk about "transitioning" your lawn to organics, which is covered at length in chapter 6. If you buy into this approach, which involves weaning your lawn off chemicals, make sure the plan is realistic and that the weaning process doesn't go on indefinitely. If you don't want any synthetic chemicals used, get this in writing and talk to the contractor about the products he or she plans to use.

How will your program build my soil?

Any contractor who is sold on a natural approach will talk excitedly about beneficial microorganisms, soil life, fungal content, and the role of calcium and compost. If your contractor talks a lot about adding nitrogen, pick a different contractor.

What is the game plan?

Traditional lawn care companies often operate according to a preset calendar. Natural lawn care companies operate based on that year's climate challenges; they make decisions according to the weather rather than making blanket applications.

What is my role in the process?

Spell out all services to be provided by the contractor, as well as what tasks you will retain if any. Does the contractor invite you to call if you see something askew in the lawn? Do you have time to mow, and the budget and space for the equipment?

How will my lawn look?

Talk about your vision for your lawn in one-, three-, and five-year increments, and make sure your contractor understands, and vice versa. A goal of no weeds or no disease is not realistic. The closer to perfection you desire, the more money and time, you're likely to spend on your lawn.

Can I get it all in writing?

Because natural lawn care doesn't lend itself to set schedules and applications, it requires more understanding on the part of the contractor and the homeowner. Many contractors talk in terms of "time and materials," which determines a preset hourly rate and charges for soil amendments, fertilizers, and so on.

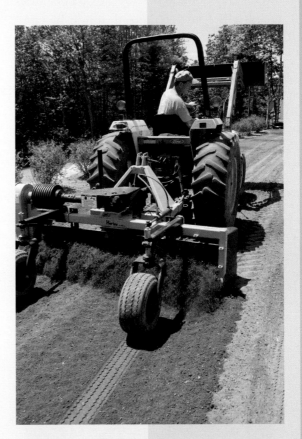

Landscape professionals use power graders to prepare soil for seed or sod.

Weeding Tools

If I could pick only one tool to pry dandelions and just about any other herbaceous weeds out of the ground, it would be a dandelion weeder, also known as a fishtail weeder or an asparagus weeder. Every shed also needs a good basic trowel, which can also be used for weeding or for plugging a southern lawn.

Hoes

Standard hoes have little function in lawn care, but a grub hoe or "grape" hoe is actually a swinging tool, much like a pickax, that is useful for digging deep into heavy soils when a pointed shovel just isn't doing the job. These can come in handy during a lawn renovation when you're trying to turn a large patch of weeds into a patch of grass.

Forks

Use a fork with heavy steel tines for breaking up clods, unearthing roots, turning the soil, and working in soil amendments. Forks work more efficiently than shovels for all these tasks, especially in heavy clay soils.

If spreading compost will be part of your annual maintenance program, you should also consider purchasing a manure or compost fork, which has thinner tines placed closer together. The light weight makes this tool ideal for shoveling compost into a wheelbarrow or for top-dressing lawns. It'll also come in handy for aerating a compost pile.

Broadcast Spreaders

Since overseeding with new grass seed is a primary component of a natural lawn care program, it will be useful to keep a broadcast spreader in your shed. It can also be used to apply fertilizers and other soil amendments. A broadcast spreader is preferable to a drop spreader because it works faster and is less prone to product overlap and "striping" of lawns.

Tarps

Your shed should have a lightweight tarp for collecting fall leaves or as a general catchall if you're transplanting a tree, moving sod, or repairing the lawn. Taking the time to put down a tarp in the beginning will save you all kinds of time in cleanup on the other end.

A fishtail weeder easily extracts the deep taproots of dandelions and other weeds.

Betsy Ross

BETSY ROSS CONSIDERS growing good, healthy grass a matter of life or death, for her farm and her way of life. She thinks the rest of us ought to think that way, too, whether we're growing a strip of lawn or thousands of acres of fields.

You might call her a flag waver.

"We believe every square foot of Texas should be healthy soil," she said. "We will go anywhere in this great state to help you make that happen."

Ross, whose family grows foraging crops for their renowned herd of grass-fed organic cattle in Granger, says the principles are the same for lawns and pastures. If you feed the soil, the soil will feed the grass; she has become a champion of applying a biological extract known as compost tea (see page 130) and has installed a large tea-brewing system to service homes and farms across the state.

"We believe that 'healthy soil' means a soil teeming with literally millions of microbes — bacteria, fungi, protozoa, nematodes — that the plants in your soil can call upon to deliver them a balanced and nutritious food supply," she said.

In her case, the healthy soil is delivering more healthy food back to her family and her customers. The Ross Farm has won widespread recognition for the most nutritious beef in all of Texas, with extremely high levels of vitamin E, beta-carotene and beneficial stearic acids. She has earned numerous vocal supporters, including Farm Aid advocate Willie Nelson and popular Texas radio host Howard Garrett, aka "The Dirt Doctor."

"Her beef is proof that there is more going on in the soil than meets the eye," said Garrett. "All her cows eat is grass; that's it. That nutrition is coming straight out of the soil."

A major benefit to the organic grass program, according to Ross, is the soil's ability to retain water. In Texas, where long-term droughts are common, lack of water can often cause crisis conditions. Homeowners facing water restrictions can still produce a green lawn by adding compost and compost tea.

"Everybody ought to be doing this. We'll show 'em how," said the grandmother, who said that, yes, she enjoys her rather famous moniker.

"It's my maiden name," she said. "My sister, Kathryn, came home from school the day I was born and guess what? The lesson at school was about Betsy Ross — so that's what they named me. I have had a lot of fun with my name through the years."

12 The Nearly No-Mow Lawn

grass lawns, even the ones we grow organically, are unnatural systems that require some level of our care. Nature, left alone, invites plenty of plant and biological diversity, with varying species living in proximity. When it works well, nature finds protective balances so no one species dominates.

If you go all the way back to chapter 1, you'll recall that part of any good natural lawn care system considers which areas of the landscape do not need to be grass and which areas will always give you a battle when you try to grow grass. The idea is to save money and time, help the environment, and protect the soil. Bare soil is defenseless against unwanted weedy intruders. As good stewards of our own landscapes, we should take the initiative to maintain at least limited control when it comes to what plants are growing where on our property.

If you've reached this point in the book and are sold on the idea of limiting your lawn's size, the good news is that the alternatives are many. Some of the most obvious, trees and shrubs or mulched beds that may incorporate flowers or vegetables, have been a part of many North American landscapes for decades. This chapter focuses on a few of the newer concepts, including "lo-mow" and ornamental grasses and rain gardens. It also reviews a small sampling of plants that make excellent ground covers in masses of their own. With these plants, you get many of the same benefits of a lawn with barely any of the same maintenance issues.

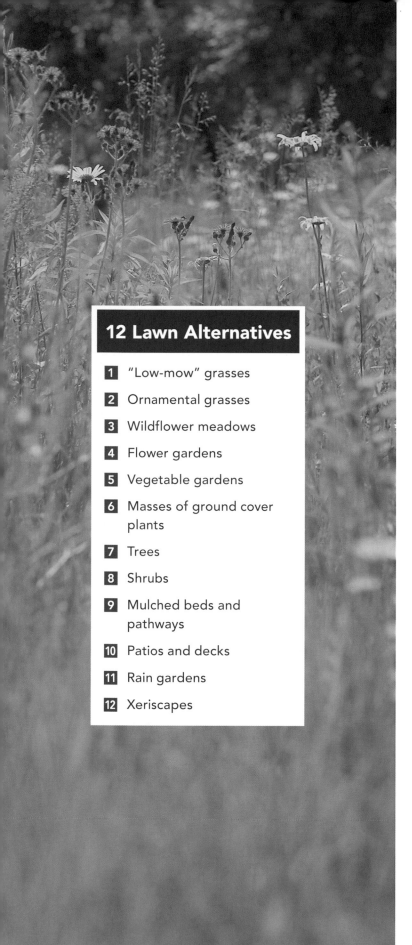

12 Lawn Alternatives

1. "Low-mow" grasses
2. Ornamental grasses
3. Wildflower meadows
4. Flower gardens
5. Vegetable gardens
6. Masses of ground cover plants
7. Trees
8. Shrubs
9. Mulched beds and pathways
10. Patios and decks
11. Rain gardens
12. Xeriscapes

The Basics

So you don't want to maintain an area of your landscape as a lawn. What do you do? If an area appears to be untouched — at least partially wooded, with plenty of trees and vegetation native to the local area — why not leave it alone? You might want to be sure the area that appears natural does not, in fact, contain the aforementioned exotic invasive species (see page 173). Otherwise, it's great to be content to let that area of your landscape grow on its own.

If, on the other hand, you or previous homeowners have maintained an area of the landscape as a lawn or garden, you should take part in the decision about the land's ongoing use. Simply letting it revert to nature is one option, but folks are rarely happy with that outcome.

Ornamental Grasses

This book discusses 16 common lawn grasses in detail in chapter 4, and yet botanists have differentiated thousands of grasses, many of which can be used in low-maintenance natural landscapes.

Ornamental grasses, so named because they're grown primarily for aesthetic appearance rather than for lawns or animal grazing, have become one of the hottest trends in recent years. Many can be planted and simply left alone all year long except for one shearing of the spent foliage in the spring. Some require little water, and others will tolerate fairly dense shade. Some grow nearly two stories high in the tropics, and others barely reach ankle high in colder climates.

No-Mow Grasses

A phrase coined by grass expert Neil Diboll, of Prairie Nursery near Westfield, Wisconsin, "no-mow" is a term applied to a group of grasses that grow low and stay low and can therefore be substituted for traditional lawn grasses in situations where a neatly manicured carpet is not the goal.

Diboll's combination of six cultivars of fine fescues can be mowed a few times a year once the grass is fully established or not at all, depending on your preference. His blend is recommended for the cooler areas of the Upper Midwest and Northeast and, like most fine fescues, will grow well in sun or partial shade.

I'll also take the liberty of borrowing and slightly altering the term for other low- or slow-growing grasses that might well give you the appearance and function you can live with, but without the maintenance that can take up so much of your life. Turn to the Low-Mow list on page 238 for just a few of the options.

Blue grama grass is one of many low-mow options.

Lawn Alternative Checklist

❑ **Trees**
Do you want shade, screening, or fruit? Do you want fast-growing species? Is your choice of tree right for the soil and sunlight?

❑ **Shrubs**
The questions are the same as with trees, along with the added question of maintenance. Most trees, other than fruit trees, require little annual maintenance, but depending on the species, shrubs require more, especially in the way of pruning.

❑ **Patios and Decks**
What is your budget? Who is your contractor? Have you checked building codes? What will be the ongoing maintenance?

❑ **Mulched Beds and Pathways**
What materials will you use? Will they retain their appearance? How will you keep weeds at bay: with landscape fabric, sprays, or flamers or by hand? How will you define the edges?

❑ **Xeriscapes**
This low-water method of landscaping is covered in detail on page 248.

❑ **Wildflower Meadows**
These are discussed in detail on page 250.

Low-Mow Lawn Grass Alternatives

Alkali grass

Puccinella distans

Specially suited for alkaline and salty soils in cool-season climates, this grass often finds its way into golf course roughs or roadside reclamations where conditions are challenging for the traditional lawn grasses. Alkali grass tends to get crowded out in situations where soils are acidic, but if you have a moist area this grass could be ideal. An improved cultivar from Colorado, 'Fults', is often used on lawns where the pH is above 7.5 and soil salts are high.

Blue grama

Bouteloua gracilis

Native to the dry plains of central North America, this highly drought-tolerant species can grow to a foot or more, or can be mowed as a lawn substitute. Considered a warm-season grass because it likes the hot weather and is slow to grow in spring, it is nonetheless hardy to Zone 3. Sometimes called mosquito grass because of the wispy appearance of its flower-heads, it grows in clumps. It prefers heavy soils. (See photo on page 237.)

June grass

Koeleria macrantha

Native to the prairies and open woods of Canada and the United States, this drought-resistant, cool-season species requires little maintenance. It prefers little to no fertilizer, occasional water, and almost no mowing. Cutting lower than 3 inches is not recommended. It may be used as a turf alternative, but given its slow growth habit, a lawn would take four or five years to fill in as a turf on its own.

Prairie dropseed

Sporobolus heterolepis

A wonderfully emerald-colored clumping grass, prairie dropseed is one of the most luxuriant cold-hardy prairie grasses for a sandy site. Often used as an edging plant in perennial gardens, where it will grow to 4 feet high, it can take high mowing in a low-maintenance lawn application. Native Americans use the seeds, which smell a bit like cilantro, to grind into flour.

Prairie sandreed

Calamovilfa longifolia

Though this native grass is used primarily for grazing and hay, it can also be included as a warm-season lawn alternative, especially for sandy sites. Incredibly drought tolerant, it's able to withstand vast extremes in climate except for floods. Left to grow to its full potential, it extends to 5 feet tall with feathery, wispy flower heads.

Sheep fescue

Festuca ovina

It was tempting to include this in chapter 4 with the lawn grasses since a few seed companies do sell this in lawn mixes and have created improved cultivars, including 'Bighorn'. It is a fescue, after all, and displays much of the same characteristic tolerance to shade and drought. This fescue — which is a native, unlike many of the common lawn varieties — is especially well suited to sandy soils in cool-season areas and is one of the few grasses that will hold their own in a gravelly site. It can be slow to get established, though.

Rain Gardens

Much as xeriscaping emerged from a municipal initiative (in that instance, to address water shortages in Denver, Colorado), the concept of rain gardens came out of Prince George's County in Maryland, where local environmentalists were looking for cost-effective, low-maintenance methods to improve infiltration for septic systems and to enhance water quality in storm water–handling installations.

A rain garden can be a homeowner's contribution to the local environment at large or a way to deal with recurrent water issues on his or her own property. Not exactly a water-saving system, and not a water garden, the rain garden has come to be defined as using native perennials and grasses to allow excess water to filter and seep back into the soil naturally. It is the horticultural opposite of the raised bed garden, which grows plants above grade, where the soil is drier and warmer. Proper rain gardens are built in low spots of the landscape to take advantage of moisture-rich areas, and they often add a completely new element to many landscapes.

Building a Rain Garden

Select a sunny area at least 10 feet away from the house, well away from any septic system, where water flows naturally during a rainstorm. At the base of slopes, next to hard surfaces like the street, driveway, or sidewalk, or naturally low areas are all potentially ideal. In choosing the site, you'll also want to think about redirecting water to that area through downspouts from the gutter

Benefits of a Rain Garden

1. Increases replenishing of groundwater
2. Reduces pollutants reaching lakes, streams, rivers, and oceans
3. Increases insect and wildlife habitat
4. Promotes healthier fish and other wildlife
5. Enhances the beauty of your property and neighborhood
6. Protects from basement flooding and storm-water overflow
7. Reduces the need for storm-water treatment structures and facilities
8. Reduces the amount of standing water in the yard
9. Reduces mosquito breeding
10. Reduces the amount of lawn to maintain
11. Increases plant diversity
12. Increases community awareness and education

system or the discharge hose from a sump pump. Make sure redirecting the water to your rain garden will be practical.

Test the soil for filtration rates. Building a rain garden over heavy clay soil is not ideal; a rain garden is not a water garden in that it does not attempt to retain water. Sandy, silty, and loamy soils are best for rain gardens.

Choose a size. The goal is to filter water efficiently, but not so fast that the plants inside the rain garden — which like a lot of water — don't get enough to drink. In other words, the area of the rain garden should be in proportion to the amount of water flowing to the site. Many rain garden planners build their gardens about 20 or 30 percent of the size of the roof on the house, which typically accounts for much of the rainwater flow during a storm. If the soil is heavy and doesn't drain quickly, the garden could be larger.

Pick the plants. Any plants that like water but can also tolerate some dry periods will work, but the true spirit of a rain garden calls for using native plants that help retain the diversity of local species and don't require a lot of maintenance. Your local Cooperative Extension Service will likely have fact sheets on ideal plants for rain gardens.

Dig the garden. Before digging, make sure no underground utility lines are in the area. Every state has a nonprofit organization that maps the locations of utilities; this information should be available from your supplier of electricity. Dig around the perimeter of your rain garden to define its shape, then remove all soil and sod to a depth of about 6 inches. The sod should be composted or used elsewhere on the property; the soil can be used to create a mounded area known as a berm around the edge of the rain garden. If the land slopes downward toward your rain garden, place the berm on the downhill side of the rain garden to help collect more water. Try to dig the base of the rain garden as level as you possibly can.

Prepare the soil. If the soil is mostly clay or sand and does not appear to have good fertility, adding 2 or 3 inches of compost to the bottom of the rain garden is a good idea. In rain gardens with a clay base, dig out at least an extra 2 or 3 inches of clay before adding the compost. You may need to dig even deeper.

Planting the garden. Plant your rain garden as you would any other garden, by blending the compost into the existing soil and watering the plantings as you go. In high-rainfall areas, some rain gardeners group plants according to their water tolerance, with grasslike rushes and reeds around the edges of the rain garden and less-tolerant plants toward the center. If your rain garden is on a slope, put the most water-tolerant plants on the uphill side of the water garden, so these plants catch the water first. Rain gardens should be mulched to reduce the impact of prolonged dry periods.

Position downspouts. If you do take steps to redirect water from your roof, leave a buffer strip of grass in place about 2 or 3 feet before the storm water enters the rain garden. This will help prevent erosion within the rain garden.

Ground Covers

The takeaway idea here is that grasses aren't the only plants that can form a carpet. Any number of shrubs, vines, and perennials will also blanket the soil. Though few invite themselves to be walked upon as readily as lawn grass, these plants will perform many of the lawn's other functions, holding and protecting the soil and beautifying the landscape. Many of these plants grow well where traditional lawns don't — in dense shade, in poor soil, in places where tree roots compete, on slopes, and in drought and heat. It's simply a matter of identifying your lawn challenge and picking an alternative plant or plants to address the situation.

The number of available plants is almost endless. The list starting on page 242, highlights some of the most popular plants for addressing problem situations. The plants are native (except for a few special ones); in general, plants that are native to your area will be better adapted to your local soil conditions and climate.

Establishing ground cover plants takes time, and some will fill in faster than others. In the meantime, you will need to maintain the ground covers by preparing the soil with compost, watering, and weeding, and likely by applying a minimum amount of fertilizer. By starting with larger plants, the process of creating a carpet can happen more quickly. For example, a 1-gallon nursery container at the garden center has probably already been growing for one to five years. The best time to start ground covers is in late summer and early fall or early spring, to avoid the stress of the first summer in the ground.

Grass alternatives known as ground covers are now commonly available at garden centers across North America.

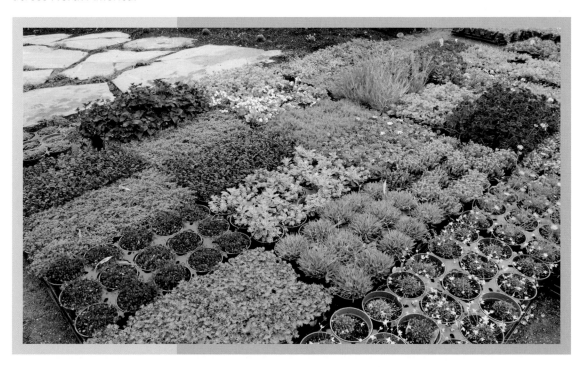

Alternative Ground Covers

DEPENDING ON NUMEROUS FACTORS, including soils, light, and your personal preferences, lawn grasses are not always the ideal plants for all parts of the landscape. Here is just a sampling of alternative plants for special landscape situations. Many of these plants, in fact, would fit into multiple categories listed below.

Shade

Liriope graminifolia — Lilyturf forms stylish flowering clumps in the shade garden and is generally tough as nails once established, which can take a year or two. Evergreen in all climates where it grows, it is also highly drought tolerant. *L. muscari* and *L. spicata* are similar in appearance and function.
Best feature: Thick, grassy foliage
Soils: Light, well drained
Zones: 5–10
Light: Part sun to mostly shade

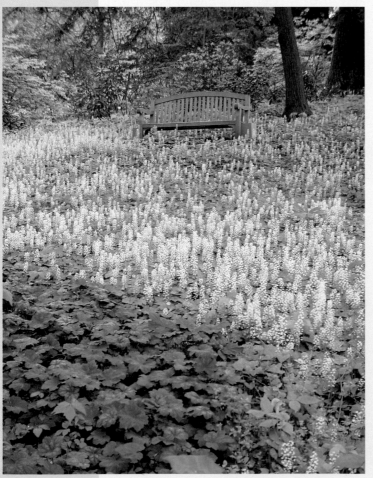
Tiarella cordifolia

Tiarella cordifolia — I fell in love with this plant at Longwood Gardens in Kennett Square, Pennsylvania. Growing there under the canopy of massive tulip trees, it forms a snowlike carpet when it flowers in spring. The handsome maple leaf foliage is attractive all summer, with good fall color in autumn, but it loses its leaves in winter.
Best feature: Spires of white flowers
Soils: Well drained, rich
Zones: 3–10
Light: Moderate shade

Pachysandra procumbens — Not to be confused with its common Japanese cousin, *P. terminalis* (known as Japanese pachysandra), this plant is commonly called Allegheny spurge. Whereas the Japanese version spreads aggressively by stolons, this native plant is clump forming. I like both plants, which are reliable performers in low light and evergreen in most climates.
Best feature: Low maintenance
Soils: Heavy
Zones: 3–10
Light: Heavy shade

Isotoma fluviatilis

Foot Traffic

Isotoma fluviatilis — Commonly known as blue star creeper because of its proliferation of small blue flowers from spring into summer, this evergreen plant stays low to the ground and is ideal for pathways around rocks or at the edge of a driveway — because it can take daily foot traffic. It will require a bit more shade in warmer climates.

Best feature: Quick establishment
Soils: Wide range
Zones: 5–9
Light: Full sun to part shade

Leptinella gruveri — Called miniature brass buttons because of its toughness, this plant can withstand a car parking on it and still bounce back. Ideal for a dark, damp area where lawn grass won't thrive, it produces a dense evergreen mat. The white flowers in spring are a bonus.

Best feature: Toughness
Soils: Moist, heavy
Zones: 7–10
Light: Moderate to full shade

Viola labradorica — One of the many violets that can be a gardener's friend or foe, this member of the family is highly useful in shady areas under trees and can tolerate reasonable foot traffic. In locations where Labrador violet really takes hold, you may need to take steps to keep it in check.

Best feature: Dark evergreen foliage
Soils: Wide range
Zones: 2–6
Light: Moderate to full shade

Viola labradorica

Alternative Ground Covers

Asarum canadense

Under Trees

Ajuga reptans — Bugleweed is one of the plants we hate to love, or learn to hate, so be careful. Some think it's a flat-out weed, and on your lawn it can be. If you need a plant for deep shade that tolerates low fertility, with the added benefit of beautiful foliage and pretty flowers, this plant does have merit. Just watch it closely.
Best feature: Purplish evergreen foliage
Soils: Wide range
Zones: 3–8
Light: Part sun to heavy shade

Asarum canadense — Wild ginger, with its glossy, evergreen, heart-shaped leaves, makes a stunning plant under trees. Not related to the common ginger, it does have an edible root and grows best where leaves have long decayed. Look for *A. caudatum*, *A. shuttleworthii*, and especially *A. europaeum*, which are similar.
Best feature: Leaves
Soils: Rich, acid
Zones: 3–7
Light: Light to moderate shade

Ferns — Too numerous to mention just one species, ferns are nature's most common plants for the forest floor. As natural gardeners, we should take the hint. You can find ferns for every climate, ferns for food, and ferns with colorful fronds. Many are evergreen, drought tolerant, and well behaved.
Best feature: Versatility
Soils: Wide range
Zones: Vary
Light: Light to heavy shade

Ferns

Poor Soils

Chamaemelum nobile — Roman chamomile is a delightfully forgiving evergreen herb to grow in sunny areas that have been neglected. A unique nonflowering cultivar known as 'Treneague' is especially good as a lawn substitute because it puts all its energy into spreading across the landscape. Wonderfully fragrant, it will start slowly but grow vigorously once established.
Best feature: Fragrance.
Soils: Wide range.
Zones: 4–9
Light: Full sun

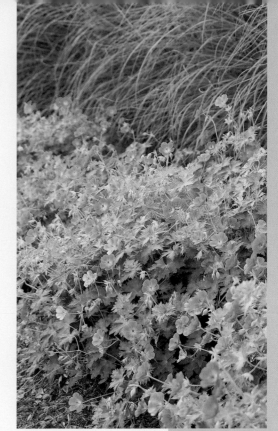

***Geranium* 'Rozanne'** — I highlight this drought-tolerant perennial geranium above all others because it's a new introduction that is as good as advertised. Its purple flowers appear from June until well after the first frost, and the plant needs scarcely any attention once it's established.
Best feature: Long bloom season
Soils: Wide range, except wet
Zones: 5–9
Light: Full sun

Geranium 'Rozanne'

***Sedum* spp.** — More than 300 species of plants belong to the sedum family, which is one of the toughest on the planet. Many flower with amazing vibrancy; others have succulent foliage and look like desert tropicals. Many gardeners plant multiple species together.
Best feature: Drought tolerance
Soils: Wide range
Zones: Vary
Light: Full sun to light shade

Sedum acre

Alternative Ground Covers

Dianthus 'Pixie'

Genista pilosa

Holding Slopes

***Dianthus* spp.** — A common resident in perennial flower gardens, this creeping plant doubles as a dynamite grass substitute on a mostly sunny slope. Tolerant of heat and humidity, dianthus also holds its foliage all winter even in a northern climate. Shear it back after the first bloom and it will reliably bloom a second time.
Best feature: Flowers
Soils: Wide range
Zones: 3–8
Light: Full sun to moderate shade

Genista pilosa — Becoming popular in the Pacific Northwest, this low-growing shrub appears at first to be a member of the juniper family, but when the plant drapes itself in stunning pea-size yellow flowers in spring, you'll know it's something quite different. Highly drought tolerant, it can take the heat.
Best feature: Flowers and foliage
Soils: Wide range
Zones: 5–9
Light: Full sun to light shade

Rubus pentalobus — Native to Taiwan, creeping rubus is durably evergreen in sun or shade, with deeply textured foliage that resembles that of lady's mantle.
Best feature: Raspberry fall foliage
Soils: Wide range
Zones: 6–8
Light: Full sun to moderate shade

Drought and Heat

Arctostaphylos uva-ursi — Bearberry is an evergreen shrub that grows only about 3 to 8 inches tall but several feet wide. Ideal for holding sunny banks, it tolerates extreme conditions of drought.
Best feature: Glossy green foliage
Soils: Poor, sandy, acid
Zones: 3–9
Light: Full sun

Thymus citriodorus — Lemon thyme is my favorite perennial, bar none. You've got to love a plant that stays evergreen all winter long in Maine yet also grows in Florida and Texas. I keep it near all my walkways because I never get tired of the fresh aroma. It will spread quickly once established
Best feature: Fragrance
Soils: Wide range
Zones: 4–10
Light: Full sun to moderate shade

Thymus citriodorus

Yucca filamentosa — Though not a ground cover, the incredibly versatile yucca provides a tropical flair to any garden, even in the North. Normally around 2 to 3 feet tall, all the pointed, rigid leaves arise from a central point in a rosette. In summer, the plant produces a flower stalk that often grows 4 feet or more
Best feature: Evergreen foliage
Soils: Poor
Zones: 5–10
Light: Full sun to moderate shade

Yucca filamentosa

Xeriscaping

This, I find, is a widely misunderstood concept. Xeriscaping begins with the acceptance that you're not going to cover your landscape with a traditional lawn, not all of it, anyway. It should not, however, be confused with "zero-scaping," which many people equate with doing nothing, or paving the property right up to the foundation. Xeriscaping is substituting drought-tolerant and primarily native plants for the thirstier plants you may be using — like your lawn grasses. It doesn't mean you're not landscaping; you're just doing it differently.

Xeriscaping also does not mean zero beauty or function. By substituting ornamental grasses for lawn grasses, for example, you can create a stunning, low-maintenance landscape that requires little water or fertilizer to be successful.

Water-conscious communities everywhere are on the xeriscape bandwagon. The town of Falmouth, Massachusetts, hired a local landscaper named Paul Miskovsky to rip out the lawn and flowers in front of the town hall. When he replaced them with ornamental grasses and perennials, many citizens were initially outraged. Now they love it. In Albuquerque, New Mexico, homeowners can earn tax credits by following xeriscaping principles; businesses in that city, where it rains less than 9 inches a year on average, can earn four times as much. The city suggests acceptable xeriscape plants, and has even hired professional landscape designers to post plans, free of charge, on its Web site to help take the guesswork out of the planting process.

Scott Calhoun's yard in Tucson, Arizona, is a model of good xeriscape design and regional appropriateness.

Falmouth, Massachusetts

LIFELONG FALMOUTH, MASSACHUSETTS, resident Paul Miskovsky was nearly drubbed out of Cape Cod when he came up with a revolutionary concept for the 3,000-square-foot area in front of Town Hall. Employing the principles of xeriscaping, his design proposed a drought-tolerant garden that would look like an idealized version of Falmouth's 17 miles of beachfront.

Selectmen, faced with budget constraints and water restrictions, immediately embraced the plan. After the garden went in, though, townspeople were up in arms. They expected sweeps of flowers; they didn't like sprigs of grass. It was one of those jobs that need to look worse before they can look better.

Miskovsky brought in 500 yards of sand as his base, but tucked 60 yards of fertile topsoil — up to 1½ feet deep — in the planting areas under the sand.

He found eight different grasses that thrive in drought and heat, along with black pines and oak trees that could go long periods without water. For a splash of color on the site, he planted several kinds of perennials, such as sedums, Shasta daisies, daylilies, and lavender. A 2-inch mulch of seaweed provided form and function.

"The appearance and color of the seaweed is great for the site," said Miskovsky. "But the best thing is that it retains moisture from any rainfall and provides all sorts of micronutrients for the plants."

By its third year, the garden had evolved to appear just as Miskovsky imagined. With careful placement of seashells and granite stones, along with seaweed on the ground and the sound of grass billowing in the air, the beautifully naturalistic Town Hall beach garden is beginning to win over the townspeople's hearts.

It's a model that should be copied all over Cape Cod and beyond, according to Brian Dale, the superintendent of parks and recreation.

"The bottom line is that the town of Falmouth is saving a lot of money each year on maintenance, water, and fertilizer," he said. "And this type of garden is helping to save the fragile environment on the island. Landscapes that require a lot of fertilizer run the risk of polluting the groundwater, not to mention wasting the [irrigation] water.

"I read the other day that half of our homeowners' water usage goes into keeping lawns watered," Dale said. "That's just too much."

For Miskovsky, the beach garden provides another benefit all gardeners enjoy.

"We don't get any weeds here," he said. "Weeds don't survive in a hot dry environment like this, but the beach grass thrives."

What more could you ask for?

Returning to the Flowery Mead

Why don't you just let your new lawn grow?" asked my mentor, horticulturist Richard Churchill, back in the mid-1990s, when he was encouraging me to kick the pesticide habit. "You might be surprised at what happens."

By then I was a licensed pesticide applicator well versed in the chemicals most commonly used to keep lawns weed-free. Sure, I had my childhood memories of my grandparents' lawn of berries and clover, and I appreciated the appearance of wildflower meadows. I even hung a nostalgic photo on my wall of my then-young daughter, who was plucking orange hawkweed from a lawn that I had not yet treated. It never occurred to me, however, to actually try to grow the plants most of my customers considered to be weeds.

The progression of that backyard seemed stunning when I took my friend's suggestion and neglected to start the mower. Week after week, month after month, colorful flowers emerged within the lawn. The tiny white bluets came first, followed by the blooms of wild strawberries and violets. Dandelions came and went, of course, followed by the most amazing carpet of daisies I had ever seen. I must have taken a hundred photos of that lawn, and even turned some of them into a calendar for my customers.

The following year seemed so sad by comparison. A few bluets peeked out, but not nearly as many as I had recalled. The strawberries and violets could barely be seen, and the dandelions, well, I had plenty . . . but my lawn produced only a few daisies, instead of the fistfuls of bouquets the year before.

The problem, I soon deduced, was the synthetic fertilizer I had applied the previous autumn. I was careful not to put down any herbicides because I wanted my wildflower meadow to reappear. The application of fertilizer had been intended to give the flowers a boost, to make them even more robust than they had been the year before. All I got, though, were more opportunities to mow the grass; the wildflowers did not appreciate the extra nitrogen, phosphorus, and potassium in that bag.

Therein lies the enigma of the elusive flowery mead. Sometimes we have to learn to live and let live, or take an entirely different tack that requires plenty of thought, preparation, labor, and adjustment of expectations.

When she was a much younger girl, my daughter, Christina, loved to play in the hawkweed that bloomed each July and August on our front lawn.

Defining the Wildflower Meadow

A wildflower meadow is simply an area of your property that is either left alone or cultivated to produce flowers. You'll need to make two kinds of decisions right from the start. The first and probably the easiest is to define what areas you're going to steal either from the grass lawn or from other gardens or woodland areas on your property. Whether you want a different appearance, less mowing, or less overall maintenance, it's fairly easy to redraw your landscape. It's a fun exercise indoors on paper in winter, or outdoors with a few lengths of garden hose to draw new boundaries. Keep sun and shade in mind; most wildflower seed mixes on the market are geared for full sun. Wildflowers grown in the shade are most often referred to as woodland gardens. Avoid planting wildflowers in areas with constant excess moisture; the plants' roots will suffer, and the foliage will be a target for slug and snail damage.

The second and more complicated decision concerns what kind of meadow you really want around your home. Growing a meadow is much like composting or gardening, or even natural lawn care in general. You can have a basic understanding with limited results . . . the lazy person's compost pile, for example, or a few flowers in a container, or a cold-turkey decision to stop spraying pesticides on your lawn. Or you can really dive into growing a meadow by understanding soil conditions, site preparation, plant selection and maintenance, and meadow evolution. It's an educational process that can take years, if you've got the interest.

Getting Started:
Tips for a Great Meadow

1 Dethatch the lawn first, to remove any dead plant debris and to scratch the soil surface to achieve good seed-to-soil contact.

2 In general, it's best to purchase seed from local or national suppliers who are familiar with your climate conditions.

3 Pick a seed mix with as many species as possible; some companies offer mixes of as many as 30 species.

4 When sowing, thoroughly mix the seed into a pail of light sand or vermiculite so you can see where you've spread the seed as you're working.

5 Water the seed frequently until you see evidence of germination, which in the case of some wildflower seeds can be a month or more.

6 Ironically, you may have more success if your grass is unhealthy at the start. The wildflowers will have less competition, and you'll be less inclined to mow while the young seedlings are growing.

7 Consider having both annual and perennial wildflowers in your meadow; that will vary the bloom times and generally keep more color in the meadow earlier and later in the season.

8 By the end of the first summer, after everything has bloomed and gone to seed, mow the meadow one more time.

Playing on the Lawn

The best reward for all our yard work, to be sure, is an awesome place to play. I don't spend the winter dreaming about the mowing and weeding I'll be doing all summer, but I do often lie awake in January enjoying the fantasy of throwing a football, baseball, or Frisbee with my young son. Lawn games, quite frankly, are the only reason I have a lawn. Those games, played with children of all ages, are also the best reason to grow lawns as naturally and safely as possible.

With the hope that many, many more people will rediscover the joys of running barefoot through their Bahia grass, here's a refresher course on some of the most popular lawn games, old and new. I won't spend too much time on the rules, though. The most fun is in making up your own.

Croquet

Like so many of our lawn games, the modern sport of croquet came to America by way of France and England. Originally called pall mall, this target game was eventually called croquet after the French word for crooked stick.

Today, you can find all the rules you want from the U.S. Croquet Association (see Resources, page 263). Three official versions of the game are known to exist, with either six wickets or nine, two to six players, and various ideal field sizes up to 100 feet long and 50 feet wide. The general idea is to carefully aim your ball so it rolls through each wicket in succession — a sort of golf-meets-billiards game — and the first player to roll his or her ball through all the wickets is the winner. Hand-eye coordination helps, but physical strength offers no particular advantage. Camaraderie and strategy play a major role in the team game, but our family has always preferred the singles version, where it's every child, mother, father, brother, sister, and grandparent for themselves. The official rules call for a measured set pattern of the wickets, but at our home my son has become the official spacer of the wickets in a sort of random chaos across the lawn.

Winning rarely seems to matter; the most fun is rolling your ball next to the opponent's ball so that it barely touches and comes to a stop. At that point you can put your foot on top of your own ball to hold it in place while you swing your mallet as forcefully as possible, thereby "sending" your opponent's ball to a far

Appendix

corner of the lawn. In the true cutthroat version, no boundaries exist. Knocking your brother's ball into the shrubs is fair game and good fun. As they say in golf, "Hit it where it lies."

Ideal lawn: Croquet aficionados will want a perfectly smooth surface, preferably a bent grass sheared to ½ inch. Backyard croquet, however, can be played on any turf mowed at about 3 inches. A few undulations and bumps, while bothersome to the serious players, will add a degree of challenge for the rest of us.

Turf impact: Low to medium

Wiffle Ball

The problem with baseball as a lawn game is that a full game has always been just about impossible to confine to the average lawn. The hard ball, when struck by a hard bat, can cause some serious harm to the windows, siding, plants, and people of an entire neighborhood. That was exactly the problem facing David N. Mullany, a former semiprofessional baseball pitcher, whose 12-year-old son was constantly in trouble for damaging school property with errant baseballs in the early 1950s in Shelton, Connecticut.

That's when David Sr. came up with an idea. He had a friend who used plastic half-balls as cases for makeup. By gluing two halves together and cutting slotted holes on one side, he eventually came up with a whole new creation: a ball that easily made batters "wiff," slang of the

day for striking out. More than a half-century later, this purely American lawn game is still going strong.

The Mullaney family Web site (see Resources, page 263) lists the official rules of play, which include an ideal field of at least 20 by 60 feet and no base running required. The true beauty of this game, though, is that any patch of turf or pavement will do just fine and just about any rules related to baseball will result in a spirited contest, whether you have one against one or nine players on a side.

Ideal lawn: Turf quality and height have little role in a successful Wiffle ball match. A pleasant barefoot pursuit, its only drawback is keeping the bases in the same spot time and time again. All that base running can make bare spots appear at first, second, third, and especially home.

Turf impact: Potentially high

Bocce

In all my research, I could never quite figure out why we Americans adopted the Italian name for a game that has been enjoyed for millennia throughout Egypt, the Far East, and France. Records at Mount Vernon show that George Washington enjoyed engaging in "bowls," the name originally brought over from England, where the oldest bowling lawn has been maintained in Southampton since 1299. That might have been a derivation of *boules,* a word coined by the French to describe their version of the game.

These days, "Bocce, anyone?" is a refined way to ask your family and friends if they'd like to roll balls across your lawn. In this, the oldest sport known to humans, a small weighted wooden or plastic ball called a pallina is rolled some distance away from the players, usually from two to eight in number. Other, larger balls are then rolled toward the pallina, with the closest balls scoring points. Knocking other players' balls away from the pallina is allowed and that, at least at my house, is where the real fun comes in. If I manage to make a close roll, my son just loves to try to blast it out of position. Official bocce players call that maneuver a "spock," and their Web site (see Resources, page 263) will tell you that bocce is "a true sport involving skill, fitness, strategy, and cunning."

Maybe in some places. The best part about bocce is that my 86-year-old grandmother can play this peaceful game with ease. As long as the pallina is rolled a reasonable distance away, she can take her aim underhanded and get the ball close. Bocce can be played in chairs with legs or wheels, and it can even be played alone as an athletic form of solitaire.

Ideal lawn: Bocce rules call for a perfectly smooth lawn, with a layout of 60 by 12 feet with backstops on each end. Grass taller than 3 inches or so will slow the roll of the ball significantly. The balls are dense, however, and will manage fine on most any turf. A few bumps and divots won't impede a friendly game.

Turf impact: Low

Badminton

Around the world, badminton is claimed to be the second most popular sport to soccer, but it has turned up less and less on American lawns since tennis increased in popularity after the 1950s. Maybe we see it as too docile. The image of proper aristocrats politely tapping the "birdie" back and forth doesn't appeal to our hyperactive X-Games culture. Badminton, though, can be as competitive as you want to make it, and in fact has been an Olympic sport since the Barcelona games in 1992. The shuttlecocks come off the rackets at speeds up to 200 miles per hour and badminton's best players, mostly from Asia these days, are some of the most finely conditioned athletes in the world.

Played one against one or two against two, the official game calls for a court 20 feet wide and 44 feet long. Smaller spaces will work just fine because the shuttlecock, which weighs only a few ounces, is no danger to surrounding plants and property.

Ideal lawn: Grass height and quality are of little importance, since a point is complete the instant the shuttlecock hits the ground. Flat areas are best, and hosts should check for potholes and bumps to avoid turned ankles. Move the court frequently to avoid compacted areas.

Turf impact: Medium to high

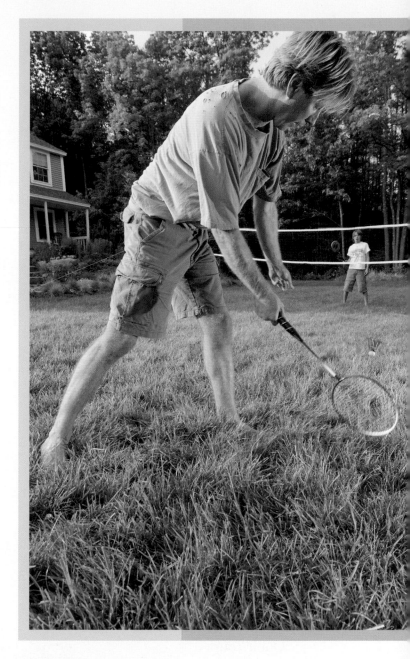

Quoits

Although this game is similar to horse-shoes and one that we may know better as ring toss, it was actually started by the ancient Romans, who found a far more friendly use for a metal weapon known as a quoit. The earliest versions were thrown sidearm like a discus, and the most skilled warriors could decapitate an enemy from a great distance. Between battles, the apparently bored soldiers came upon the idea of sticking a stake in the ground and tossing their quoits underhanded toward the target.

These days, myriad variations of the game can be found in sporting goods stores and toy departments across the land. Quoits, usually called rings, are made from rope or plastic and can be enjoyed by toddlers barely out of a crib or nursing home residents who take aim at the target from their wheelchairs.

The true sport of quoits, in which metal pins are set into the ground about 20 feet apart, is still enjoyed in many pockets of the United States, most notably in eastern Pennsylvania, where the United States Quoiting Association (see Resources, page 263) runs the National Quoit Tour.

Ideal lawn: Turf type plays no role in quoits since this is a total target game. As in horseshoes, hosts often construct "pits" filled with mud or sand around the stakes, although hammering a stake directly onto the lawn works just fine.

Quoits do leave divots when they land, and players and spectators often cause bare patches by playing repeatedly from the same locations.

Turf impact: Potentially high

Disc Golf

Another uniquely American game, this sport has become immensely popular in recent years. Giant courses have been set up across the country, with more than 3 million participants, and unlike the game of "ultimate" — which requires constant running after the disc and a high level of fitness — disc golf can be enjoyed by the most docile of players.

The game is, simply, aiming a Frisbee at a target. A tree, lamppost, rake, or hoe handle will all work equally well. Players keep score to see how many shots it takes to go from target to target. Larger lawns and yards can make the game more interesting, and you can purchase fancy target poles to catch the Frisbee if you want to get serious. As with so many lawn games, however, a lot of space and money really aren't necessary.

Ideal lawn: Turf height and quality are not a factor in disc golf, or any sort of Frisbee playing, for that matter.

Turf impact: Low

Acidity/acid soil. A factor of soil biology that refers to a measurement on the pH scale from 0 to 14, with anything less than neutral (7.0) being acidic.

Aerate. On lawns, a function of poking or cutting holes in the turf to allow water, air, nutrients, and other amendments to get down to the roots; in compost tea, to add oxygen or air movement.

Aerobic. A condition of soils or compost tea that indicates good air or oxygen movement, or the presence of beneficial soil bacteria.

Aggregate. Individual clumps of soil that collectively reveal soil structure.

Alkalinity/alkaline soil. A factor of soil biology that refers to a measurement on the pH scale from 0 to 14, with anything more than neutral (7.0) being alkaline.

Amoeba. A single-celled organism that lives in the soil.

Anaerobic. A condition of soils or compost tea that indicates poor air or oxygen movement or the lack of beneficial soil bacteria.

Annual. A plant that germinates, grows, sets seed, and dies all in one season; it also means yearly, as in an annual application of fertilizer.

Available nutrient. Any element that exists in a form that can be used by plants; elements such as nitrogen, potassium, and phosphorus may exist in the soil without being available to plants due to various soil conditions.

Bacteria. Microorganisms in the soil that can be either beneficial or harmful.

Basin. A dug-out area that serves as a water reservoir.

Bioassay. A soil test that measures the bacterial and fungal relationships in the soil.

Black water. Water from toilets, sinks, and dishwashers, which should not be used to water the lawn unless treated.

Blend. A combination of two or more cultivars of the same grass species planted together.

Burn. A toxic grass condition in which excessive nitrogen has been applied to the lawn, usually resulting in dehydration and yellow or brown patches.

Cation exchange capacity. A measure of the positive or negative charge of soil that predicts the soil's ability to hold nutrients and water.

Chemical. In this text, refers to a synthetic system of horticulture. Products and amendments may have been created in a laboratory; actions may consider only their impact on the plant, overlooking their influence on soil, water, and air quality. This approach follows formulaic instruction, and often treats plant care as a symptom rather than as part of an entire ecosystem. A chemical lawn system has the potential to harm life, both above- and belowground.

Ciliates. Microscopic creatures that feed on soil bacteria.

Clump-forming. Grasses that grow in bunches or mounds without sending out root runners known as either rhizomes or stolons.

Compaction. A description of soil structure in which aggregates are tightly packed, often inhibiting grass growth.

Compost. Decomposed organic matter that is the basis for organic soil management.

Compost tea. Compost that has been brewed or steeped in water, which can then be used to treat soil and plants as a beneficial inoculant and food source.

Cool-season grass. An evergreen grass that grows in northern regions of North America, typically USDA Zones 1–7.

Core aeration. An aeration technique that cuts a grass and soil plug out of the ground with knifelike cylinders on a drum.

Crown. The central point of growth on a grass plant where the roots and shoots meet, typically at the soil surface.

Cultivar. A named variety within a species of plants; the word is used interchangeably with *hybrid*.

Dethatch. The process of removing thatch from lawns, ideally with a bamboo rake or a specialized machine with revolving metal tines.

Diatomaceous earth. Remains of algae mined from the ocean floor that can be used to control insects including grubs, chinch bugs, and slugs.

Dormant/dormancy. A lawn condition that is a sleep response to excess heat or drought, and often results in a brown appearance.

Endophytes. Fungi that exist with perennial ryegrass and fescues — as well as bluegrass and bent grass in the near future — that give the grasses disease and insect resistance but are toxic to foraging animals and birds.

Enzyme. A complex protein in grasses that controls growth rates and microbial activity.

Evapotranspiration. A combined measurement of evaporation of water from the soil and the transpiration of water through plants.

Fish emulsion. By-product of fish processing used as high-nitrogen fertilizer.

Flagellates. Microscopic creatures that feed on soil bacteria.

Fixing. A process by which atmospheric nitrogen is stored in the roots of plants belonging to the legume family, such as clover and bird's-foot trefoil.

Fungi. Soil organisms that break down organic matter and toxins and attack other species.

Germination days. The expected number of days until a seed sprouts.

Germination rate. The percentage of seed that sprouts within a given batch.

Grade. On a lawn, a measurement of the downhill slope.

Gray water. Water from the washing machine, bathtub, and bathroom sink, which may be reused to water lawns.

Herbicide. Any substance used to kill weeds or unwanted plants.

Humus. The most stable form of organic matter that exists in soil.

Humic acids. Also called humates and fulvic acids, these are soil conditioners that increase microbial activity, water retention, and disease resistance and promote good structure.

Larva/larval stage. The early stage of insect life characterized by wingless bodies. Grubs, the larval stage of many types of beetles, often cause lawn damage.

Legume. A family of plants, including peas, beans, and clover, capable of storing atmospheric nitrogen in their roots.

Lignin. A complex compound found in grass roots that resists decomposition.

Leaf. Plant foliage; in grass plants, leaves contain two parts, the sheath at the base and the blade that extends outward and upward.

Macronutrients. Nitrogen (N), phosphorus (P), and potassium (K), the three elements listed on the front of all fertilizer bags, which are used in relatively high percentages by plants.

Microbe/microorganism. Microscopic living material in plants and soil, including bacteria, fungi, algae, protozoa, ciliates, flagellates, nematodes, arthropods, and amoebae.

Micronutrients. Boron, chlorine, copper, iron, manganese, molybdenum, and zinc, which are essential but used in extremely low percentages by plants.

Mixture. A combination of two or more grass species planted together.

Mulch. Any natural or man-made material placed on top of the soil to retain moisture, suppress weeds, or prevent erosion, or for aesthetics.

Mulching mower. A grass-cutting machine with special blades to finely chop grass, so the grass remain on the lawn.

Mycorrhizae. Forms of fungi that grow in a beneficial association on or in plant roots; they occur naturally and may also be inoculated into roots to encourage disease resistance, water retention, and overall vigor.

Nematodes. Microorganisms in the soil that can be either beneficial or harmful.

Nonselective. A material such as a weed killer or pest control that indiscriminately kills all plants or insects; a selective weed killer will eliminate target plants but allow others to live.

Organic. In this text, refers to elements within a natural system of horticulture. Any products and soil amendments within the system must be derived from plants, animals, or minerals; any actions should consider their impact on soil, water, and air quality and the overall health of the earth. This approach requires careful observation and strives for a balance that gives us results we desire, while making certain not to override nature. A successful organic system improves life, both above- and belowground.

Ornamental grass. Grass plants grown for pure aesthetics, rather than for a lawn or forage crop.

Overseeding. The process of spreading seed over an existing lawn to fill in thin areas, to rejuvenate the lawn, or — especially in the South — to plant cool-season species for green winter color.

Perennial. A plant the lives for multiple years.

Pesticide. Any material used to combat insects, diseases, or weeds in the lawn or garden.

Photosynthesis. The essential life-supporting process by which a plant uses its own chlorophyll plus sun, carbon dioxide, and water to create carbohydrates for food.

Plug. A small piece of sod used to introduce grass into a new lawn area or to patch an existing lawn area.

Porosity. A description of a soil's ability to absorb water; porous soils allow water to pass through quickly.

Preemergent. A weed control, such as corn gluten, that does not allow weed or grass seeds to germinate.

Protozoa. Soil microorganisms that accelerate decomposition by feeding on bacteria, fungi, and plant residue.

Rain barrel. A vessel for gathering natural precipitation, typically in conjunction with a downspout from a house's gutter system.

Rain garden. A natural garden utilizing native plants created in a low area of the yard to encourage gathering of storm water.

Rhizome. An underground stem from a grass plant that will send off shoots and roots and allow the plant to creep.

Rhizobia. Bacteria that live in a symbiotic relationship with leguminous plants that results in nitrogen fixation.

Scalp. To cut the lawn too short by removing most of the top growth of the grass plant.

Secondary nutrients. Calcium, magnesium, and sulfur; essential elements that are used in moderate percentages by plants.

Sheath. The base of the leaf of a grass plant that encircles the stem.

Sod-forming/sod. A grass that weaves together with rhizomes and/or stolons to form a collective mat; strips of grass that are sold in the lawn care industry to establish lawns quickly.

Soil conditioner. Any material designed to improve or change the characteristics of soil, such as humic acids to improve fertility and drainage.

Soil probe. A hollow tube inserted into the soil to provide a quick profile of root depth, soil texture, structure, and moisture.

Species. A classification in the naming of plants and animals within which all members share most, but not all, of the same characteristics.

Sprig. A grass cutting that can be planted to establish a new lawn, or to repair an existing lawn.

Stolon. An aboveground stem from a grass plant that will send off shoots and roots and allow the plant to creep.

Structure. The physical constitution of soil material as expressed by aggregate size, and impacting density and porosity.

Synthetic. Any material derived from a man-made source, typically involving a laboratory setting.

Texture. The feel of soil based on relative amounts of sand, silt, and clay; a relative description describing the soil characteristics, such as heavy clay or sandy loam.

Thatch. A layer of undecomposed but dead or dying grass stems, roots, stolons, and rhizomes that, if allowed to become too thick, may lead to insect and/or disease problems and other lawn ailments.

Top-dress. Evenly spreading any material over the surface of the lawn, usually not more than a ½ in thickness.

Topsoil. Generally the upper layer of soil containing enough organic matter to support growth.

Transition zone. An area of the nation between cool-season and warm-season that may support the growth of either of those categorizations of grasses or other grasses uniquely suited to that area.

Transpiration. The process by which plants and animals lose water, as vapor, into the atmosphere.

Turfgrass. A grass commonly used to grow lawns.

Warm-season grass. A grass that grows in southern regions of the country, typically USDA Zones 6–10, that will go dormant and turn brown in winter.

Xeriscaping. An alternative form of landscaping that uses drought-tolerant grasses, perennials, shrubs, and trees.

Zone. A measure of the average climatic condition of a geographic area as it relates to low temperature. Most references define 10 distinct zones.

Recommended Reading

Bormann, F. Herbert, Diana Balmori, and Gordon T. Geballe.
Redesigning the American Lawn.
Yale University Press, 2001.

Easy Lawns: Low Maintenance Native Grasses for Gardeners Everywhere.
Brooklyn Botanic Garden, 2001.

Ellis, Barbara, and Fern Marshall Bradley.
The Organic Gardener's Handbook of Natural Insect and Disease Control.
Rodale Press, 1996.

Hastings, Chris.
Southern Lawns: A Step-by-Step Guide to the Perfect Lawn.
Longstreet Press Inc., 2000.

Hill, Lewis, and Nancy Hill.
Rodale's Successful Organic Gardening: Lawns, Grasses & Groundcovers.
Rodale Press, 1995.

Hynes, Erin.
Rodale's Successful Organic Gardening: Controlling Weeds.
Rodale Press, 1995.

Jenkins, Virginia Scott.
The Lawn: History of an American Obsession.
Smithsonian Books, 1994.

McCaman, Jay L.
Weeds and Why They Grow.
Self-published, 1994.

Pfeiffer, Ehrenfried E.
Weeds and What They Tell.
Biodynamic Farming and Gardening Association, 1981

Pollan, Michael.
Second Nature. Grove Press, 2003.

Sachs, Paul D. Edaphos
Dynamics of a Natural Soil System.
The Edaphic Press, 1999.

Standards for Organic Land Care: Practices for Design and Maintenance of Ecological Landscapes.
Northeast Organic Farmers Association. www.nofa.org.

Steingraber, Sandra.
Living Downstream: A Scientist's Personal Investigation of Cancer and the Environment.
Vintage Books, 1998.

Trenholm, Laurie E., and J. Bryan Unruh.
The Florida Lawn Handbook.
University Press of Florida, 2005.

Wargo, John.
Risks from Lawn-Care Pesticides.
Environmental and Human Health Inc., 2003.

Waters, Charles.
Weeds: Control Without Poisons.
Acres U.S.A., 1999.

Resources

Grass Seed Suppliers

**Jonathan Green Lawn
and Garden Products**
800-526-2303
www.jonathangreen.com

OutsidePride.com
877-255-8470
www.outsidepride.com

Pawnee Buttes Seed
800-782-5947
www.pawneebuttesseed.com

Pennington Seed
800-285-SEED
www.penningtonseed.com

Seedland
888-820-2080
www.seedland.com

Superseedstore.com
716-683-0683
www.superseedstore.com

Compost Tea Supplies, Fertilizers, and Organic Resources

Some of these companies
may sell products that are
not organic in nature, in
addition to organic products
recommended for natural
lawns.

Bradfield Organics
800-551-9564
www.bradfieldorganics.com

Earth Tea Brewer
541-767-2744
www.composttea.com

Fertrell Company
717-367-1566
www.fertrell.com

Gardeners Supply Co.
802-660-3500
www.gardeners.com

GardensAlive
513-354-1483
www.gardensalive.com

Growing Solutions
541-343-8374
www.growingsolutions.com

**Harmony Farm Supply &
Nursery**
707-823-9125
www.harmonyfarm.com

McGeary Organics
717-394-6843
www.mcgearyorganics.com

Midwest Bio-Systems
800-335-8501
www.aeromasterequipment.com

North Country Organics
802-222-4277
www.norganics.com

Organic Growers Supply
207-873-7333
www.fedcoseeds.com

Organica
631-544-0348
www.organica.net

Peaceful Valley Farm Supply
530-272-4769
www.groworganic.com

Planet Natural
406-587-5891
www.planetnatural.com

Seven Springs Farm
800-540-9181
www.7springsfarm.com

Sustainable Growth
888-922-GROW
www.sustainablegrowth.com

Algae Products

Microp
800-221-7645
www.soiltechcorp.com

Wetting Agents

Aquabond
800-956-0063
www.poulengerusa.com

AquaMaxx
866-361-4977
www.aqua-maxx.com

Organic Water Wizard
888-892-8375
www.uwaterless.com

PennMulch
800-233-1067
www.lebsea.com

High-Calcium Limestone

Old Castle Stone Products
800-526-1753
www.oldcastle.com

MK Minerals
785-537-8902
www.mkminerals.com

Organic Pest and Weed Controls

Cedarcide
559-320-0166
www.cedarcide.com

Cutting Edge Formulations
866-906-WEED
www.naturesavenger.com

Dr. T's Nature Products
800-299-6288
www.animalrepellents.com

Extremely Green Gardening Company
781-878-5397
www.extremelygreen.com

Green Light Company
210-494-3481
www.greenlightco.com

Natura
800-523-2680
www.naturaproducts.ca

St. Gabriel Laboratories
540-672-0866
www.milkyspore.com

Woodstream Corporation
717-626-2125
www.saferbrand.com

Rain Garden Information

www.raingardennetwork.com
www.raingardens.org
www.raingarden.il.gov

Wildflower Seed

The American Meadows Company
802-951-5812

The Lady Bird Johnson Wildflower Center
512-292-4100
www.wildflower.org

The New England Wild Flower Society
508-877-7630
www.newfs.org

Additional Online Information

National Sustainable Agriculture Information Service
www.attra.org

National Turfgrass Evaluation Program
www.ntep.org

Organic Materials Review Institute
www.omri.org

Lawn Games

Disc Golf Association
831-722-6037
www.discgolfassoc.com

The United States Quoiting Association
610-473-8473
www.usqa.org

U.S. Bocce Federation
510-229-2157
www.bocce.com

U.S. Croquet Association
561-478-0760
www.croquetamerica.com

USA Badminton
719-866-4808
www.usabadminton.org

Wiffle Ball Inc.
203-924-4643
www.wiffle.com

Safe Lawns

In July of 2005, I joined with a number of organizations to help form SafeLawns.org, with the following mission statement: *To create a broad-based coalition of non- and for-profit organizations committed to educating society about the benefits of organic lawn care and gardening, and affecting a quantum change in consumer and industry behavior.* The SafeLawns.org Web site includes how-to instructional videos, links to sources of materials and landscape professionals, as well as other information about making the transition to natural, organic lawn care.

Acknowledgments

Nothing is ever undertaken alone in this life, and this book, especially, is the result of a lifetime of collaboration among friends, family, and professional colleagues.

It begins with a nod to my grandparents, Henry and Clarida VanDyne, whose dairy farm in Bradford, Maine, gave me an appreciation of insects, lawn flowers (they're not weeds!), and manure between my toes. Every member of my immediate family has contributed support, emotionally and in numerous other ways, and I thank all the Tukeys — Charlotte, my mother; along with Randy, Jill, Lynn, Tara, Marion, and Chet — the Hoffmanns, the Boardways, Paul, my father, and Marny. When you do something like this, your wife and children inevitably sacrifice the most. Katie, Christina, and Duke, I love you and I promise life won't always be this crazy. Special thanks to my sister, Donna Morin Miller, who helped immeasurably in the early days of research when this seemed especially daunting. Thank you Tim Rhys, Mike Young, Mike Stone, and Erik Heitmann for your friendship.

I haven't given up the day job, which is publishing and editing a magazine known as *People, Places & Plants,* as well as producing a television show for HGTV by the same name. While I spent a year of my life chronicling what I know about lawn care, the amazingly dedicated folks affiliated with *PPP* — Rick Churchill, Paul Shampine, Anita Dafonte, Rich Miller, Cameron Bonsey, Joline Cloutier, Brett Plymale, Molly O'Neil, Michael Feeney, Deb Bridges, Emily Rollock, Roger and Elisabeth Swain, and our editor extraordinaire, Allen Lessels — held things together. We're in this together at *PPP;* this is your book, too.

Then there are the people who helped, not because they're related or because they work for the company, but because they too wanted to get out good information and do the right thing. At the head of that line is the organic land care guru from Connecticut, Todd Harrington, my primary in-the-field consultant. You should see the organic lawns he has created through the years. I also want to acknowledge the pioneering work of Charles Waters, Ehrenfried E. Pfeiffer, Jay L. McCaman, Phil Catron, Patricia Beckett, Chip Osborne, Nancy Alderman and the folks at EHHI.org, R. R. "Ronny" Duncan, Dr. Michael Surgan, Eliot Coleman, F. Herbert Bormann, Dr. David Pimentel, Dr. Sandra Steingraber, Dr. Elaine Ingham, and countless others.

I applaud the folks at Storey, especially Dan Reynolds and Pam Art, for giving life to this project. Special thanks go to our art director, Mary Velgos, designer, Kristy MacWilliams, and publicist, Wes Seeley, for taking this book under their wings. Though I never met her, I appreciate the feedback of Susan Lang of California, who helped give the editing process a good solid West Coast perspective. I'm thrilled that Storey hired my longtime friend and colleague, John Ewing, as the primary photographer for the book. John has always been the consummate professional.

I'll conclude this inadequate acknowledgment with a public hug and professional bow to the book's editor, Carleen Perkins. When you have self-edited for as long as I have, accepting criticism isn't always easy. Carleen stood her ground, yet welcomed discussion. She worked with the project, never against it, and for that she will forever have my respect.

Index

Page numbers in *italics* indicate photographs or illustrations. Page numbers in **bold** indicate tables.

Other Storey Titles You Will Enjoy

Deckscaping, by Barbara W. Ellis.
How to transform any deck from an overly exposed flat stretch of space to a cool,
private expansion of the house's living area with trellises, lighting, plantings, and
furniture.
176 pages. Paper with flaps. ISBN 1-58017-408-6.
Hardcover with jacket. ISBN 1-58017-459-0.

Down & Dirty!, by Ellen Zachos.
A fun way for a new generation of gardeners to get started — more than 40 simple
projects to ensure success and build confidence.
256 pages. Paper. ISBN 1-58017-641-0. Hardcover. ISBN 1-58017-642-9.

Grasses, by Nancy J. Ondra.
Full-color photographs and illustrated plans for 20 gardens designed to highlight the
beauty of grasses in combination with perennials, annuals, shrubs, and other garden
plants.
144 pages. Paper with flaps. ISBN 1-58017-423-X.

The Homeowner's Complete Tree & Shrub Handbook, by Penny O'Sullivan.
The new bible of tree and shrub selection and care, showing hundreds of plant possi-
bilities in full-color photographs.
384 pages. Paper. ISBN 1-58017-570-8. Hardcover with jacket. ISBN 1-58017-571-6.

The Lawn & Garden Owner's Manual, by Lewis and Nancy Hill.
Advice to keep every part of the garden fresh and lively — complete with maintenance
charts, schedules customized by climate, and troubleshooting advice.
192 pages. Paper. ISBN 1-58017-214-8.

The Vegetable Gardener's Bible, by Edward C. Smith.
A reinvention of vegetable gardening that shows how to have your most successful
garden ever.
320 pages. Paper. ISBN 1-58017-212-1.

Watering Systems for Lawn & Garden, by R. Dodge Woodson.
Explanations in clear nontechincal language and step-by-step installation instructions
for all types of irrigation systems.
144 pages. Paper. ISBN 0-88266-906-0.

These and other books from Storey Publishing are available
wherever quality books are sold or by calling 1-800-441-5700.
Visit us at *www.storey.com.*